STANDOFF
AT HIGH NOON

ANOTHER BATTLE OVER THE TRUTH
IN THE MYTHIC WILD WEST

BILL MARKLEY
KELLEN CUTSFORTH

TWODOT®

GUILFORD, CONNECTICUT
HELENA, MONTANA

A · TWODOT® · BOOK

An imprint and registered trademark of Globe Pequot, the trade division of
The Rowman & Littlefield Publishing Group, Inc.
4501 Forbes Blvd., Ste. 200
Lanham, MD 20706
www.rowman.com

Distributed by NATIONAL BOOK NETWORK

British Library Cataloguing in Publication Information available

Library of Congress Cataloging-in-Publication Data available

ISBN 978-1-4930-5335-3 (cloth)
ISBN 978-1-4930-5336-0 (electronic)

CONTENTS

INTRODUCTION

THE HISTORY OF THE OLD WEST IS FILLED WITH STORIES OF HARDSHIP, courage, and perseverance as well as treachery, cowardice, and failure. Most stories have more than one side to them. In our previous book, *Old West Showdown*, we told the stories of ten controversial Old West events and characters from two opposing points of view: who started the gunfight near the O.K. Corral, were Wild Bill Hickok and Calamity Jane lovers, did Pat Garrett really kill Billy the Kid, and more. Readers must have liked *Old West Showdown* so much (or maybe loved to hate it) because we were asked to write a sequel with ten more controversial Old West stories. So here it is, *Standoff at High Noon*. We will again explore ten stories from two opposite viewpoints.

We kick off the first chapter with a real barnburner. How did Davy Crockett die at the Alamo? There are two opposing positions—the first is he was killed fighting and the second is he either surrendered or was captured and then executed. After covering this story, we might not be allowed to cross the border into Texas.

The second chapter is about Sacagawea, the Shoshone woman who traveled with Meriwether Lewis and William Clark's Corps of Discovery to the Pacific Ocean and back. Where and when did she die? Many historians believe she died in 1812 at Fort Manuel in present-day South Dakota, while the Shoshone people believe she returned to the tribe and lived to a ripe old age on the Wind River Reservation in Wyoming.

The third chapter delves into the horrors of the snowbound Donner Party. In 1846, a wagon train bound for California became stranded in the Sierra Nevada Mountains and ran out of food. Horror stories of cannibalism swept the country. However, did they all resort to consuming human flesh?

Next, Wild Bill Hickok made his way to the gold camp of Deadwood in Dakota Territory's Black Hills. On August 2, 1876, Hickok was playing cards in Number 10 Saloon when Jack McCall approached him from behind and shot him in the back of the head. Was McCall a disgruntled gambler as most believe or a paid assassin?

Everyone knows Lakota and Cheyenne warriors wiped out Lieutenant Colonel George Armstrong Custer and the men of the Seventh Cavalry in his immediate command at the Little Big Horn on June 25, 1876, in present-day Montana. However, could there have been a different outcome if General George Crook had continued his advance after the Battle of the Rosebud—instead of taking a break hunting and trout fishing in the Big Horn Mountains?

Robert Ford shot and killed the outlaw Jesse James in his St. Joseph, Missouri, home on April 3, 1882. Or did he? There are those who believe it was all a hoax.

Tragically, the Hunkpapa Lakota leader Sitting Bull was killed by Indian police at his Grand River home on the Standing Rock Reservation in South Dakota on the morning of December 15, 1890. There was controversy right from the start as to the disposition of his body that was buried at Fort Yates, North Dakota. Years later, Sitting Bull's nephew Grey Eagle was angry that Sitting Bull's grave was in bad shape and no one was caring for it. On the night of April 8, 1953, he and a group of South Dakotans disinterred Sitting Bull's bones, took them to the South Dakota side of the reservation, and reinterred them in a new grave. North Dakotans were outraged and then claimed the South Dakota contingent removed the wrong bones.

Everyone loves a good lost treasure/lost mine story with a dash of murder and mayhem. We will wrangle over the existence of America's most infamous lost treasure—Arizona's Lost Dutchman Mine.

Wyoming ranchers were concerned about cattle rustling and the introduction of sheep. Stock detectives were hired to look out for the big ranchers' interests. One of the most well-known stock detectives was Tom Horn. Kels Nickell had introduced sheep into Wyoming's Iron Mountains, which was cattle country. On July 18, 1901, his son, fourteen-year-old Willie Nickell, was shot and killed. Tom Horn became the number one suspect in the case and paid the ultimate price. Did Horn really commit the cold-blooded murder or was it someone else?

Finally, we all know Butch Cassidy and the Sundance Kid died on November 6, 1908, in South America during a shootout with the Bolivian army, or at least that's the way it has been portrayed by Paul Newman and Robert Redford in the popular movie of the same name. However, maybe it was not them. Maybe it was another two guys.

So, there's the rundown of the ten chapters. We will each take an opposing point of view on every story. Each chapter is a stand-alone story divided into three parts. The first part sets the stage and relates the facts as most historians agree upon. The second part will be one of us taking one side of the story, and the third part is the other of us taking an opposing view to the story. We'll let you know who takes what position. For instance, in the case of the death of Davy Crockett, Bill takes the position Davy went down swinging, and Kellen takes the position Davy was executed after the Alamo had been taken.

Our hope is that by telling two sides to these stories, it will expand your interest in the history of the Old West. If you do not like our conclusions, we hope you'll conduct your own research and come to your own conclusions.

Are you ready? Then go ahead. Enter our world of *Standoff at High Noon*.

—Bill and Kellen

CHAPTER 1

THE MANY DEATHS OF DAVY CROCKETT

JUST THE FACTS

From February 23 to March 6, 1836, a thirteen-day siege took place at the Alamo Mission near what is today San Antonio, Texas. Nearly 1,400 Mexican soldiers eventually attacked around 260 Texian, Tejano, and immigrant defenders of the Alamo. The defenders fought against overwhelming odds and were eventually overrun by the larger Mexican force. President General Antonio Lopez de Santa Anna had given orders to leave no survivors, and many of the occupants of the Alamo were put to death. It is considered by most historians one of the most pivotal battles during the Texas Revolution.[1]

Among the men killed at the Battle of the Alamo were Americans William Travis, James Bowie, and Davy Crockett. The battle began because Texian immigrants and revolutionaries had, through some small skirmishes, driven most of the Mexican military and authorities out of what is present-day Texas. With Santa Anna in power, he mercilessly taxed Mexicans and Texians alike. Receiving no benefits from the taxation, they revolted. Santa Anna was determined to establish control in Mexico and retake Texas while dealing swift justice to the Texians that he saw as pirates attempting to secede Texas territory from Mexico.[2]

Between February and March 1836, Santa Anna launched an offensive against the Texian soldiers and Texian-controlled facilities. Two of the largest engagements that occurred during this offensive were the Goliad Campaign and the Battle of the Alamo. In the early days of the Texas

Revolution, Texian troops had laid siege to San Antonio de Béxar, where the Alamo Mission stood. Most of the Texians involved in the siege were volunteers. After defeating the Mexican soldiers in several minor skirmishes, the Mexicans retreated to Béxar and eventually into the Alamo. After an assault by the Texians they surrendered. After capturing Béxar, Sam Houston, who had helped organize Texas's provisional government, had become a top-ranking official in the Texian Army. He instructed Jim Bowie, along with thirty men, to take out all the artillery from the mission and destroy the complex.[3]

However, Bowie felt that after pushing out the Mexican forces and occupying Béxar, the only way to save Texas and the revolution was to hold Béxar and keep Santa Anna from retaking it. Santa Anna believed he could use Béxar strategically as a stronghold to command troops against the Texians.[4] Initially, there were about one hundred Texians garrisoned at the Alamo. When Bowie and William B. Travis arrived at the mission, they brought reinforcements, swelling the troop totals to around 250 men.[5]

Many of the men who arrived at the Alamo as reinforcements were recruits who loved Bowie for his fighting prowess and voted him to be their leader. At the time, the US government had a treaty with Mexico. Supplying troops and munitions to the Texians at the Alamo or during the revolution would have been an act of war, so the established American government tried extremely hard to not become involved in the Texas revolt, though many congressmen supported it.[6]

As Bowie arrived at the Alamo with his men, Santa Anna marched his troops inland through Texas. Most of Santa Anna's men were raw and could not properly fire their weapons. They received much of their training on the march to Béxar. The Mexicans also did not have enough mules to carry all their supplies. These hardships were made even more taxing with some of the Mexican soldiers suffering from dysentery and Indian attacks from hostile Texas tribes. These complications slowed their march, causing Santa Anna to take an extremely long time to reach the Rio Grande River. Even with these issues, the Mexicans' numbers were still about two thousand strong when they reached the outskirts of San Antonio de Béxar.[7]

Before the Mexican troops arrived at the Alamo, however, the Texian soldiers joined the residents of Béxar in a fiesta celebrating George Washington's birthday. The men and women in the town partied the night away. Aware of the festivities, Santa Anna meant to launch his attack during the distraction, but heavy rains halted this attempt.[8] Following the fiesta on February 23, Santa Anna's troops made their way into San Antonio de Béxar and began to surround the Texians, who, alerted to the Mexican Army's presence, hurriedly huddled into the Alamo.[9]

It soon became apparent to the Texian occupants of the Alamo that Santa Anna was going to show no mercy to them. Accompanying William Travis and Jim Bowie inside the mission was Davy Crockett, a former Tennessee frontiersman and congressman in the US House of Representatives. Known to many as the "Gentleman from the Cane," Crockett was well known for opposing many of President Andrew Jackson's policies, which eventually led to his defeat at the polls in 1831. He had been reelected to represent the state of Tennessee in Congress in 1833, only to lose again in 1835. Following his defeat, Crockett famously said, "You all can go to Hell and I shall go to Texas." Crockett had arrived in the Mexican state of Tejas in early 1836 and soon joined the Texas Revolution.[10]

During the first week of Santa Anna's siege, the Mexican troops fired cannonballs into the Alamo's plaza. The Texian forces inside, for a time, returned fire. Jim Bowie, who had fallen gravely ill and required bed rest, left William Travis in sole command of the Texian resistance. Travis quickly realized that the Alamo defenders needed to conserve their ammunition and ordered his men to cease firing. In the ensuing days, small skirmishes broke out between Mexican scouts and Texian troops. As the Mexican scouts tried to station themselves in small shacks near the Alamo, the defenders ventured out to burn the shacks. Several shots were exchanged, and the first casualties of the battle were recorded.[11]

Santa Anna eventually received multiple reinforcements at the beginning of the siege, which swelled his troop numbers to nearly thirty-one hundred. Seeing the growing number of Mexicans outside their walls, Travis ordered three men, including Davy Crockett, to leave the sanctuary of Alamo. Crockett and his compatriots were sent to find Colonel James Fannin's three hundred troops, who were supposed to be heading their way from the nearby town of Gonzales. Unfortunately for the Alamo defenders, those reinforcements never arrived. Fannin's contingent of troops had disbanded after marching only a mile outside Gonzales with no word being sent to the Alamo defenders. Fannin blamed the retreat on his officers, while those officers, in turn, blamed Fannin for aborting their mission.[12]

Whatever the case, Crockett and the other scouts discovered only a small group of about fifty Texians who had come from the town of Goliad after detaching themselves from Fannin's aborted reinforcement contingent. On March 4, Crockett and the new group of Texians entered the Alamo and took up defensive positions inside the mission.[13] Late the following evening, the Mexicans ceased their bombardment of the Alamo Mission and began making final preparations for an all-out assault. Santa Anna strategically sent five hundred Mexican cavalry troops to positions around the Alamo to prevent the escape of any of the mission's defenders.[14]

Santa Anna then positioned fourteen hundred Mexican troops into four separate columns with experienced soldiers on the outside of each column to ensure the inexperienced recruits were kept in line. Early on the morning of March 6, the Mexican columns quietly advanced on the Alamo. Three Texian sentinels sleeping outside the walls were immediately killed by the advancing Mexican troops. After this action, the Mexican buglers sounded off, waking the sleeping Texians within the Alamo and signaling the attack had begun.[15]

As the shooting commenced, the tightly packed Mexican columns did not allow for troops in the back rows to fire easily. Many of the raw recruits fired into the backs of their own comrades, injuring and, in some cases, killing the men in front of them. When the Texian troops saw the compact columns of Mexicans below them, they loaded their cannons with scraps of metal and blasted the attacking troops, wiping out whole portions of their contingent. Though the Mexicans suffered heavy losses during this initial phase, their overwhelming numbers pushed up against the Alamo's walls and forced the Texians to lean over the walls to fire down upon the invaders. This action exposed many of the Texians to return fire. William Travis, who had leaned over the wall to fire his shotgun, was mortally wounded.[16]

As the Mexican troops pressed up against the Alamo's walls, they found them to be soft and they began to dig in footholds to scale the mission's north wall. Seeing the bulk of his army amassing there, Santa Anna sent multiple troops to the area in hope of breeching their defense. The Mexicans stormed into the Alamo as most of the Texian forces fell back toward the barracks and church. The fighting intensified with shots exchanged at close range, and hand-to-hand combat broke out. The Texians who fell back from the walls had their own cannons turned against them. As some of the Alamo defenders tried to escape toward an open prairie, they were cut down by the awaiting Mexican cavalry.[17]

Reportedly, the last Texians to die during the assault were eleven men manning two twelve-pounder cannons in the Alamo's chapel. At the end of this fierce fighting, 257 of the 260 Alamo occupants had been killed. These casualties included such famous men as William Travis, James Bowie, and Davy Crockett. In the years following the battle, much speculation and controversy has swirled around exactly how these men met their fate, especially Crockett.

DAVY CROCKETT DIED FIGHTING AT THE ALAMO—BILL MARKLEY

I do have a bias. I am one of those baby boomers who grew up idolizing Davy Crockett. I loved Walt Disney's *Davy Crockett* miniseries (1954–1955) with Fess Parker playing Davy along with his sidekick Georgie Russell played by Buddy Ebsen. I proudly wore my Davy Crockett coonskin cap as I sang Davy Crockett's theme song. I passed on the coonskin cap to my son, but I still have my Davy Crockett mug prominently displayed in my office. When John Wayne's movie, *The Alamo*, was released in 1960, my parents took my brother and me to the drive-in theater where I was awed by the battle scenes. To be honest, I liked Fess Parker's version of Davy better than I did John Wayne's—not to say I don't like John Wayne. So, with that out of the way, let's look into the accounts of Davy Crockett's death and why I believe he went down fighting.

Davy Crockett was a nationally known personality at the time of his death. He was well liked by many but was also disliked by Jacksonian Democrats as he had opposed some of President Andrew Jackson's policies such as the forced removal of Indian tribes to Indian Territory.

Whether people liked or disliked Crockett, they followed accounts of his actions and what he said just like pop culture stars today.

I take the position there are no verified first-hand accounts of how Davy Crockett died at the Alamo. There are two schools of thought on how he died. The first is he was killed during the fight. The second is he surrendered or was captured and executed shortly after the fight. Most of the information I use in this analysis was developed by historian Bill Groneman and others. I am merely passing along what they have researched before me. So, let's go ahead and examine the sources for Davy Crockett's death and their claims of how he died.

First, did Davy Crockett really die at the Alamo? Soon after the fight, newspapers proclaimed he was still alive. The March 26, 1836, edition of the *Morning Courier and New York Enquirer* stated, "Colonel Crockett . . . is *not* dead, but still alive and grinning." Additional newspapers reported the same, saying he would soon return from hunting in the Rocky Mountains.[18]

Other newspapers reported Crockett was at the Alamo but survived. The May 12, 1836, edition of the Bellows Falls *Vermont Chronicle* repeated, "Col. Crockett. The Cincinnati Whig publishes a statement showing that the Col. was not dead—that after the Mexicans had left St. Antonio, he was found alive among heaps of slain and conveyed to comfortable lodgings and was said to be doing well."[19]

When Crockett failed to return, it was obvious these reports were wrong.

On February 6, 1840, William C. White, an American living in Mexico, wrote a letter to the *Austin City Gazette* claiming Davy Crockett was alive and being held captive in Mexico. White had visited Guadalajara where he heard about an American prisoner of war working in the Salinas mine. White received permission to meet with the American. White offered to deliver a message for the prisoner, who responded, "I know that, so let us go about it: My name is David Crockett. I am from Tennessee and I have a family there. They think I am dead and so does everyone else; but they are mistaken. I should have written to them, as the overseer told me I might write, if I could get any person to take a letter for me . . . and thanks be to God, I have got one at last." The newspaper did print a disclaimer: "The letter comes from an unknown source, and may or may not be true." Congressman John Wesley Crockett, Davy's oldest son, learned of White's letter and asked the US ambassador to Mexico to investigate whether his father was being held prisoner. The ambassador wrote back that he had discussed the matter with a Mexican officer "of high rank" who turned out to be Colonel Juan Nepomuceno Almonte, who had been at the battle of the Alamo. Almonte believed Crockett had been killed at the Alamo. His cook, a black American, Ben Harris, had identified Crockett's body after the battle.[20]

Two American survivors from inside the Alamo as well as a resident of San Antonio de Béxar stated they had seen Davy Crockett's body. They did not witness how he had died but did see his body.

Joe, Colonel William Travis's black slave, had fought alongside Travis at the Alamo's north wall until Travis was killed. Joe retreated along with other defenders as Mexican soldiers scaled and captured the wall. He took shelter in a room from where he continued to fight until the battle was over. Mexican officers were attempting to spare the lives of black slaves, and Joe was fortunate Captain Manuel Barragán saved him along with a white man named Warner or Warnell. When Barragán brought them to Santa Anna, he ordered Warner shot. Santa Anna told Joe to show them the bodies of Travis and Crockett. Bowie had already been identified. He showed the Mexican officers Travis's body and then found Crockett's. Joe later reported Crockett's body and the bodies of some of his friends lay together surrounded by over twenty dead Mexican soldiers.[21]

Santa Anna wanted additional confirmation of the Texan rebel leaders' bodies and had Francisco Antonio Ruíz, San Antonio's acting alcalde (mayor), brought into the Alamo. Santa Anna told Ruíz to show them Travis, Bowie, and Crockett's bodies. He identified them, including Crockett's, later saying, "Toward the west in a small fort opposite the city, we found the body of Col. Crockett." Ruíz's statement, translated by J. A. Quintero, appeared in the 1860 *Texas Almanac*. Some historians believe Ruíz's statement meant the location of Crockett's body was between the Alamo's western wall and west of the Alamo's church building.[22]

Susanna Dickinson and her fifteen-month-old daughter, Angelina, took shelter in the Alamo church's sacristy. Toward the end of the fight, her husband, Captain Almeron Dickinson, an artillery officer, ran into the church and said, "Great God, Sue, the Mexicans are inside our walls! All is lost! If they spare you, save my child!" He kissed her, drew his sword, and ran out into the fight. Mexican soldiers chased three unarmed gunners into the church and shot them down in front of Susanna. Soldiers bayoneted one of them named Walker, lifting his body in the air on their bayonets until an officer stopped them. Susanna and Angelina were spared. After leaving the church, she later recalled, "I recognized Colonel Crockett lying dead and mutilated between the church and the two-story barrack building, and even remember seeing his peculiar cap lying by his side."[23]

Counting Ben Harris mentioned earlier, four witnesses who knew Davy Crockett identified his body at the Alamo. However, none of them saw how he died.

Six accounts tell of Crockett dying in battle. Two of them are by Andrea Castañon de Villanueva, one by Sergeant Felix Nuñez, another by Captain Rafael Soldana, one by an unidentified Mexican captain, and one by Enrique Esparza, who was an eight-year-old boy in the Alamo at the time of the attack.[24]

Andrea Castañon de Villanueva said she was at the Alamo; however, Susanna Dickinson disputed her claim. Other survivors said they did not see her but would not challenge her claim. Villanueva said she was caring for the ill Jim Bowie when Mexican soldiers burst into the room. She tried to protect Bowie, but they bayonetted him.[25]

Villanueva told varying accounts as to what had happened during the attack on the Alamo. She recounted two different versions of Davy Crockett's death. In her 1889 account, she said, "He looked grand and terrible standing in the door and fighting a whole column of Mexican infantry." He fired his last shot, then swung something at the oncoming Mexicans. "A heap of dead was piled at his feet and the Mexicans were lunging at him with bayonets." Finally, they were able to kill him. In her 1890 account, Villanueva told a completely different story, saying Crockett was one of the first to be killed. Unarmed, he was running from the church to the wall when he was shot and killed.[26]

Sergeant Felix Nuñez was the next to describe the death of Crockett. There is no information on Nuñez other than from his account. Nuñez told his story to Professor George W. Noel, who then gave the story to an unidentified reporter for the *San Antonio Express*, which published it in 1889. Nuñez did not name Crockett but described a man who most agree must have been him—a tall man wearing a buckskin coat and "a round cap without any bill, and made of fox skin, with the long tail hanging down his back." Mexican soldiers took aim at him but could not hit him. The man was an expert shot, killing at least eight Mexicans before a lieutenant "dealt him a deadly blow with his sword, just above the right eye." The man, who was the last to be killed, fell to the ground and was stabbed by twenty bayonets.[27]

Captain Rafael Soldana was in Corpus Christi at the end of the Mexican War when he gave his account to Creed Taylor, who then told it to James T. DeShields. Soldana described the final assault on the walls and then into the Alamo. Speaking of a man he called Kwockey, whom most agree was Crockett, he said, "Kwockey was killed in a room of the mission." As soldiers tried to enter the room, he knifed them. They could not shoot him because of how he had positioned himself in the room behind the door; they could not bring their guns to bear on him. Finally, someone was able to shoot him in the right arm, making it useless. "He then seized his long gun with his left hand and leaped toward the center of the room where he could wield the weapon without obstruction, felling every man that came through the doorway. A corporal ordered the passage cleared of those who were being pressed forward, a volley was fired almost point blank and the last defender of the Alamo fell forward—dead."[28]

Enrique Esparza was an eight-year-old boy in the Alamo at the time of the attack. In 1907, Charles Merritt Barnes interviewed Esparza about the fight at the Alamo, and it appeared in the May 19 issue of the *San Antonio Express*. Esparza said:

> *[Crockett] was everywhere during the siege and personally slew many of the enemy with his rifle, his pistol and his knife. He fought hand to hand. He clubbed his rifle when they closed in on him and knocked them down with its stock until he was overwhelmed by numbers and slain. He fought to his last breath. He fell immediately in front of the large double doors which he defended with the force that was by his*

side. Crockett was one of the few who were wide awake when the final crisis and crash came. When he died there was a heap of slain in front and on each side of him. These he had all killed before he finally fell on top of the heap.[29]

There are those who hold an alternate position on the death of Davy Crockett—that he surrendered to Mexican troops or they captured him and then they immediately executed him. Santa Anna had ordered all Alamo defenders to be killed. Early newspaper reports in the United States stated all had been killed at the Alamo and those taken prisoner had been executed. There are seven accounts stating Davy Crockett, or a man taken to be him, was executed. The first account was by an unidentified witness, the second alleged to be by Colonel Juan N. Almonte, the third by Colonel Fernando Urriza, the fourth by Sergeant Francisco Becerra, the fifth by General Martín Perfecto de Cós, the sixth by Colonel José Juan Sanchez-Navarro, and the seventh by Lieutenant José Enrique de la Peña.[30]

The first account of Crockett's execution was told by an unidentified witness to an unnamed reporter, possibly William H. Attree. It was published in the July 9, 1836, issue of the *Morning Courier and New York Enquirer*, the same newspaper that reported Crockett "still alive and grinning" back on March 26.[31]

The newspaper story related that "after the Mexicans had got possession of the Alamo, the fighting had ceased, and it was clear daylight, six Americans were discovered near the wall yet unconquered." The Mexican troops had them surrounded. General Castrillón ordered them to surrender and promised them his protection. Castrillón took the six men to Santa Anna. The story continues:

> *"His Excellency" [was] surrounded by his murderous crew, his syco-phantic officers. DAVID CROCKETT was one of the six [prison-ers]. . . . Nothing daunted, he marched up boldly in front of Santa Anna, looked him steadfastly in the face, while Castrillón addressed "His Excellency," "Sir here are six prisoners I have taken alive; how shall I dispose of them?" Santa Anna looked at Castrillón fiercely, flew into a most violent rage, and replied, "Have I not told you before how*

to dispose of them? Why do you bring them to me?" At the same time his brave officers drew and plunged their swords into the bosoms of their defenseless prisoners!! . . . This was the fate of poor Crockett, and in which there can be no mistake. Who the five others were, I have not been able to learn. . . . There are certain reasons why the name of the narrator of these events should not be made known. I will only repeat that he was an eye-witness.[32]

The editor of the *Morning Courier and New York Enquirer* was James Watson Webb. When US Congressman David Crockett visited New York City in 1834, Webb escorted him to the city's Five Points neighborhood. Webb was a charter member of the New Washington Association.[33]

The New Washington Association's members were New York investors who had established the town of New Washington on the east side of Galveston Bay in Texas. After the fall of the Alamo, the Mexican army confiscated the association's goods and burned New Washington to the ground.[34]

On April 21, 1836, Sam Houston's Texans defeated the Mexican Army at the Battle of San Jacinto and captured Santa Anna. At the time of the *Morning Courier and New York Enquirer* story on Crockett's execution, Santa Anna was still in the hands of the Texans. He would not be returned to Mexico until November 1836.[35]

The *Morning Courier and New York Enquirer* execution story of Crockett and the others was reprinted by newspapers across the country, fueling indignation and anger at Santa Anna. It was in the best interest of the New Washington Association that Santa Anna not regain power and that Texas become independent of Mexico.[36] Was it possible the *Morning Courier and New York Enquirer* made up the story of Crockett's execution to further its own agenda? I believe this Crockett execution story was fiction and created to use as propaganda.

The second account of Crockett's execution was a letter published in the September 7, 1836, issue of the *Detroit Democratic Free Press*. The letter was written by George M. Dolson, an orderly sergeant from Cincinnati, Ohio, in the Texan army to his brother. It was dated July 19, 1836, and sent from Galveston Island, Texas. In his letter, Dolson said he was employed as an English and Spanish interpreter for Colonel James Morgan, who was in charge of that area. He said he acted as translator in a private meeting between Colonel Morgan and Colonel Juan Nepomuceno Almonte.[37]

Dolson's letter printed in the newspaper stated:

The Mexican was then requested to proceed with the statement according to promise; and he said he could give a true and correct account of the proceedings of Santa Anna towards the prisoners who remained alive at the taking of the Alamo. This shows the fate of Colonel Crockett and his five brave companions.

The letter went on to state Crockett and the five men surrendered to General Castrillón, who promised them protection and led them to the tent of Santa Anna. Dolson's letter continued:

Colonel Crockett was in the rear, had his arms folded, and appeared bold as the lion as he passed my informant (Almonte.) Santa Anna's interpreter knew Colonel Crockett, and said to my informant, "the one behind is the famous Crockett." When brought to the presence of Santa Anna, Castrillón said to him, "Santa Anna, the august, I deliver up to you six brave prisoners of war." Santa Anna replied, "Who has given you orders to take prisoners, I do not want to see these men living— shoot them." As the monster uttered these words each officer turned his face the other way, and the hell-hounds of the tyrant dispatched the six in his presence, and within six feet of his person. Such an act I consider murder of the blackest kind. Do you think that he [Santa Anna] can be released?[38]

The letter went on to state that all the money in Mexico and Europe could not ransom Santa Anna before "Texas will have released him out of his existence." In the end, the Dolson letter stated Santa Anna should be tried as a felon.[39]

Several things were going on here. Colonel James Morgan was a charter member of the New Washington Association and was its agent

and manager in Texas. Colonel Almonte had led the pillaging and burning of New Washington. General Castrillón had been killed at the Battle
of San Jacinto and could not be asked to provide an account if Crockett
had been captured and executed. Santa Anna never mentioned in any
of his writings capturing and executing Crockett. It's interesting that
Orderly Sergeant Dolson recently of Cincinnati, Ohio, would have been
proficient enough in Spanish to be used as an interpreter instead of other
Americans who had been in Texas long term and would have a better
knowledge of Spanish. Finally, Almonte was not being held at Galveston Island. He and Santa Anna had first been held on board the ship
Independence, then at Velasco, after that at Bell's Landing in Columbia,
Texas.[40]

One final thought—Almonte did not see Crockett executed. When
the US ambassador to Mexico had asked about Crockett being held
captive in Mexico, Almonte had to refer to his cook, Ben Harris, who
had identified Crockett's body after the battle. The Dolson letter has the
appearance of being fabricated to stir up resentment against Santa Anna.
I believe this Crockett execution story was fiction and created to use as
propaganda.

The third account some believe refers to the execution of Davy Crockett is Nicholas Labadie's memoir published in the 1859 *Texas Almanac*.
Labadie wrote that in a private interview Colonel Fernando Urriza told
him, "I was then acting as Santa Anna's secretary, and ranked as Colonel."
Urriza told Labadie of an execution after the Alamo had been taken.
Labadie recorded Urriza saying, "I observed Castrion [sic] coming out of
one of the quarters, leading a venerable-looking old man by the hand; he
was tall, his face was red, and he stooped forward as he walked. . . . [Cas-
trillón] said: 'My General, I have spared the life of this venerable old man
and taken him prisoner.' Raising his head, Santa Anna replied, 'What
right have you to disobey my orders? I want no prisoners,' and waving his
hand to a file of soldiers he said, 'Soldiers, shoot that man,' and almost
instantly he fell, pierced with a volley of balls."[41]

Later in the interview Labadie asked Urriza, "What was that old
man's name?"

"I believe they called him Coket," Urriza responded.[42]

Bill Groneman and other historians have called Labadie's account questionable. Written twenty-three years after the fall of the Alamo, it was controversial at the time of publication over another story. John Forbes, who was Commissary General of the Texas Army at the time of the Battle of San Jacinto, sued Labadie over his allegation Forbes murdered a Mexican woman. Years later the suit was dismissed. There is no collaborative information that this interview ever took place or that Urriza was a witness to any executions. Urriza never mentioned this account in his writings or to anyone else. Labadie writes that Urriza said, "I believe they called him Coket." There is no identification as to who "they" were.[43]

At the time of his death at the Alamo, Davy Crockett was forty-nine years old. Accounts portray him in good health before the fall of the Alamo. I am not sure a healthy forty-nine-year-old man would be considered a venerable old man. Would Davy Crockett be the type of stooped-forward man to be led by the hand? By the time Labadie wrote his memoir, the Crockett execution story had been floated in all the newspapers. I believe this Crockett execution story was fiction, or at best, embellished to identify Crockett as the venerable old man executed.

The fourth account is by Sergeant Francisco Becerra. His account was given in a speech by John S. Ford at the Austin Public Library in 1875. The Becerra account states when the Mexican troops entered the Alamo he found two men. General Martín Perfecto de Cós knew one man, who was William Travis. Travis identified his companion as Colonel Crockett. Becerra accompanied General Cós and Generals Almonte and Tolza, who took Travis and Crockett to Santa Anna to ask that they be spared:

Santa Anna was very much enraged. He said:—"Gentleman generals, my order was to kill every man in the Alamo." He turned, and said:— "Soldiers, kill them." A soldier was standing near Travis, and presented his gun at him. Travis seized the bayonet, and depressed the muzzle of the piece to the floor, and it was not fired. While this was taking place the soldiers standing around opened fire. A shot struck Travis in the back. He then stood erect, folding his arms, and looked

calmly, unflinchingly, upon his assailants. He was finally killed by a
ball passing through his neck. Crockett stood in a similar position. They
died undaunted like heroes.[44]

According to Becerra, eight Mexican soldiers were killed and wounded by their fellow soldiers firing at Travis and Crockett. Becerra said, "I did not know the names of two Texans, only as given by Gen Cos. The gentleman he called Crockett had a coat with capes to it."[45]

Becerra's account was published in the April 1882 edition of the *Texas Mute Ranger*. There are problems with this account. Becerra said the Mexican Army lost over two thousand men killed, but that was more men than attacked the Alamo. Becerra has both Travis and Crockett executed, but Joe, Travis's slave, said Travis was killed in the fight on the Alamo's north wall. According to John S. Ford, someone prepared Becerra's account from notes, read them to him in English, which he understood, and again in Spanish. Becerra then "endorsed them as a true version of the affair." However, Becerra told Ford, "He did not know them [Travis and Crockett] personally and might be mistaken as to their identity."[46]

I believe Becerra's account, at best, was an embellishment adding in Travis and Crockett's names.

The next account is allegedly by General Martín Perfecto de Cós given to Doctor George M. Patrick when Cós was being held prisoner by the Texans at Anahuac. According to this account, Cós found "a fine looking and well-dressed man" who had been locked up alone. The man told him he was David Crockett, a representative to the US Congress. He had been exploring Texas and had been in San Antonio when the fighting broke out and took shelter in the Alamo. Crockett said he did not take part in any of the fighting. Cós took Crockett to Santa Anna. Cós gave a lengthy introduction of Crockett to Santa Anna and asked that he be spared. "Then he [Santa Anna] replied sharply, 'You know your orders'; turned his back upon us and walked away. But as he turned, Crockett drew from his bosom a dagger, with which he smote at him with a thrust, which, if not arrested, would surely have killed him; but was met by a bayonet-thrust by the hand of a soldier through the heart; he fell and soon expired."[47]

Cós allegedly gave this account to George Patrick in 1836. Patrick then told it to William P. Zuber, who did not write it down until in a 1904 letter to Charlie Jeffries, which was later published in the 1939 book *In the Shadow of History*. Zuber himself did not believe the story, writing in his letter, "This story by Cos, though a gross falsehood, shows what Santa Anna would have done if it were true." Neither Cós nor Patrick left any separate record of this account.[48]

I believe the Cós story is nothing more than fiction.

The sixth account is allegedly by Colonel José Juan Sanchez-Navarro. It first came to light in 1936 and was published in 1938. In Navarro's journal, he writes about the Mexican troops swiftly taking the Alamo and then, "By six thirty in the morning none of the enemy existed. I saw actions that I envied, of heroic valor. Some cruelties horrified me, among others the death of an old man they called 'Cocran' and of a boy approximately fourteen years old."[49]

Some historians use this as additional proof of Crockett's execution. Again, does "Cocran" really mean "Crockett"? Would Crockett at age forty-nine be considered an old man? The narrative does not say Cocran was executed, but that could be inferred. "They" who identify Cocran are not named.[50]

Navarro's journal is written in two ledger books that record government information during the years 1831–1839. The records do not pertain to the Mexican Army while in Texas. The journal is written on portions of pages that had been left blank between data entries. Navarro was well off and could have afforded to buy his own journal book instead of using a government book that could have been taken away at any time for government purposes.[51]

Bill Groneman believes the Navarro journal is a twentieth-century forgery. Someone could have acquired the ledger books and then wrote their version of events in the blank spaces. On April 5, 1836, an anonymous Mexican soldier published an account of the capture of the Alamo in the newspaper *El Mosquito Mexicano*. Groneman believes portions of the newspaper account are so similar to what was written in the ledger books that the forger had used the newspaper account to write the

Navarro journal. The letter published in the newspaper made no mention of the death of old man Cocran.[52]

Carlos Sanchez-Navarro published the journal in 1938, but he did not state where or how he had obtained the ledger books. The University of Texas eventually acquired the ledger book journal. As of 1999, Bill Groneman was unaware of any forensics testing conducted on the books to determine the authenticity of the journal.[53]

Based on the information I have read, I believe the Navarro journal is not real.

Many historians believe Lieutenant José Enrique de la Peña wrote the seventh account of Crockett's death. After the Mexican troops captured the Alamo, the Peña memoir relates,

Some seven men had survived the general massacre and guided by General Castrillón, who sponsored them, were presented to Santa Anna. Among them was one of great stature, well-formed and regular features.

The text goes on to describe "the naturalist David Crocket [sic]" and stated that he had been traveling through the country when the fighting broke out and he took refuge in the Alamo. Santa Anna directed troops to shoot the seven men. The officers of the troops hesitated to give the order. Then, other officers who wanted to flatter Santa Anna positioned themselves in front of the prisoners,

And sword in hand they threw themselves upon these unfortunate defenseless ones, in the same way that a tiger throws itself upon its prey. They tormented them before they were made to die, and those unfortunate ones died moaning, but without humiliating themselves to their executioners.[54]

Most historians who ascribe to the theory that Davy Crockett was executed after the capture of the Alamo use Peña's account as proof. Bill Groneman and a few others believe it is a modern-day forgery. Let's look at the facts that Groneman has documented.[55]

There is no record of the Peña account before 1955. Jesús Sanchez Garza edited and self-published Peña's documents in Spanish. Its title in English is *The Rebellion of Texas: Unpublished 1836 Manuscript by an Officer of Santa Anna*. It was first published in Mexico in March 1955. Garza made his living buying and selling old books, documents, coins, and currency. He did not say from whom or how he had obtained the Peña documents. The original documents were purchased and are now housed at the University of Texas at Austin. In 1975, Carmen Perry translated the Peña documents into English, and Texas A&M published them in the United States.[56]

Peña's account has factual errors such as the manner of Travis's death. Peña has Travis retreating, firing, retreating and firing before he was killed. Joe, Travis's slave, said Travis died in the first fight along the Alamo's north wall. It appears some of the information in Peña's account may have been pieced together from other accounts. There is no information that anyone has ever tried to determine if the Peña documents are authentic.[57]

I agree that, as James Donovan pointed out in his book, *The Blood of Heroes*, the biggest problem with the document is that it is not an original holograph, an original journal written in Peña's hand. It was written by at least three different people.[58]

The account of Crockett's execution was written in a different hand and on a different piece of paper. James Donovan states,

> *The brief account of Crockett's execution is contained on a single slip of paper—the verso of folio 35—and was not only written on a different kind of paper from the rest of the manuscript (consisting of 105 folded "quartos" of four pages each) but was also written in a different hand. Folio 35 was tucked into the manuscript just as several other slips of paper were—suggesting that it was one of many accounts, rumors, and stories obtained from other sources and inserted where it belonged chronologically, rather than with accounts of episodes witnessed by de la Peña himself.[59]*

Bill Groneman has written, "At worst the Peña document is a twentieth-century fake . . . at best it is now a memoir padded with researched material. If that is so, we do not know if the references to Crockett and the executions were researched from newspaper articles circulating at the time. What it is not is a firsthand eyewitness diary—the quality for which it received all of the attention in the first place."[60]

Based on the information at hand, I believe the Peña memoir account of the execution of Davy Crockett was collected from one of the early newspaper stories previously mentioned, embellished, and inserted into the Peña document.

In 1956, the pulp magazine *Man's Illustrated* printed a story by Jackson Burke, "The Untold Secret of the Alamo," purporting to be based upon Santa Anna's handwritten account of the capture of the Alamo. According to this story, just before Crockett was executed, he told Santa Anna that thirty Alamo defenders had mutinied. No evidence of this has ever been found. There is no documentation of this particular account. The story was again reprinted in the April 1960 issue of *Man's Conquest*, another pulp magazine, as "The Secret of the Alamo." The story appears to be fiction.[61]

No official Mexican Army document mentions the execution of Crockett. Santa Anna, Colonel Almonte, and Santa Anna's secretary, Ramón Caro, all wrote accounts of the Battle of the Alamo after their return to Mexico. None of them mention the execution of Davy Crockett. General Vicente Filisola, who was second in command to Santa Anna, collected verbal and written information from soldiers and officers who were at the Alamo and wrote a detailed account of the siege and capture. There is no mention of Crockett's execution. Santa Anna wrote a report of the battle for the Alamo on the same day of its capture, March 6, 1836. He did not mention the execution of Davy Crockett, but he did say Crockett was "among the corpses." After Santa Anna's capture, he was questioned for two hours and never said anything about a Crockett execution. During the seven months Santa Anna was in Texas and the United States there was never any mention of the execution of Crockett. In his later memoirs, Santa Anna wrote concerning the defenders of the Alamo, "Not one soldier showed signs of desiring to surrender."[62]

I do not believe there is any clear-cut evidence to prove Davy Crockett was executed after the Alamo's capture. I'll go ahead and state for the record I like Enrique Esparza's account that Davy Crockett died swinging his rifle like a club, fighting off his attackers to the last.

I think if Davy could know about all the hoopla made over how he died, he would be rightly amused. However he died, and however all the other people on both sides died, their deaths were tragic. They should all be considered honorable.

It's fitting to end with Davy's favorite saying, "I leave this rule for others when I'm dead, 'Be always sure you're right—THEN GO AHEAD!'"[63]

A HERO DEFINED—KELLEN CUTSFORTH

"Davy! Davy Crockett! King of the Wild Frontier!" Or so the old Disney theme song goes from the popular 1950s television program *Davy Crockett*. Fess Parker's portrayal as Crockett helped transform Davy into a larger-than-life folk hero for generations of Americans. However, Crockett, without the help of modern entertainment television, had built quite the reputation as a frontiersman, soldier, and politician. Because of his exploits, he was celebrated in stage plays and other print media during his lifetime.

Crockett had been a member of the Tennessee militia in 1813. As a Tennessee backwoodsman, he made a quality scout and knew how to handle a musket. He participated in the Creek War until December 1814. Andrew Jackson, in control of the US military during the War of 1812, which was taking place at the same time the Creek War was raging, asked for the help of the Tennessee militia. So, Crockett reenlisted but saw little action in this campaign.[64]

Following his military service in the Tennessee militia, he began his political career. He was appointed justice of the peace, then was elected lieutenant colonel of the Fifty-seventh Regiment of the Tennessee militia. By the 1820s, Crockett won a seat in the Tennessee General Assembly, where he honed his skills as an orator, and, by the early 1830s, he was elected to represent Tennessee in the halls of the US Congress in the House of Representatives.[65]

During his terms in the Tennessee General Assembly, Crockett fought to lower taxes on poorer settlers. When he eventually won a seat in the US Congress, Crockett challenged President Andrew Jackson's policies, especially the Indian Removal Act. Because of his vociferous dissent against the legislation and against President Jackson himself, Crockett became a target of the president's proponents, which made it difficult for him to win reelection. Eventually in 1835, Crockett lost his final reelection attempt to represent Tennessee in the US Congress and decided that he would pull up stakes and head to the Mexican state of Coahuila y Tejas, which was becoming embroiled in what would be known as the Texas Revolution.[66]

After Crockett left the Volunteer State, he made his way to Texas, where he hunted buffalo during December of 1835. Many Texians believed Crockett had only come to Texas to hunt and not join the revolution. After spending time in the country and hunting game, however, David decided to join up with the Texas volunteers for six months. Crockett was soon joined by several other Tennesseans. The former frontiersman arrived in San Antonio de Béxar in early February 1836.[67]

Supposedly, Crockett was asked to take an officer's role amongst the Texian troops posted at the Alamo, but he declined. Davy, instead, would enlist as a "high private." Crockett threw himself into the Texas revolutionary cause. He would celebrate George Washington's birthday with the rest of the Béxar residents on February 22 and would also be surprised by Santa Anna's arriving Mexican forces.[68]

Crockett hunkered down alongside the defenders inside the Alamo as Mexican troops besieged the small mission for nearly two weeks. The former Tennessee frontiersman also did his duty when he sneaked out of Béxar in search of Fannin's reinforcements that never fully arrived.

As the fight for the Alamo raged on that fateful day in early March, it is impossible to follow all the movements of the mission defenders and the Mexican attackers. David Crockett certainly participated in the heavy action as most of the Alamo inhabitants were forced into fighting as the Mexicans breeched the Alamo walls and poured into the interior of the mission. There is no supporting evidence that definitively states David Crockett did not participate in the fighting. In fact, Crockett most likely fought as hard as any of the men inside the Alamo. The defenders, which included Crockett, were able to fight and repel the Mexican forces on two separate occasions.[69]

When the Mexicans breached the walls of the Alamo, complete havoc was unleashed. The Texians had to fall back toward the center of the complex to continue to defend and to not be overrun. When the defenders were completely engulfed by the Mexican soldiers streaming into the mission, they had to make a split decision to either drop their arms and throw themselves on the mercy of the invading army or fight knowing their deaths were inevitable.

It does not take a brain surgeon to realize the inhabitants of the Alamo were beaten when the Mexicans breached the walls. The Texian defenders knew the odds, too, and they knew they were not in their favor. Seeing thousands of Mexican troops with sharpened bayonets and firing their rifles, Crockett and sixteen of his Tennessean compatriots repelled many of the attacks on the Alamo's west wall but had to eventually fall back to the center of the mission.[70]

By most accounts, this is where David Crockett and his Tennessee boys met their end. For years, stories of his final moments circulated in newspapers and amongst the public. Crockett's bloody body was identified by William Travis's slave, Joe, who fought during the battle, was captured, and then was released by the Mexican forces. Joe was told by Santa Anna to identify the bodies of Bowie, Travis, and Crockett.[71]

In early accepted accounts, Joe walked through the mass of bodies and identified Jim Bowie, whom most of the Mexicans knew by reputation. He was found in his bed where he took down a couple of Mexican troopers before he was overwhelmed. Joe also identified William Travis's corpse near the Alamo wall where he had been killed trying to fire down upon invading Mexican forces. Finally, Joe supposedly identified Crockett, whose body was alongside those of some of his friends.[72]

Eulalia Yorba, a Tejana woman who survived the battle, said she saw Davy covered in blood, having "died of some ball in the chest or a bayonet thrust." Crockett was supposedly surrounded by several dead Mexican troops.[73] This version of Crockett's death was the accepted history for several decades following the outcome of the Texas Revolution.

Then, in 1955, a diary was uncovered by researcher J. Sánchez Garza and published in Mexico. This document told a different story of Davy's demise. The "diary" apparently belonged to José Enrique de la Peña, who was a lieutenant in the Mexican Army during the Texas Revolution and served in the Battle of the Alamo. Within the pages of the diary, Peña described the engagement at the Alamo and how the Texians were able to wipe out entire companies of Mexicans with their cannons at the beginning of the battle.[74] More stunningly, he alleged that David Crockett did not die taking several Mexicans with him but was one of a few Texians captured and eventually executed on Santa Anna's orders. Peña said Crockett and the other captured men were executed with swords.[75]

When the Mexican assault on the Alamo began on March 4, one of Santa Anna's generals, Manuel Fernández Castrillón disagreed with the attack feeling heavy artillery should be brought up to the front to support their advancing troops. But Santa Anna was in a hurry to have a glorious victory. Castrillón also disagreed with Santa Anna's earlier "red flag declaration" that stated no mercy be given to their Texian opponents. When the fighting ended at the Alamo, Santa Anna entered the fort at 6:30 a.m. He was soon approached by General Castrillón towing seven bloody prisoners behind him. One of these men was Davy Crockett.[76]

In Pena's diary, the Mexican lieutenant gave a solid accounting of Crockett writing he was, "one of great stature, well proportioned, with regular features, in whose face there was the imprint of adversity, but in whom one also noticed a degree of resignation and nobility that did him honor." When Santa Anna saw the prisoners, he was furious. He ordered Castrillón to execute them, but the general balked at the order. After Castrillón's defiance, Mexican officers fell upon the defenseless Texians and slaughtered them with their swords.[77]

Originally, Lieutenant José Enrique de la Peña did not know who Crockett was when he was executed. When the Mexican soldier realized who Davy was, he wrote, "[the man] was the naturalist David Crockett, well known in North America for his unusual adventures."[78]

Interestingly in 1934, before the discovery of the Peña diary, artist John W. Thomason Jr. painted an illustration featuring Crockett. In the image, he portrayed a large group of Mexican soldiers leading a shirtless, captured Davy Crockett with bandaged head to his execution. This is just more evidence that supports the common knowledge that Crockett was captured and later executed.

The validity of Peña's diary has been challenged by a few historians over the decades. Questions have been raised about the diary's provenance because there is no reference to it until 1955. Coincidentally, this also happened to be the height of Crockett's popularity because of Disney's, *Davy Crockett: King of the Wild Frontier* television program which was airing at the time.

There are also some quality questions revolving around the handwriting in the Peña's diary. It is believed by some historians that the known samples of the Mexican lieutenant's handwriting do not match any of the diary entries. Along these lines, the diary pages are also believed to be comprised of several different types of paper.[79] These are certainly good points, however most historians believe in the validity of the Peña diary and refute these various points. They do so because José Enrique de la Peña's accounts of the battle have been found to be historically accurate and corroborated by various eyewitnesses.[80]

The fact remains that the entries in the José Enrique de la Peña's diary are quite believable. His description of the intense fighting during the battle remain consistent with descriptions from separate survivor accounts that have been authenticated. His descriptions are often quoted by multiple authors and historians and are believed to be solid firsthand accounts of the Alamo Battle. These aspects alone give credence to the Crockett capture story being true[81]

Amongst all this controversy, however, is perhaps the one question that is rarely if ever approached. What does it matter if Davy was captured and executed or not? Does it make him any less of a patriot and symbol of the Texas Revolution? Does it make him any less a defender of the Alamo than Travis, Bowie, or any of the other men who perished in the face of those insurmountable odds?

By all accounts, Crockett fought just as fiercely as any man who met his end that fateful day, and according to José Enrique de la Peña he died with his honor intact. More than likely, when Crockett was captured, he was surrounded by an overwhelming enemy and realized there was no chance of escape and no chance of winning a fight. His only real option was to surrender. So, that begs another question. Are any of the soldiers who faced similar odds during the Civil War, World Wars, or other similar conflicts cowards because they threw up their hands for mercy? Most would say no.

At the conclusion of the Battle of the Alamo, Davy Crockett had zero quit in him. He was defiant when interrogated by Santa Anna, and, when he was run through with a Mexican saber he accepted his death and met his end like a man. Because David Crockett died after being captured at the Alamo his reputation and legacy should not be tarnished. He fought and ultimately died at one of the most remembered and inspiring battles in American history.

CHAPTER 2

WHERE AND WHEN DID SACAGAWEA DIE?

JUST THE FACTS

Sacagawea is possibly one of the best known American Indian women's names in history, but other than her role assisting Meriwether Lewis and William Clark's Corps of Discovery in their expedition across the North American continent and back, little is known about her.

Today, her name is spelled several different ways: Sakakawea, Sacajawea, and Sacagawea. The members of Lewis and Clark's expedition spelled it phonetically, "Sahcagahweah." The Hidatsas say it means "Bird Woman." The Shoshones say it means "Boat Launcher."[1]

If it was not for black Haitian freedom fighters, Sacagawea might have been unknown to history. France had controlled Haiti, the western half of the island of Hispaniola in the Caribbean Sea. French planters brought in African slaves to work their sugar cane plantations, and sugar production became a major part of the French economy. In 1791, the slaves rebelled and expelled their French overlords, inflicting a severe blow to the French financial system.[2]

Napoleon Bonaparte seized control of France in 1799. To help revive France's economy, in 1802 he sent troops to Haiti to regain control, reinstall sugar production, and with it—slavery. A combination of Haitian armed resistance and swarms of mosquitoes bringing yellow fever decimated the French army.[3]

Napoleon had concluded a secret deal with Spain to return New Orleans and the Louisiana Territory to France. The United States found out about the deal and wanted to buy New Orleans. Knowing he could not control Haiti and realizing Louisiana was an economic drain to France, Napoleon offered to sell the United States not only New Orleans but the entire territory, encompassing more than 827,000 square miles. After intense negotiations, the United States bought the Louisiana Territory for fifteen million dollars in 1803.[4]

President Thomas Jefferson commissioned a military expedition named the Corps of Discovery to find out what the country had bought. Its mission was to proceed up the Missouri River to its source and find a passage to the Pacific Ocean that might be useful to promote trade with China. The corps was to inform the local inhabitants they were now part of the United States and that the United States desired peace. Lewis and Clark were to record their actions and determine prospects for trade, as well as take notes on the people and their customs and scientific observations of flora, fauna, natural resources, and topography. Jefferson placed Meriwether Lewis in command, and Lewis selected William Clark to be second in command. However, Lewis treated Clark as co-leader.[5]

France officially transferred the Louisiana Territory to the United States on March 10, 1804, and the expedition began its journey up the Missouri River on May 14. They initially started out with forty-two men, their numbers fluctuating over the course of the expedition.[6]

On October 25, 1804, after 164 days and 1,510 miles, the Corps of Discovery reached the Mandan and Hidatsa villages where the Knife River enters the Missouri in present-day North Dakota. The Mandan and Hidatsa villages were the major trading center on the Northern Plains. Their combined populations were estimated at thirty-five hundred people. Many tribes came there to trade for everything and anything—corn, horses, buffalo robes, and white-man manufactured goods, including guns. The Hudson Bay Company and the North West Company as well as independent traders out of Canada visited the villages.[7]

Lewis and Clark planned to winter over here and began building Fort Mandan downstream and across the Missouri River from the villages. On November 4, a French-Canadian independent trader, Toussaint Charbonneau, paid Lewis and Clark a visit as the men were working on the fort and its cabins. Lewis and Clark needed an interpreter who could speak Hidatsa, and Charbonneau could do so. Accompanying

Charbonneau were his two wives, both of whom belonged to the Shoshone tribe. One of these women was Sacagawea. This was good fortune for the Corps of Discovery. Clark wrote in his journal that day, "We engau [sic] him [Charbonneau] to go on with us and take one of his wives to interpret the Snake [Shoshone] language."[8]

Toussaint Charbonneau was born about 1758 in Montreal, Canada. As a young man, he worked for the North West Company trading with Indian tribes and later branched out on his own as an independent trader. Charbonneau was one of the first white traders in the Knife River villages.[9]

Charbonneau's two wives were members of the Shoshone tribe. The Shoshones, sometimes known as the Snake Indians, called themselves *Newe*, "the People." They were divided into three major groups. Charbonneau's two wives were members of the Northern Shoshones whose territory was roughly present-day western Idaho. The Northern Shoshones hunted, fished, and gathered plants and vegetables for food. They had horses and traveled east to the plains to hunt buffalo.[10]

About four years before the Corps of Discovery reached the Knife River villages, Hidatsa raiders had captured Sacagawea and the other Shoshone girl at Three Forks on the Missouri River in present-day Montana. Charbonneau acquired the two girls from their captors, and they became his wives. When Charbonneau agreed to sign on as interpreter with the Corps of Discovery, he chose to take Sacagawea with him. At the time, she was about fifteen years old and six months pregnant.[11]

Lewis and Clark had learned the Shoshones had horses, and acquiring horses from them would be important for the Corps of Discovery in its journey from the headwaters of the Missouri River to the Pacific coast. They believed it was fortunate to have Sacagawea along to assist in communicating with the Shoshones.[12]

On November 20, Charbonneau and his wives relocated to the fort and erected their dwelling about sixty yards outside its walls. Lewis and Clark also hired the free trader René Jessaume, of French and Indian descent, to translate Mandan for them while they stayed at Fort Mandan.[13]

Translations were cumbersome for the Corps of Discovery. British fur trader Charles MacKenzie visited Fort Mandan and wrote in his journal, "Sacagawea spoke a little Hidatsa in which she had to converse with her husband who was a Canadian and did not understand English. [René Jessaume] who spoke bad French and worse English, served as interpreter to the Captains, so that a single word to be understood by the party required to pass from the natives to the woman, from the woman to the husband, from the husband to [Jessaume, from Jessaume] to the Captains."[14]

On February 11, 1805, Sacagawea gave birth to a baby boy, whom they named Jean Baptiste after Toussaint's father. This was Sacagawea's first child, and according to Lewis "her labour [sic] was tedious and the pain violent." To ease the pain, Jessaume made her drink a concoction of dried crushed rattlesnake rattles mixed with water that seemed to ease the pain, and the baby was delivered ten minutes after she drank the potion. Clark later gave the baby the nickname "Pomp" or "Pompy."[15]

On April 7, the thirty-one men, one woman, and one child of the Corps of Discovery proceeded into the unknown, up the Missouri River in two pirogues and six canoes.[16] Sacagawea along with her infant son participated in all the adventures and trials the men of the Corps of Discovery experienced on their journey to the Pacific Ocean and back.

Lewis and Clark had bought a tepee for their use, and throughout the trip, the people who slept in the tepee were Lewis, Clark, the interpreter George Drouillard,[17] Charbonneau, Sacagawea, and little Pomp. Throughout the trip, this group would set up camp together.[18]

On April 9, Lewis wrote that when they stopped for dinner, Sacagawea took a stick and prodded the earth around driftwood and found large caches of roots that mice had stashed underground. Lewis said the roots tasted like Jerusalem artichokes.[19]

The Corps of Discovery had not been on the river too many days when trouble hit. On April 13, they were near the mouth of the Little Missouri River. The sails were set, and Charbonneau was at the helm of the white pirogue, the most stable of the two. On board were nonswimmers, Sacagawea, and the baby as well as Lewis and Clark's most important instruments and papers. A sudden squall struck, blowing the pirogue sideways. Charbonneau panicked and steered the wrong way, bringing the boat broadside to the wind. Lewis instantly ordered the sails brought in and Drouillard to take the helm. The men quickly acted, averting disaster. Lewis believed if they had capsized, the nonswimmers, Sacagawea, and the baby "would most probably have perished, as the waves were high, and the perogue [sic] upwards of 200 yards from the nearest shore."[20]

Clark was in the habit of hiking along the riverbank and from time to time invited Charbonneau and Sacagawea to join him.[21]

It was toward evening on May 14. Lewis and Clark were both together on the riverbank. The white pirogue was out in the river sailing about three hundred yards distant from them. Charbonneau was again steering the boat when a sudden squall hit. Charbonneau turned the boat into the wind so the sails violently luffed, ripping the square sail rope out of the hands of the man in charge of it. The wind hit the sail, blowing the boat over on its side, swamping it. Charbonneau let go the tiller, crying to God for mercy. Pierre Cruzatte, who was in the bow, shouted at Charbonneau to take hold the tiller and control the boat or he would shoot him. Charbonneau settled down and did as he was told. The men quickly hauled the sails from the water and righted the boat. The water in the boat was within an inch from the top of the gunwale. Cruzatte ordered the two nonswimmers to bail while he and two other men rowed the boat to the nearest shore. During all this turmoil, Sacagawea calmly held onto Pomp in his basket while retrieving important items floating away from the boat. Lewis wrote about Sacagawea, "The Indian woman to whom I ascribe equal fortitude and resolution, with any person onboard at the time of the accedent [sic], caught and preserved most of the light articles which were washed overboard." In honor of Sacagawea's dedication to saving their items from being lost during the accident, Lewis and Clark later named a river after her.[22]

Sacagawea survived additional mishaps. During the night of May 17, an overhanging tree caught on fire and almost burned down their tent while she and the others were sleeping inside. From June 10 through June 20, she became very ill with a pelvic inflammation. Clark and Lewis tried various remedies on her. Clark blamed Charbonneau, writing, "If She dies it will be the fault of her husband." However, by June 20, she had recovered. On June 29, while accompanying Clark on one of his hikes away from the river, Charbonneau, Sacagawea, who was carrying Pomp, and Clark just barely escaped being swept away in a flash flood.[23]

By July 27, the Corps of Discovery reached Three Forks where the Jefferson, Madison, and Gallatin Rivers join together to form the Missouri. They had entered country Sacagawea recognized. It was here five years earlier that a Hidatsa war party had attacked the Shoshone party Sacagawea was with. She and other women tried to escape but were captured three miles upriver and taken away.[24]

Lewis and Clark were hoping they would be able to acquire horses from the Shoshones to help in their crossing of the mountains. On August 9, Lewis, Drouillard, and two other men headed out from the main party to find the Shoshones. On August 12, they crossed over Lemhi Pass in the Beaverhead Mountains, the continental divide and boundary between present-day Montana and Idaho. On their descent of the western slopes, they met Shoshone women who guided them to their village where they received a friendly reception by their leader, Cameahwait. Lewis convinced Cameahwait and fifteen other Shoshone men and women to come with him and meet the others of his party now on the Jefferson River.[25]

Lewis, Cameahwait, and their party reached the location on the river where they were to rendezvous with Clark and the rest of the Corps of Discovery, but they were not there. The next morning, Saturday, August 17, Lewis sent Drouillard and a Shoshone warrior riding downriver to find Clark and his party. Other warriors joined them in their quest, but they did not have far to go.[26]

Clark, Charbonneau, and Sacagawea carrying Pomp were walking upriver ahead of the boats. Charbonneau and Sacagawea were a hundred yards ahead of Clark when he saw Sacagawea "begin to dance and show every mark of the most extravagant joy, turning round him [Charbonneau] and pointing to several Indians." They were Drouillard and Sacagawea's fellow Shoshones.[27]

Clark, Charbonneau, and Sacagawea walked toward the rendezvous location. The Shoshones who accompanied them "sang aloud with the greatest appearance of delight." As the party reached the camp, a woman broke from the crowd when she and Sacagawea recognized each other. The two women "embraced with the most tender affection." They had been childhood friends and were separated when the Hidatsa war party had attacked and captured Sacagawea.[28]

While Sacagawea caught up with her friends, Lewis introduced Clark to Cameahwait. They sat in a tent where the Shoshones performed welcoming ceremonies and then the smoking of the pipe, after which Sacagawea was called to help with translating.[29]

Sacagawea entered the tent and sat down. As she started to translate, she recognized Cameahwait. He was her brother. She jumped up and embraced him. Weeping uncontrollably, she threw her blanket over him. Cameahwait, too, was moved but tried to show less emotion in front of the white strangers. They conversed and then Sacagawea returned to her seat where she resumed her interpretations, but her tear-filled emotions would overwhelm her throughout the process.[30]

After the meeting, Cameahwait informed her of their family's situation. All were dead except for him and a brother as well as a small nephew who was the son of their eldest sister. Sacagawea immediately adopted the boy.[31] None of the journals make mention of Sacagawea's nephew, so he must have been left with the Shoshones as it would have been a huge responsibility to take another child along on the expedition.

The meeting later resumed. Conversation was cumbersome. A Shoshone would speak, Sacagawea would translate to Charbonneau in Hidatsa, Charbonneau would translate to Francois Labiche in French, and then Labiche would translate to Lewis and Clark in English. When Lewis and Clark spoke, the process was reversed. It took time to converse, and there was plenty of room for misunderstandings to occur.[32]

A potentially disruptive issue arose in Cameahwait's village. Before Sacagawea was captured, she had been betrothed to a man twice her age. The man, who currently had two wives, was living in the village and now claimed Sacagawea belonged to him. However, he decided he did not want her when he learned Sacagawea had a child by another man.[33]

While they spent their time with the Shoshones to prepare for the next leg of their journey, Sacagawea and Charbonneau assisted Lewis in learning and recording Shoshone lore and customs. However, Lewis and Clark's main concern was bartering for horses and learning the best route through the mountains to the Columbia River. By August 29, through Sacagawea's assistance and Charbonneau's translations, the Corps of Discovery had acquired twenty-nine horses but at high prices.[34]

On September 1, 1805, led by a Shoshone guide Lewis and Clark nicknamed Old Toby, the Corps of Discovery members rode their newly acquired horses into the rugged western mountains on the next leg of their journey.[35]

After much hardship and the death of seven horses, the Corps of Discovery entered Ross' Hole in modern-day Ravalli County, Montana, where they met the Salish people, whom they referred to as Flathead Indians. Fortunately, a Shoshone boy, who could speak the Salish language, was living with them, and was added to the translator communication chain. The Salish owned five hundred horses, and Lewis and Clark were able to trade for more horses. When the Corps of Discovery continued their journey following the Bitterroot River on September 6, they had thirty-nine horses, one mule, and three colts. Using the Lolo Trail, it took them three weeks to cross over the Bitterroot Range. Sergeant Patrick Gass called them "the most terrible mountains I ever beheld."[36]

On Sept 20, Clark and a party of hunters were well in advance of the rest of the Corps of Discovery when they reached their first Nez Perce Indian camp. No one knew the Nez Perce language; however, Drouillard was able to communicate using sign language. They made two thirty-five-foot-long canoes out of cottonwood trees, and on October 7, 1805, leaving their horses in the care of the Nez Perce, they began paddling down the Clearwater River, reaching its confluence with the Snake River on October 10.[37]

Even though Sacagawea did not know the Nez Perce language or any of the northwest coast tribe languages, Clark believed the villagers they encountered along the way were peaceful since "the wife of Shabono [Charbonneau] our interpetr [sic] we find reconsiles [sic] all the Indians, as to our friendly intentions, a woman with a party of men is a token of peace."[38]

On October 16, the Corps of Discovery reached the Columbia River and began paddling downriver. There were times when they had to make difficult decisions to portage along treacherous rapids or run them. When they came upon Indian villages, they stopped, informing the inhabitants they were now part of the United States, distributing gifts, and making a record of the tribes. More and more they were finding the people they encountered had white-man goods from trading with sailing vessels. As they got closer to the coast, the Columbia widened, and they experienced fog setting in from the ocean.[39]

On November 7, they had their first sight of the Pacific Ocean, Clark writing in his journal, "Ocian in view! O! the joy." They were equally excited to hear the roar of breakers hitting the shore. However, they were not at the ocean proper; they were at the Columbia River estuary. On November 17, Lewis led a small party ahead to Cape Disappointment to see the Pacific Ocean, then on November 18, Clark led a second party to the same spot. Clark's group included Charbonneau but not Sacagawea.[40]

On November 24, the Corps of Discovery needed to determine where to build their winter camp. Lewis and Clark decided to let everyone vote on where to spend the winter. The choices were to stay where they were on the north shore of the Columbia River estuary where there was plenty of deer, move to the south shore where they were told there was plenty of elk, or move upriver to the falls and be in position to begin their return trip as soon as the snow in the mountain passes melted. It was a momentous vote, not on what was voted, but who voted—everyone, including Clark's slave York and Sacagawea, who specified the location should have plenty of wapato, a plant with an edible root.[41]

The vote was to cross to the south shore. They found a good location on what is today the Lewis and Clark River about three miles upriver from its mouth. On December 7, the entire Corps of Discovery reached the site of what would be named Fort Clatsop after a neighboring tribe, and they began chopping down trees and preparing for its construction. By December 23, the men were still working on the fort, but enough was completed that they could move into their unfinished cabins. Charbonneau and Sacagawea with little Pomp had their own room, one of four in one of two large structures within the palisade.[42]

As part of their Christmas festivities, the Corps of Discovery members gave each other presents. Sacagawea gave Clark a Shoshone cloak she had made out of two dozen white weasel tails.[43]

The Clatsops told Lewis and Clark of a large whale washed up on shore near what is today called Tillamook Head. Clark put together a twelve-man party to go with him to the whale and bring back blubber and oil. Charbonneau and Sacagawea were not included in the party. Sacagawea was upset they were not going. She told Clark she had traveled all this way with them and had not yet seen the ocean. She wanted to be included in the party to see the ocean and the whale. Clark agreed to include Charbonneau, Sacagawea, and their son.[44]

Clark's party left on January 6, 1806, in two canoes, but high winds from the northwest were so bad they put into shore and hiked cross-country to the coastline. On January 8, they reached the whale, or what was left of it. Tillamook Indians had stripped the flesh from the whale and were in the process of boiling blubber when Clark's party arrived. They measured the length of the skeleton to be 105 feet. Clark was able to buy three hundred pounds of blubber and a few gallons of oil, but at high prices.[45] No one recorded what Sacagawea thought of her first sight of the expanse of the Pacific Ocean, the rugged coastline, or the whale skeleton.

The Corps of Discovery prepared to retrace their trip back up the rivers, across the mountains to the Missouri River tributaries, and then back to St. Louis. On March 23, 1806, they piled into their canoes and paddled eastward up the Columbia River.[46]

Their only means of interaction with the river tribes was sign language, and they were experiencing communication problems along the way until April 28 when they encountered the Walla Walla tribe. Sacagawea discovered the Walla Wallas were holding a fellow Shoshone woman captive, and through her they were able to communicate with the Walla Walla people.[47]

On May 4, they met their first band of Nez Perce Indians. When they reached a village near the confluence of the Snake and Clearwater Rivers, the Nez Perce there held a male Shoshone captive who they used as part of the communication link through Sacagawea to Lewis and Clark. The Nez Perce informed them a large amount of snow had fallen in the Bitterroot Mountains making them impassible until June. The Corps of Discovery would have to wait on the western side until snowmelt occurred.[48]

Sacagawea and Charbonneau had other worries. Their son, Jean Baptiste, was very sick with diarrhea, a high fever, and a swollen neck and throat. Lewis tried a variety of remedies on him. Some days it appeared he was getting better; other days he was worse. Both Lewis and Clark wrote in their journals they were worried Pomp was going to die, but by May 22, he was returning to good health.[49]

On June 10, 1806, the Corps of Discovery set out to cross the Bitterroots. However, deep snow forced them to turn back. On June 24, they made the attempt again and this time succeeded, crossing to their old camp, Traveler's Rest, near present-day Missoula, Montana, in six days.[50]

Lewis and Clark had made the decision to split their command to explore more territory. On July 6, Lewis and most of the Corps of Discovery headed north to recover their cached supplies and pirogues as well as explore the Marias River, return to the Missouri, and continue downriver to its juncture with the Yellowstone River. Clark, with nine men along with Carbonneau and his family, would proceed downriver along the Yellowstone where they would meet the rest of the Corps of Discovery at its confluence with the Missouri.[51]

Clark planned to head north and cross at Flathead Pass to reach the Yellowstone, but Sacagawea persuaded him to go by way of the southerly Bozeman Pass, cutting the distance and saving time. Clark wrote, "[Sacagawea has] been of great Service to me as a pilot through this Country."[52]

It wasn't an easy journey for Clark's party. They were beset by accidents and injuries. Indians stole their horses, which were never to be recovered, so they built canoes to continue their journey.[53]

On July 25, 1806, downriver from present-day Billings, Montana, they stopped and explored two-hundred-foot-high sandstone cliffs where Clark carved his name and date. He named the formation Pompy's Tower after little Jean Baptiste Charbonneau. The name was later modified to Pompey's Pillar.[54]

They reached the Missouri River on August 7. The mosquitoes were so bad that Clark's party did not wait for Lewis and the rest of the Corps of Discovery but left them a note at their prearranged meeting location and continued down the Missouri River. Lewis caught up with them on August 12, in present-day Mountrail County, North Dakota.[55]

On August 14, 1806, the Corps of Discovery reached the Mandan and Hidatsa villages at the Knife River. "Those people were extreamly

[sic] pleased to See us," Clark wrote. Charbonneau, Sacagawea, and little Pomp were home, ending their adventures with the expedition.[56]

As the Corps of Discovery prepared to embark downriver on August 17, Clark paid Charbonneau $500.33⅓ for his horse, tepee, and services. Lewis and Clark also gave him their bellows and blacksmith tools. Clark was very fond of little Pomp and offered to take him along to St. Louis and raise him as his own son. Charbonneau and Sacagawea said they would bring him to Clark when he was older.[57]

Clark wrote a letter to Charbonneau, stating, "Your woman who accompanied you that long dangerous and fatigueing rout [sic] to the Pacific Ocian [sic] and back diserved [sic] a greater reward for her attention and services on that rout than we had in our power to give her."[58]

SACAGAWEA LIVED TO A RIPE OLD AGE WITH THE SHOSHONES—BILL MARKLEY

Many believe Sacagawea eventually returned to her people, the Shoshones, and lived to a ripe old age at Fort Washakie on the Wind River Reservation in Wyoming.

After the Corps of Discovery returned in 1806 to the Hidatsa and Mandan villages on the Knife River in what is now North Dakota, Toussaint Charbonneau and his wife Sacagawea, along with their son Jean Baptiste, would have rejoined Charbonneau's second wife, Otter Woman, at their home in the Hidatsa village. Otter Woman was also Shoshone and about the same age as Sacagawea. She had been captured along with Sacagawea, and Charbonneau had acquired her at the same time as Sacagawea, eventually making both his wives.

There is no record exactly when, but Charbonneau with at least Sacagawea and Jean Baptiste arrived in St. Louis where Clark gave them assistance. The first record of the Charbonneaus in St. Louis is on December 28, 1809, when a Catholic priest baptized Jean Baptiste.[59]

In the Spring of 1811, Charbonneau and Sacagawea returned up the Missouri River onboard Manuel Lisa's keelboat, leaving Jean Baptiste behind in St. Louis to be raised by William Clark. Manuel Lisa, one of the principal partners in the St. Louis Missouri Fur Company, had hired Charbonneau as an interpreter. Lisa had also hired a Pittsburgh lawyer, Henry Marie Brackenridge, to act as a hunter. Brackenridge was a fellow passenger aboard the keelboat. Concerning Sacagawea, he wrote in his journal on April 2, 1811, "She had become sickly and longed to revisit her native country."[60]

Lisa's party was on its way to his trading post, Fort Mandan, which he had built in 1809, ten miles upriver from the Hidatsa and Mandan villages. They arrived at the fort on June 26, 1811.[61]

With the outbreak of war between Great Britain and the United States in June 1812, many tribes sided with the British, making it unsafe for American fur traders. Abandoning his Hidatsa and Mandan trading post, Lisa built a new one, Fort Manuel Lisa, in 1812, on the west bank of the Missouri River north of the Grand River in present-day South Dakota.[62]

Lisa again employed Charbonneau at his new fort. On December 20, 1812, John Luttig, working as a clerk at the fort, wrote in his journal, "This Evening the Wife of Charbonneau a Snake Squaw died of a putrid fever she was a good and the best Woman in the fort, aged about 25 years she left a fine infant girl."[63]

Luttig did not name Sacagawea. The "Wife of Charbonneau" could just as equally have been Otter Woman. Historians have not found any written recording of what happened to Otter Woman.

On the cover of an account book for the years 1825 to 1828, William Clark wrote a list of the Corps of Discovery members and whether they were dead or alive. Beside "Se car ja we au" he wrote "Dead."[64] Could William Clark have been wrong? Yes. Where did he get his information? If someone told him the "Wife of Charbonneau" was dead, he could have assumed it was Sacagawea who had died and not Otter Woman.

Similar mistakes had been made. A mistake was made that Charbonneau was dead. While Fort Manuel Lisa was still in operation, the Hidatsas and Mandans had wanted to continue trade with the St. Louis Missouri Fur Company, so Manuel Lisa sent Charbonneau up the river to trade. John Luttig wrote in his Fort Manuel Lisa journal, "Monday the 1st of March, 1813 clear and cold, after dinner Charbonneau and Leclair set off for their Stations at the Bigbellies [Hidatsa] took some Powder and Ball to complete his Equipment, they were escorted by 5 of our Men, untill [sic] he would be out of Danger, at Sunset it began to Snow."[65]

Two days later Luttig wrote, "Wednesday the 3d, clear and cold, . . . at noon 7 Rees arrived from above, as also our party which had escorted Charbonneau, with Latour, Machecou, Duroche, and Laderoute 2 Squaws and 3 Children."[66]

On March 5, 1813, Indians attacked Fort Manuel Lisa, killing fifteen men. Lisa and the survivors abandoned the fort and headed downriver where he constructed a new fort before returning to St. Louis. Lisa and his men must not have heard from Charbonneau or had received information that he was dead. On August 13, 1813, a St. Louis orphan's court document was signed appointing John C. Luttig, whose name was crossed out and written above it William Clark, "guardian of the infant children of Tousant Charbonneau deceased to wit: Tousant Charbonneau, a boy about the age of ten years; and Lizette Charbonneau, a girl about one year old." Their father, Charbonneau, turned up later very much alive.[67]

Jean Baptiste Charbonneau was Sacagawea's first child and was eight years old at the time of the orphan's court document. Jean Baptiste was already under the care of William Clark in St. Louis. The "Wife of Charbonneau" who died at Fort Manuel Lisa was the mother of Lizette. So, who was the mother of the ten-year-old boy, Toussaint Charbonneau? Is it not possible Toussaint and Lizette were the children of Otter Woman and it was she who died at Fort Manuel Lisa and not Sacagawea?

Dr. Grace Raymond Hebard spent years researching Sacagawea's life and believed it was Otter Woman and not Sacagawea who died at Fort Manuel Lisa in 1812. Dr. Hebard was a respected professor of political economy and western history as well as librarian and trustee at the University of Wyoming.[68]

In 1907, Dr. Hebard presented her findings in the *Journal of American History* in her article "Woman Who Led the Way to the Golden West: Pilot of the First White Men to Cross America." Hebard believed Sacagawea had returned to the Shoshone tribe and was buried at Fort Washakie on the Wind River Reservation, Wyoming, in 1884.[69]

Dr. Hebard's finding created quite a stir among historians. In 1924, the Commissioner of Indian Affairs asked Dr. Charles Eastman to investigate whether Sacagawea died in 1812 at Fort Manuel Lisa or in 1884 at Fort Washakie. Dr. Eastman, a well-known Santee Dakota physician and author, reviewed documents and conducted interviews with Indians and whites. He concluded Sacagawea was buried at Fort Washakie on the Wind River Reservation.[70]

In 1933, Dr. Hebard expanded on Eastman's and her findings in her book *Sacajawea: A Guide and Interpreter of the Lewis and Clark Expedition, with an Account of the Travels of Toussaint Charbonneau, and of Jean Baptiste, The Expedition Papoose.* Hebard's account of what happened to Sacagawea follows below.

When William Clark left Charbonneau and his family at the Knife River villages in August 1806, he had left Charbonneau and his family a standing invitation to come to St. Louis. At some point during the years 1807 to 1808, Charbonneau took Clark up on his invitation, arriving in St. Louis with his wife Sacagawea and her son Jean Baptiste as well as his wife Otter Woman and her son Toussaint.[71]

At first, Charbonneau possibly worked for a fur trading company in territory inhabited by Comanches as well as other tribes in present-day Arkansas. On October 30, 1810, he bought land from William Clark, but soon decided to sell it back to Clark on March 26, 1811. He embarked on Manuel Lisa's keelboat for the Mandan and Hidatsa villages and that is where Henry Brackenridge wrote about Charbonneau and his wife in his April 2 journal entry.[72]

Brackenridge wrote Charbonneau's wife had "accompanied Lewis and Clark to the Pacific," which indicates she was Sacagawea, but Dr. Hebard wrote that Brackenridge was mistaken, that Charbonneau's wife was Otter Woman and Sacagawea had remained with Clark in St. Louis to care for both Jean Baptiste and Toussaint. The reason for this was Jean Baptiste was six years old and too young to be left in St. Louis without his mother's care.[73]

Eastman reported that when he interviewed Wolfe, Chief of the Hidatsas, and a Mrs. Weidemann, they both stated Charbonneau had three wives, a Mandan wife and two Shoshone wives. When he left the Knife River villages for St. Louis, he took the two Shoshone wives with him and when he returned, it was with only one Shoshone wife, who died on December 20, 1812.[74]

When it was wrongly feared Charbonneau was dead in 1813, only Lizette and Toussaint needed to be provided guardianship as Sacagawea was still alive in St. Louis, and Jean Baptiste was under her care.[75]

In July 1816, Auguste Chouteau hired Charbonneau to trade with the Indian tribes along the Arkansas and Platte Rivers. By 1820, Charbonneau also had with him a Hidatsa wife, Eagle Woman. Charbonneau continued working at various jobs, trading, guiding, and interpreting, taking his wives and two sons with him.[76]

On one of his trading expeditions, Charbonneau and his family were somewhere in present-day western Oklahoma and Kansas. Charbonneau decided to take another wife, marrying a young Ute girl. She and Sacagawea did not get along. Both Jean Baptiste and Toussaint were away from Charbonneau's camp when Sacagawea and the new wife entered into a dispute, with Sacagawea emerging as the winner. Charbonneau found out and whipped Sacagawea in front of the new wife. Humiliated, Sacagawea left Charbonneau for good. When his two sons returned to camp, they learned what their father had done. They too left him and never had anything to do with him again.[77]

Sacagawea eventually joined a Comanche band. The Comanches and Shoshones are kindred people with similar traditions and language so Sacagawea could communicate with them and fit in. The Comanches originated in modern-day Wyoming. In the early nineteenth century, their territory had expanded to the southern plains but still extended up into Wyoming's Wind River area, abutting Shoshone territory.[78]

Sacagawea married a Comanche with a name in English meaning Jerk Meat. Together they had five children, but only a son named Ticannaf and the youngest, a daughter named Yaga-wosier (Crying Basket), survived. Jerk Meat was killed in battle, and after that, his family made life so difficult for Sacagawea that she told the band she was leaving to find her own people.[79]

No one believed she would actually leave, but she did, taking Yaga-wosier with her. The band looked for her in vain. She became known as Wadze-wipe, Lost Woman.[80]

It's possible she reached the Shoshones in the early 1840s when the tribe was under the leadership of Washakie. Accounts say that she arrived with two adopted daughters and several horses.[81]

Among the Shoshones she found her son Jean Baptiste, who would come and go over the years, and her nephew she had adopted back in 1805 when she met her brother Cameahwait and learned her older sister had died. Her adopted son, Shoo-gan, was called Bazil by the whites. He was a sub-chief under Washakie and was related to him. Bazil was interested in agriculture and learned irrigation and other farming techniques from Mormon farmers who settled around Fort Bridger. By 1856, he was raising wheat and vegetables.[82]

Sacagawea was at the 1868 Fort Bridger council where the Shoshones signed a treaty with the US government. Working through Bazil, Sacagawea had great influence with the Shoshones. She sat with the women where she gave a short speech. Dr. Hebard wrote, "For it is certainly evident that Sacajawea proved of the greatest value to the whites through her influence with her own people. She was able to understand the white man's point of view and present this to the Indians, at the same time successfully interpreting the Indian's point of view to the whites. Her own people respected her council, and the whites valued her understanding and influence."[83]

In 1871, Sacagawea went with her people to live in the Wind River Valley, which was within the Wind River Reservation where she lived until her death in 1884. According to F. G. Burnett, a federal government agricultural agent, "Sacajawea was of the greatest help to the Indian agents.... Sacajawea and Bazil, both able to speak English and Shoshone, were of invaluable service as interpreters to the agent during a long and important period of this reservation life."[84]

Many white people attested that the Sacagawea of Lewis and Clark's expedition and the Sacagawea of the Wind River Reservation were the same person. One of those was Charles William Bocker, an early Wyoming pioneer. Bocker wrote that he worked at Fort Bridger off and on starting in 1865. Sacagawea spent time at Fort Bridger, and one day Judge W. A. Carter introduced Bocker to Sacagawea, whom he judged to be about seventy years old at the time. He said she was good-looking for her age, could ride horses with the best of them, and could speak a little English. "At this time one of the Carters or Mr. [Dick] Hamilton spoke to me about this Indian woman having been on an expedition with the white men. . . . Everybody all around everywhere knew it, and it was common talk. [Jim] Bridger knew it, Carter knew it, Hamilton knew it, the white man knew it, the Indians knew it."[85]

James I. Patten, a teacher at Wind River Reservation, knew Sacagawea and had conversations with her. She told him about being a part of Lewis and Clark's expedition. In written testimony Patten stated, "I had read one of the publications of the Lewis and Clark expedition, and was entirely convinced from their description of the Shoshone Indian woman guide whom they called Sacajawea in the journals or in the book which I read, that the Sacajawea of the reservation and the Indian guide of the expedition were one and the same person."[86]

Many Shoshones attested that the Sacagawea of Lewis and Clark's expedition and the Sacagawea of the Wind River Reservation were the same person. James McAdams was a member of the Shoshone tribe and great-grandson of Sacagawea. She told him she had gone with white soldiers to the Pacific Ocean and that he had relatives with the Comanches. McAdams lived with Sacagawea from the age of six until 1881, when he was sent to the Carlisle Indian School in Pennsylvania. While he was there, he talked with fellow students who were Comanches. He related that his great-grandmother had said he had relatives with the Comanches. Together they figured out that Sacagawea was the person the Comanches knew as Lost Woman.[87]

Sacagawea died in April 1884. Reverend John Roberts with the Episcopal Church at the Wind River Indian Reservation conducted Sacagawea's burial service on April 9, 1884. In the parish records he listed her as Bazil's mother and that she was one hundred years old. In 1909, Reverend Roberts identified Sacagawea's gravesite at the Fort Washakie cemetery where a cement marker was erected at her grave.[88]

Today, many Shoshone graves surround Sacagawea's grave maker in Sacajawea Cemetery outside of Fort Washakie, on the Wind River Reservation in Wyoming. The inscription on her plaque reads:

SACAJAWEA
DIED APRIL 9, 1884
A GUIDE WITH THE
LEWIS AND CLARK
EXPEDITION
1805–1806
IDENTIFIED, 1907 BY
REV. J. ROBERTS
WHO OFFICIATED AT
HER BURIAL

THE DEATH OF 1812—KELLEN CUTSFORTH

It is quite accurate to say that little, if anything, is known about Sacagawea before her encounters with famed explorers Meriwether Lewis and William Clark. However, there do exist some scraps of information pertaining to her early beginnings. Sacagawea was a Lemhi Shoshone woman believed to have been born in 1788. Around twelve years of age, she was kidnapped, along with many other Shoshone girls, by Hidatsa Indian raiders. During this raid, several Shoshone men, women, and young boys died.[89]

At the young age of thirteen, Sacagawea was sold by the Hidatsas to a French-Canadian trapper from Quebec named Toussaint Charbonneau. This Frenchman had been living in the Hidatsa village for a time and had numerous dealings with the Indians. Before Charbonneau purchased Sacagawea, he bought another kidnapped Shoshone girl from the Hidatsa who is referred to as Otter Woman, though no one knows her real identity.[90]

Otter Woman is believed to have been born in 1786 or 1788. She was originally the wife of a Shoshone man named Smoked Lodge. Most likely, though it is not confirmed, Otter Woman was abducted by the Hidatsa as well, somewhere around the end of the eighteenth century. Following this event, Otter Woman was sold and forced into a nonconsensual marriage with Toussaint Charbonneau. Unlike Sacagawea, however, Otter Woman did not accompany the Corps of Discovery on the expedition that included explorers Meriwether Lewis and William Clark.[91]

Though there is little left on the historic record concerning Sacagawea's life after she acted as a guide for the Corps of Discovery, much speculation and controversy has arisen over her death. Unfortunately for those who would say otherwise, there is ample evidence that the most well-known Indian guide in American history died from a brutal illness in 1812.

All the storm swirling around Sacagawea's death stems directly from a Wyoming historian named Grace Raymond Hebard and an article she wrote for a 1907 issue of the *Journal of American History*. Within the article, Hebard theorized that Sacagawea did not perish in 1812 but survived for more than seventy years, eventually dying from extreme old age on April 9, 1884, while residing at the Wind River Indian Reservation in Wyoming.[92]

When this woman—whom Hebard speculated to be Sacagawea and who was sometimes referred to as Porivo by the people at the reservation—passed, her lifeless body was found by her adopted son Bazil. The boy told Reverend John Roberts, a missionary who oversaw the funeral proceedings for Porivo, that his adoptive mother was one hundred years old. Interestingly, when Roberts entered this woman's name into the Parrish Register of Burials he referred to her simply as "Bazil's Mother," not Sacagawea. According to her writings on the subject, however, Hebard believed this Indian woman was Sacagawea.[93] Unfortunately for her, there are many problems with this hypothesis.

Consulting the few verified historic documents available relating to Sacagawea, one can begin by looking at the journal of Henry Brackenridge. Brackenridge was a fur trader living at Fort Manuel Lisa Trading Post on the Missouri River in 1811. Within his journal, he made an entry concerning Sacagawea and her husband Toussaint Charbonneau.

Brackenridge wrote, "We had on board a Frenchman named Charbonneau, with his wife, an Indian woman of the Snake nation, both of whom had accompanied Lewis and Clark to the Pacific, and were of great service. The Woman, a good creature, was of a mild and gentle disposition, greatly attached to the Whites, whose manners and dress she tries to imitate, but she had become sickly, and longed to revisit her native country; her husband, also, who had spent many years among the Indians, had become weary of civilized life."[94]

Brackenridge identified Charbonneau as having only one wife with him when they met. He also makes note that this wife was the one who accompanied Lewis and Clark on their expedition with the Corps of Discovery. It is an accepted fact that only Sacagawea was with Charbonneau and the corps, not Otter Woman. Armed with this information, it is only logical to conclude that the wife described by Brackenridge in his journal was Sacagawea. Brackenridge also detailed the state of Sacagawea's health, writing that she was "sickly," which foretells future events.

Accompanying these descriptions, Brackenridge also noted that Charbonneau's wife is a woman of the Snake nation, to which the Shoshone people were sometimes referred. It is also a fact that Sacagawea was of Shoshone heritage. Otter Woman's origins, much like her name, are still up for debate.[95]

Following this meeting a year later in 1812, John Luttig, a clerk at the Manuel Lisa Fort Trading Post, jotted down a historic entry in his journal. He wrote, "This evening the wife of Charbonneau a Snake Squaw [Shoshone woman], died of a putrid fever she was a good and the best wom[a]n in the fort, aged abt 25 years she left a fine infant girl."[96] After the writing of this journal entry, any mention of Sacagawea's death disappears from the historic record until the 1907 Hebard article.

Many historians have torn apart Hebard's conclusions regarding Sacagawea's death. These historians were suspicious at the utter lack of primary resources, like the Luttig and Brackenridge journals, backing Hebard's assertions, and the dates she gave in her writings do not align with the known facts about Sacagawea's life.

If Sacagawea did live to be one hundred years old as reported by her supposed son Bazil, that would have meant she was born in 1784, not 1788. Hebard stated that Sacagawea was five years old when she was abducted by the Hidatsa raiders. If this were true, she would have only been ten years old when her first child was born. This makes no sense.

Interestingly, Luttig's journal was not published until 1920, while Hebard's "findings" were first published in 1907. Even though Luttig's journal, an actual firsthand account by someone who knew Charbonneau and Sacagawea, contradicted her theory, Hebard continued to push the nonsensical notion that Sacagawea lived into extreme old age. She published a book in 1933 about her theory.[97]

Within the pages of Hebard's book, she quoted Brackenridge's journal, writing, "In 1811, Brackinridge [sic] states that Sacagawea and Charbonneau were seen on the Missouri river." Hebard herself admitted the woman Brackenridge identified on the Missouri River, near Fort Manuel Lisa, was indeed Sacagawea.[98] If she accepted Brackenridge's identification then she would also have to accept Sacagawea's "sickly" state. Yet, Hebard continued to insinuate Sacagawea lived on past the time John Luttig proclaimed she died. This is nothing more than an instance of picking and choosing facts while attempting to prove a desired narrative is true. Hebard's writings are a false narrative devoid of any real historic research.

Then, in 1924, Charles Eastman, a Sioux Indian, physician, and author, was hired by the Commissioner of Indian Affairs to verify Hebard's work. After some more highly questionable research, Eastman concluded Hebard was telling the truth about Sacagawea having lived well into her nineties and being buried at the Wind River Reservation. Not long after the submittal of his report, however, Eastman's own research came under the scrutiny of historians. Most of Eastman's report relied on hearsay delivered through secondhand and even thirdhand accounts of stories passed down from one elderly person to another, again, disregarding primary resources and relying more on oral traditions.[99] Eastman's report simply does not survive scrutiny. There is no factual basis for Charles Eastman's findings nor for the article Grace Hebard wrote.

Following these thought lines, Eastman's report included a transcription from teacher and Indian Agent James I. Patten on the 1877 census roll of inhabitants on the Wind River Reservation. The roll identified the woman Hebard believed to be Sacagawea simply as "Bazil's Mother." However, Patten took creative liberty interpolating "Sacajawea" next to this entry. Perhaps more damning of Eastman's report is the information he decides to leave out.

In his review of Hebard's work, Charles Eastman blatantly omitted Henry Brackenridge's identification of Charbonneau's wife on the Missouri River as the woman who accompanied Lewis, Clark, and the Corps of Discovery, disregarding her sickly condition in the process. He goes on to conclude that Charbonneau's wife who died from a "putrid fever" in Luttig's account was Otter Woman and not Sacagawea.[100] This is complete bunk, just another instance of picking and choosing facts and statements one wants so they can arrive at a desired conclusion, amounting to nothing more than a boldfaced lie.

Further information refuting the idea Sacagawea lived past her midtwenties comes from William Clark's own accounts. In the early 1950s, an artifact collector from Chicago had most of his historic materials reviewed by Dale L. Morgan of the Bancroft Library at the University of California. Morgan discovered an account book covering the years 1825 to 1828 once owned by explorer William Clark. On the cover of the account book, Clark listed the names of the members from the Corps of Discovery.[101]

Next to each name, William Clark noted whether the individual was living or dead. For Sacagawea's entry he wrote, "Se car ja we au. Dead." At this point, it is important to reiterate Clark had become the guardian of Sacagawea's little boy Pompy (little Pomp) and acted as his father. He was also a good friend of Sacagawea and would most likely have had knowledge of her life.[102] Is it so farfetched to think Sacagawea's close friend and guardian of her child would know whether she was dead or not?

Yet, conspiracy theorists persist by pointing to previous excavation attempts over the years looking to uncover a grave for Sacagawea in Fort Manuel Lisa and the surrounding areas and finding none. However, Indian ethnologists have pointed to the fact that the Hidatsas, a people with whom Sacagawea had spent a great portion of her short life, were known for placing their dead on raised platforms in the woods instead of burying them. In this circumstance, any of Sacagawea's remains would have been taken by animals or scattered to the wind.[103]

From the Brackenridge and Luttig journals to William Clark's own accounts, there are ample primary resources proving Sacagawea perished in 1812, long before the year 1884. In Hebard and Eastman's accounts of Sacagawea's death, most everything is backed by oral histories and traditions that have proven, on more than one occasion, to be completely unreliable.

Most historians, throughout their professional careers, strive to discover new information concerning significant historic individuals or events. Whether it is through the publishing of a newly discovered diary or by digging deep into census records or personal correspondence, historians are always on the lookout for a unique kernel that will give their life's work status and significance. Grace Raymond Hebard was no different. She desperately wanted to have something new to report on one of the most significant individuals in American history, but in this circumstance the facts just do not support the theory.

In fact, there is literally nothing other than Grace Raymond Hebard's musings pointing to Sacagawea's death taking place in 1884. Hebard once said about the scrutiny imposed by historians on her findings that they were viewed with "ridicule, doubt, suspicion, [and] denial."[104] Looking at how loosely she played with the facts of this case, it is little wonder most historians met her findings with scorn.

CHAPTER 3

DONNER PARTY CANNIBALISM

JUST THE FACTS

In the spring of 1846, a contingent of pioneers, with almost five hundred wagons in tow, departed from Missouri following the Oregon Trail with hopes of migrating to California.[1] A body of these migrants, who became known as the Donner Party, comprised thirty-two members of the Reed and Donner families and their employees. They were all led by George Donner, patriarch of the Donner family.[2] Soon after leaving Independence, the Donners and Reeds joined a man named William H. Russell, who was leading a group of fifty wagons overland. Along the way, the Donner, Reed, and Russell contingent was joined by several other families.[3] In all, there were over eighty migrants in the Donner wagon train heading west.

After following the train of five hundred wagons along the overland passage for a time, the Donner Party elected to take a new route referred to as the Hastings Cutoff. This alternate route was claimed by Lansford Hastings, the path's originator, to be a "worked out new and better road to California."[4] Unbeknownst to the Donner Party, the cutoff would rain down upon them a great deal of hardship before they ever reached the Sierra Nevada.[5]

The Hastings Cutoff forced the Donner Party to cross the Wasatch Mountains and the Great Salt Lake Desert in Utah. They also had to trek through present-day Nevada, where, along the path, they lost several livestock and wagons and, more importantly, time. Following proven and established routes, the normal trip leaving Missouri usually took four to six months' travel time. The Hastings route, with its wandering way and wretched terrain, slowed the Donners to a crawl and put them on course to run headlong into a cruel and bitter winter.[6]

When they eventually reached the Sierra Nevada range in early November, some of the members of the wagon train had already died in the desert and the Wasatch Mountains. These tribulations caused many of the pioneers to break into small, separate factions. Accompanying those hardships, an unexpected, heavy snowfall trapped the Donners near Truckee Lake (later renamed Donner Lake). Stuck in the high Sierras, the party began to run low on provisions for both people and animals. Eventually, the families and small groups joined the main Donner contingent.[7]

Though they attempted to forge ahead, the snow fell steadily, accumulating over four feet and making the trail nearly invisible and difficult to travel. Sixty members of the surviving families set up camp near Truckee Lake, using an abandoned cabin and building two more to ride out the winter. Farther up the trail near Alder Creek, the Donners constructed tent shelters for twenty-one people. With little to forage, the animals began to starve and freeze. As provisions ran low for the families, they turned to eating the frozen oxen and horse carcasses.[8]

So much snow fell it reached to the shelter roofs, and they had to dig entrances from the snow surface down to the shelter doors.[9] That winter, ten major snowstorms generated deep snowpacks at the Alder Creek camp (ten to twelve feet), Truckee Lake camp (fifteen to twenty feet), and what would become known as Donner Pass (more than twenty feet).[10]

Throughout the brutal winter, there were multiple attempts made to rescue the stranded pioneers. Some men from the families attempted to ride out of the mountains to find help in the towns at the foot of the Sierra Nevadas. After securing the help of some townsmen, it took until February for a small band of rescuers to make it to the separate camps. What they found was heart wrenching. Several of the pioneers had perished from starvation and the freezing cold, while the living were emaciated, malnourished, and dying from multiple ailments. After giving the people some food, the small rescue party was able to extract twenty-three of the migrants from their predicament.[11]

This group passed a second rescue party, which was ascending the mountains to try and save the remainder of the stranded emigrants, and extracted seventeen members of the doomed wagon train. A third, and final, rescue party arrived at the camp of the remaining depleted and dying pioneers. This party pulled four children from the living nightmare and carried them down the mountainside.[12]

Several adults who were too weak to make the trip out of the Sierra Nevadas were left behind. Two separate relief parties were organized to try and extract the remaining survivors, but they were turned away by harsh winter storms. In April of 1847, a salvage party assembled and made the trek to the Truckee and Alder camps. This group found a lone survivor named Lewis Keseberg. On April 29, 1847, Keseberg was the last surviving member of the Donner Party to descend the mountain. Several testimonials from survivors, newspaper stories, and historic documents have noted that some members of the Donner Party participated in cannibalism to survive.[13] Of the eighty-seven emigrants who entered the Wasatch Mountains on their way to the Sierra Nevada, only forty-eight survived. The saga of the Donner Party is seen as one of the most horrendous tragedies in American history.

EATERS OF MAN—KELLEN CUTSFORTH

The Earp brothers won the gunfight at the O.K. Corral. George Armstrong Custer and his entire Seventh Cavalry command were wiped out at the Battle of the Little Big Horn. Members of the Donner Party turned cannibalistic to endure winter in the Sierra Nevada. These have been accepted facts for over 150 years of Western history. However, recent revisionist historians have challenged the long-held notion that the Donners, and those who traveled with them, committed cannibalism to survive starvation.

It is unbelievable that the actions of the Donner Party are even under discussion or that there is any controversy surrounding them. As recently as 2010, however, "scientists" who reported on a bone analysis of remains done at the Alder Creek encampment said they found no physical evidence of cannibalism. This was interpreted by members of the press as "[there was] no Donner Party cannibalism."[14]

These researchers buoyed their theory by stating that Donner Party survivors denied cannibalism occurred and that journalists sensationalized the story to sell newspapers. The researchers in 2010 were backed by digs done in 2003 and 2004 at Alder Creek that reported no "physical evidence" of cannibalism by the Donners. Both digs did an intense examination of the bones and the site and noted that few if any had anything resembling teeth marks or gnawing or biting of the remains.[15]

The idea that there was mass denial of cannibalism by the survivors of the Donner tragedy is completely absurd. At least eight separate survivors, including the final man from the mountain, Lewis Keseberg, wrote about the cannibalism or verbally admitted they had partaken in the consumption of human flesh. Along with accounts from the survivors, members of the rescue parties noted seeing multiple signs of cannibalism, including Donner survivor Jean Baptiste Trudeau carrying a severed human leg over his shoulder when they arrived in camp.[16]

Further bolstering the reports of the Donner Party's cannibalism, on December 16, 1846, a group of seventeen men and women set out to find help amid the deteriorating situation at the multiple camps in the Sierras. Unfortunately for them, this contingent of pioneers became known as the "Forlorn Hope." Of the seventeen who set out, two turned back immediately. Only seven of the remaining fifteen survived, and, of the dead, all but one was cannibalized. All the surviving members of the Forlorn fully admitted this.[17]

Two men and the five women of the Forlorn Hope arrived at a spot known as Johnson's Ranch on January 17, 1847. They all related their stories of starvation and cannibalism, along with the desperate situation of the people camped at Truckee Lake and Alder Creek, to the settlers at the ranch. The first relief party was assembled after hearing about their horrendous ordeal. Accompanying the confessions and eyewitness accounts of the encampment's cannibalism, newspapers published the horrendous stories in early 1847.[18]

After these stories made their way to the greater public, donations began to pour in with hopes of organizing a larger relief effort. The second relief effort, composed of more rescuers, reported the same grisly findings that the first relief did. They found human bones sawed and sitting by open cooking fires. This gory scene also included the discovery of a corpse lying in one of the cabin's doorways stripped of its flesh.[19]

The second relief party found even more gruesome sights at the Alder Creek encampment. They gave detailed descriptions of unearthed graves with mutilated bodies as well as stripped and cooking human bones at the hearth. When the second rescue party departed, they took seventeen emigrants with them and left behind eleven, most of which were either too sick or emaciated to leave the encampment.[20]

The third relief group, when it arrived, found even more disturbing sights of mutilation and cannibalization of corpses. Virtually only a few hours after the rescue party arrived at the encampments, they took the four remaining children and left the rest of the emaciated, sick, and starving pioneers behind. It would not be until over a month, on April 21, 1847, when a fourth party would return to Alder and Truckee encampments. This group, however, would only be sent to try and salvage the Donner's property for their surviving children.[21]

When the salvage crew arrived, they found "human bodies terribly mutilated, legs, arms, and sculls [sic] scattered in every direction." They also found the Alder and Truckee encampments devoid of life. While packing up the salvageable goods, members of the team were shocked to find Lewis Keseberg still alive and in one of the makeshift cabins. It appeared he had subsisted the whole winter completely on human flesh.[22]

Keseberg admitted to the salvagers that he had recently consumed the corpse of Tamsen Donner, the Donner family matriarch. Keseberg also freely confessed to having boiled the flesh from the bones of several of the deceased Donner party members. After following the salvage crew down the mountainside, Keseberg was asked by a woman at Sutter's Fort what human meat tasted like, and he replied that "it was better than chicken."[23]

In the summer of 1874, Brigadier General Stephen W. Kearney and an entourage of men rode through Donner Pass and found the campsites still strewn with human wreckage. Several members of Kearney's crew testified they witnessed sawed and split skulls (apparently so the brains could be consumed) and hacked bones lying strewn about the deteriorated campgrounds. Seeing the desecration of the Donner Party member's skeletons, Kearney ordered his men to bury the remains. Following orders, the men collected as many of the bones and body parts as they could, piled them in one of the ramshackle cabins, and burned them.[24]

In the months after Kearney's visit, human souvenir hunters and animal scavengers tore through the camp and either dragged the remains away or took some of the bones and bits of skull as tokens of the tragedy. It was not until the archaeological digs of 2003 and 2004 that the fact of cannibalism was challenged. Those archaeologists found over sixteen thousand pieces of bone at the Alder Creek campsite. Most of them were too small to be examined properly.[25]

The bone fragments the archaeologists were able to get results from ended up being all animal remains. None were human in origin. This "discovery" has led skeptics to theorize there was no cannibalism at the Donner campsites, which is utterly absurd. The bones they found were mostly from the animals that the Donner Party members brought with them. The starving pioneers ate most of these animals to survive, boiling or scorching most of the bones to eat. They even boiled the oxen hides into an edible jelly-like paste.[26]

When the Donner contingent boiled, reboiled, and burned the animal bones, they became calcined. This caused the remains to lose their organic constituents and to not decompose. The human bones were treated differently than the animal bones. Because the human remains were not boiled multiple times and charred, they decomposed naturally upon burial. These facts were verified during the archaeological digs conducted in 2003 and 2004, when the researchers discovered there was no organic content in the unearthed fragments.[27]

Furthermore, in 1847 relief party member Nicholas Clark shot and killed a bear cub, which was treated similarly to the consumed human remains. When all the archaeological digs were conducted, they did not find any bear bones at the campsites. It is also reported that a dig conducted in 1984 by Donald L. Hardesty at one of the pioneers' makeshift cabins, the team found three human bone fragments. But they were so deteriorated and decomposed that evidence of cannibalism could not be found.[28]

Before the archaeological dig in 2004, historic human remains detection dogs were brought to the Donner site for a thorough inspection of the grounds. The dogs, trained to alert at the scent of human remains that can remain in the earth for centuries, signaled an alarm at several spots at the Alder Creek encampment. By intense archaeological research, one of the main areas the dogs alerted has been proven to be the hearth. This spot has been identified by historic documents and eyewitness accounts as where much of the cooking of human flesh took place.[29]

Based on all the evidence from historic records, eyewitness accounts, the alerting corpse dogs, and the 1984 discovery of human bone fragments, it is clear the Donner Party committed cannibalism. It is not the evidence that was found that is most telling, it is what the archaeologists did not find that tells the true tale. The almost near lack of human remains is most important. According to historic records, diaries kept by Donner members, and eyewitness reports, the human remains consumed at both the Truckee and Alder campsites were not boiled and reboiled then charred like the animal remains.

This means all organic matter was removed from the bones in question allowing them to remain. The human bones, however, were not treated in the same manner as the animals and disintegrated naturally, which is in concert with the reports from the survivors. This fact, coupled with the sheer admittance of cannibalism from multiple Donner Party survivors, is proof that humans ate humans. Anything else brought forth by revisionist historians is nothing more than fake news.

NOT ALL RESORTED TO CANNIBALISM—BILL MARKLEY

Yes, you have been hungry, but have you ever been starving-to-death hungry with no prospect of food in sight? Have you seen your children starving to death and there was nothing you could do?

There is no denying that cannibalism did occur during the Donner Party's ordeal. The families of the Donner Party were just regular people heading to California with hopes for a better life. However, circumstances, some they could control and others beyond their control, led to tragedy in the Sierra Nevada. Was cannibalism as widespread as some claim? No. A number of survivors did not resort to cannibalism. Let's look a little further in detail as to what happened.

On July 31, 1846, a party of emigrants led by sixty-two-year-old George Donner made its fateful decision to leave the established and relatively safe Oregon Trail at Fort Bridger in present-day Wyoming and take the new Hastings Cutoff, which was supposed to save them three hundred to four hundred miles and about a month in travel time. In reality it would add more miles and weeks to their journey. From the time the seventy-four people, many of whom were children, left Fort Bridger, they were beset by delays and troubles. Others would join them along the way, increasing their number to over eighty.[30]

They lost time and expended energy as they blazed a new trail through the Wasatch Mountains, reaching the Great Salt Lake on August 25. That evening, Luke Halloran died. Luke was a single man who had been extremely sick, so much so that his former traveling companions had left him behind. George and Tamsen Donner had pity on him and took him along with them. When they buried Luke along the Great Salt Lake, they found fifteen hundred dollars in coin in his possessions, which Luke had left to the Donners.[31]

They next had to cross the Great Salt Desert. Extreme temperatures and lack of good drinking water further stressed the people and their livestock. Thirty-six head of oxen died crossing the salt flats, and four wagons had to be abandoned along with possessions that had been hauled over thirteen hundred miles.[32]

By the time they crossed the desert, it was early September, and they could see snow had fallen in the mountains ahead. Virginia Reed later wrote they took stock of their provisions and found they did not have enough food supplies to make it all the way through the mountains to California.[33]

The Donner Party was beyond the point of no return. They did not have enough supplies to turn back and hope to survive. The Lansford Hastings Party was ahead of them somewhere on the trail and knew the Donner Party was following behind. The decision was made to press on and get as close to California as possible with the hope that those in advance would alert Californians to their plight and send help if they did not arrive.[34]

Trying to beat the weather, they pushed westward into the mountains with nineteen wagons, traveling throughout the day, through the night, and into the next day. Animals became exhausted, and some had to be left behind.[35]

They reached a meadow with water and rested. On September 11, 1846, realizing they would not be through the mountains before more snow would fall, they sent Charles Stanton and William McCutchen, riding two horses, ahead to California to bring back supplies.[36]

On September 26, the Donner Party left the Hastings Cutoff and was back on the established California Trail. The cutoff was supposed to have saved them time and miles, but in reality, it had cost them one month of time and added 125 miles to their trip.[37]

Once on the California Trail, they made good time. They had stripped down their belongings to the essentials and were traveling twenty miles a day. Two friendly Indians visited them. The emigrants thought they could trust them, but the Indians left, stealing two oxen and supplies.[38]

October 5, 1846, was a tragic day. The oxen teams of James Reed and John Snyder became entangled. A violent quarrel erupted between Reed and Snyder, ending with Snyder striking Reed several times with the butt of his bull whip and Reed driving his knife into Snyder's chest, killing him.[39]

The emigrants held a meeting to determine Reed's fate. Lewis Keseberg, a recent immigrant from Germany, wanted to hang Reed and propped up his wagon tongue from which to hang him. Keseberg held a grudge against Reed for temporarily banishing him from the wagon train. One story had it Keseberg had robbed an Indian grave along the Platte River. Another story said Reed had spoken harshly to Keseberg for beating his wife. They made the decision to exile Reed from the party and allowed him to ride ahead, westward, on his worn-out horse, taking nothing with him. The emigrants assured him they would care for his wife Margret and their four children. Margret sneaked weapons, ammunition, and food to him, and he was joined by Walter Herron, one of his teamsters. Even with Reed being able to hunt and kill a few animals, the two men would just barely be able to reach Sutter's Fort in California on October 28.[40]

After Reed had gone, the Donner Party continued westward and came upon a message Reed had left them to be on the lookout for hostile Indians. Shortly after that they found the skeleton of an emigrant who had died from an arrow wound.[41]

Indians soon began harassing them, running off horses and shooting arrows into the oxen. Some of the travelers were becoming hardened by their desperate circumstances. By October 9, the party had split in two, with the Donner and Murphy families a day ahead of the others. Lewis Keseberg, who had been hauling "old man" Hardcoop in his wagon, left him behind on the trail. A rider went back and recovered Hardcoop, but again Keseberg left him behind. Some wanted to go back and get him, but the others would not wait for them, so no one turned back to get him. No one ever saw Hardcoop again.[42]

The two groups came together on October 10, and on October 13 they reached Humboldt Sink after losing two animals along the way. Indians attacked again, killing twenty-one animals, including all of those belonging to William Eddy and Jacob Wolfinger. The people butchered the dead animals. There was no time to preserve the meat so they ate what they could, abandoned Eddy and Wolfinger's wagons, and continued on their trek, now down to fifteen wagons.[43]

Wolfinger wanted to cache his goods. Rumor had it he was wealthy and had a large amount of gold coins. Fellow Germans Augustus Spitzer and Joseph Reinhardt volunteered to stay behind and help him as the party proceeded along the trail. On October 16, Spitzer and Reinhardt rejoined the party, now following the Truckee River westward. The two men said Indians had attacked, killing Wolfinger and burning the wagons. The Donner family took care of Wolfinger's distraught wife, Doris. Some were suspicious of Spitzer and Reinhardt's story.[44]

On October 19, the travelers finally had something to celebrate. Charles Stanton arrived from Sutter's Fort in California, with seven pack mules loaded with provisions.[45] William McCutchen had become ill and remained behind. Two of Sutter's Indian vaqueros Luis and Salvador, had accompanied Stanton to help with the emigrants' rescue. They also had the additional good news that Reed and Herron had made it to Sutter's Fort.[46]

The emigrants reached Truckee Meadows, where they camped five days, resting the livestock and gearing up for their final sixty-mile push through the Sierra Nevada to California. On October 21, tragedy struck. Brothers-in-law William Pike and William Foster were sitting on a log beside each other in front of a fire. As Pike stood to get more firewood, he handed his pepperbox pistol to Foster. It accidently discharged, firing into Pike's back and killing him. Pike's wife, Harriet, was now a widow with two small children, and Foster was the only adult male in the extended twelve-member Murphy family. Snow fell in Truckee Meadows as they buried Pike.[47]

At their first evening camp after leaving Truckee Meadows, an Indian shot arrows into their cattle herd, wounding nineteen animals, until William Eddy shot him. It snowed each day as they pressed on. A Donner wagon broke an axle on October 27. As George Donner worked to replace the axle, a chisel he was using slipped and cut a major gash into the back of his hand. The Donner family lagged behind caring for George and fixing the wagon, while Patrick Breen led the rest of the party toward the mountain pass.[48]

On October 31, Breen's advance party was in sight of the pass when a major snowstorm hit. A foot of snow fell during the night as the wind blew it into drifts ten feet high. The next day, the travelers attempted to cross over the pass but had to turn back. There were several more attempts to cross, but all failed. Their only hope now was the possibility of a thaw or that a rescue effort would be launched from California.[49]

The Breen party set up camp on the eastern shore of Truckee Lake, where they improved an abandoned cabin and built two additional cabins to house roughly sixty people. The cabins were built at a distance from each other as factions had developed among party members. The camp was spread out over roughly a half mile.[50]

The Donner group, consisting of twenty-one people, was farther back down the trail when the first major storm had hit. When they learned the Breen party had turned back, the Donners established camp where they were, erecting three crude canvas and brush huts at Alder Creek, seven miles northeast of Truckee Lake.[51]

More than half of the eighty-one people trapped were under the age of eighteen, a quarter of them were under the age of five, and six were babies.[52]

Both camps sent out hunters, but game was scarce. They began slaughtering some of the oxen for food. It was now cold enough that the meat would not spoil.[53]

Exiled James Reed and Walter Herron had reached Sutter's Fort in California, where Reed began acquiring supplies and pack animals. On October 30, Reed and the now-recovered William McCutchen set out to take the much-needed food to the stranded emigrants. Unfortunately, extreme weather conditions in the mountains took a toll on their animals. The two men were eventually reduced to carrying what they could on their backs as they broke through heavy snow. Reed and McCutchen turned back when they reached shoulder-high drifts and realized they could become casualties themselves.[54]

November 12 was a clear day, and fifteen Truckee Lake Camp people tried to get through the pass, but ten-foot-deep, soft snow blocked their way, forcing them to turn back. William Eddy went out hunting on November 15 and killed a grizzly bear estimated at eight hundred pounds, which added to their food supplies.[55]

There was another long thaw. On November 21, twenty-two Lake Camp people with seven mules made it over the pass. Slogging through the deep snow exhausted them. Charles Stanton, and Sutter's Indian vaqueros Luis and Salvador, who had brought the rescue provisions, worried about the deteriorating condition of Sutter's mules and refused to go any farther, so the group returned to the cabins.[56]

Snow and rain continued to fall through November. Some of the livestock wandered off in a snowstorm, died, and were buried under snow, never to be found by the emigrants. Some of the Lake Camp people began making snowshoes for their next attempt to cross the pass, fourteen pairs all together.[57]

By mid-December, the people were getting weaker. At the Adler Creek Camp, Jacob Donner, the sixty-five-year-old brother of George, died along with Sam Shoemaker, James Smith, and Joseph Reinhardt. Reinhardt confessed on his deathbed he was involved in the death of Jacob Wolfinger at Humboldt Sink. Twenty-four-year-old Bayliss Williams was the first to die at the Lake Camp.[58]

On December 16, there was a break in the weather and a group of seventeen people—ten men, five women, and two boys—left, attempting to reach California. They each took a six-day supply of food. Years later, author Charles McGlashan, in his book *History of the Donner Party*, would call them the Forlorn Hope.[59] At the end of the first day, eleven-year-old William Murphy and thirty-year-old "Dutch Charley" Burger turned back, but the rest pressed on through deep snow and hardship. On the sixth day, December 21, Charles Stanton, who had returned with supplies for the emigrants, was in a weakened condition. He told the others to go on and he would catch up later. He never did. On the seventh day, the fourteen remaining people were out of food, except for William Eddy, who nibbled on a little bear meat his wife had hidden in his pack. They began to discuss that the only way to survive was cannibalism. One idea was for the men to have a shootout. The loser would be eaten.[60]

A snowstorm hit and they had to hunker down until it abated. Patrick Dolan and two other men died on Christmas Day. The next day, hunger won out over the taboo of eating human flesh. The Forlorn Hope party butchered Dolan, then roasted and ate his flesh. Over the next weeks, other members would die, and their flesh helped sustain the lives of the survivors. On January 12, 1847, emaciated and frostbitten, five women and two men, William Eddy and William Foster, staggered into an Indian village where they were welcomed and given acorn bread to eat.[61]

Back at the mountain camps the situation continued to deteriorate. Snow kept falling and accumulating, piling up to nine feet deep. After the oxen were eaten, the emigrants killed and ate the family dogs and boiled cow hides for nourishment.[62]

On January 4, 1847, Margret Reed, her daughter Virginia, Eliza Williams, and Milt Elliot made the attempt for California but could not get through the drifts, and all returned by January 8. By the end of the month, Levinah Murphy had lost her sight, one-year-old Lewis Keseberg died on January 24, and sixteen-year-old John Landrum Murphy died on January 31.[63]

In California, funds were raised, and volunteers were found to mount what would be called the first rescue party. On February 4, Aquilla Glover and Dan Tucker, leading a seven-member rescue team bearing food packs, left Johnson's Ranch in the foothills of the Sierra Nevada. Reaching the Lake Camp on the evening of February 19, 1847, the rescue party found the emigrants in a starving, weakened condition. There had been more deaths in both camps, including Milt Elliott and Eleanor, William Eddy's wife.[64]

The rescuers gathered the strongest of the survivors from both camps to escort them out of the mountains. Twenty-three would attempt the escape. Fourteen were under the age of sixteen, and some of these were infants. Most left behind were too weak and sick or stayed to care for those unable to leave. Rescuers believed and told survivors there were more rescue parties on the way. Seventeen people remained at the Truckee Lake cabins: five adults—Lewis Keseberg, Patrick and Margaret Breen, Levinah Murphy, and Elizabeth Graves—and twelve children. Twelve people remained at the Adler Creek camp: adults Betsy, George, and Tamsen Donner; sixteen-year-old Jean Baptiste Trudeau; and eight children. George's hand wound had never healed and was so infected he was incapacitated.[65]

The rescue party with their charges left the Lake Camp on February 22, but soon they had to bring back eight-year-old Patty and three-year-old Thomas Reed, who were in no shape to make the trip.[66]

The conditions were grueling for the rescue party. Along the way, John Denton died and then also Ada Keseberg, the three-year-old daughter of Lewis and Phillippe. On February 26, they found food the rescue party had cached. Death claimed one final victim. The rescue party had fed the refugees, but sparingly. Too much food on an empty stomach could kill. Twelve-year-old William Hook, Betsy Donner's son by her first marriage, was still hungry. During the night, he broke into the food supply and ate his fill. He became ill and hours later died. Eighteen Donner Party survivors would make it out of the mountains alive—eighteen people who did not have to resort to cannibalism.[67]

James Reed had been determined to rescue his family still snowbound in the mountains. He had been busy organizing what was called the second rescue party. Reed's expedition, which included William McCutchen, left Yerba Buena on February 7, 1847, a few days after Glover's expedition had entered the mountains. Selim Woodworth, a midshipman, was leading what would be called the third rescue party and had left Yerba Buena the same time as Reed but was lagging behind.[68]

On February 27, Reed and the second rescue party met the first rescue party as it descended through the mountains. They gave baked bread to the survivors, and James Reed was reunited with his wife and two children, but little Patty and Thomas were still at the Lake Camp.[69]

Back at the mountain camps, those who had remained behind were running out of food. On February 23, Patrick Breen wrote in his journal that he had to shoot Towser, the family dog, so they could eat. Wolves prowled about the camps intent on digging up bodies.[70]

It was February 26 at the Lake Camp when Patrick Breen wrote in his journal that Levinah Murphy talked about butchering the body of Milt Elliot to eat him. Breen, who lived with his family in a separate cabin, wrote, "I don't [believe] that she has done so yet, it is distressing. The Donnos [sic.] told the California folks that they [would] commence to eat the dead people 4 days ago, if they did not succeed that day or next in finding their cattle then under ten or twelve feet of snow & did not know the spot or near it, I suppose they have done so ere this time." On February 28, an Indian passed by the Lake Camp and left six bulbous roots for Patrick Breen to eat.[71]

As Reed's rescue party advanced through the snow, in places thirty feet deep, Charles Cady, Nicholas Clark, and Charles Stone, who were in the best shape, pressed ahead of the rest of the party, reaching the Lake Camp the morning of March 1, 1847. They distributed food to the survivors, then Clark and Cady proceeded on to the Alder Creek Camp.[72]

James Reed and William McCutchen along with the rest of the rescuers arrived later that day. Reed was relieved to find his two children Patty and Tomas alive in the Breen cabin.[73]

They found horrible conditions in Levinah Murphy's cabin. Murphy and Lewis Keseberg, the only adults in that cabin, were weak and incapacitated, unable to care for the smaller children, who had not been out of bed for days. Keseberg had an old foot injury that was taking a long time to heal. The rescuers joined in helping Stone wash the filth off the children and two adults.[74] Jessy Quinn Thornton, who wrote about the Donner Party in *Oregon and California in 1848* (published in 1849), said Reed and McCutchen saw a friend's mutilated body in the snow by the cabin door and human remains inside the cabin.[75]

Thornton also wrote, on approaching the Alder Creek Camp later that afternoon, that Clark and Cady said they saw sixteen-year-old Jean Baptiste Trudeau carrying one of Jacob Donner's legs. When the boy saw them, he threw the leg into a hole in the snow. When they looked in the hole, they saw Donner's head, which had been cut from the body. The arms and legs were removed as well as the body cut open and heart and liver removed. They then said they saw children sitting on a log eating Donner's half-roasted heart and liver.[76]

On March 2, Reed left four men at the Lake Camp to get all who could travel ready to go. Reed and three others went to the Alder Creek Camp. Reed first visited Jacob Donner's shelter, where Jacob's wife Betsy lay close to death. She told Reed she had allowed the children to eat all the food and she would rather die than eat her husband's flesh.[77]

Reed visited George Donner's shelter. George was incapacitated. The wound to his hand had not healed and now his arm and shoulder were infected. His wife Tamsen, who was healthy, refused to leave his side. Decisions were made. George, Tamsen, and their three youngest daughters would remain at the Adler Creek Camp. Reed would take three older children all from Jacob and Betsy's family. The remaining nine survivors—three adult Donners, Trudeau, and five Donner children—would remain with supplies and two of the rescuers, Cady and Clark, who would care for them. Everyone expected Woodworth's relief party to arrive shortly.[78]

It was midday March 3 at the Lake Camp when Reed left Charles Stone to care for those who could not travel. Reed left behind a week's supply of food, which was thought should take care of them until Woodworth arrived. The Lake Camp people remaining behind were Levinah Murphy, her ten-year-old son Simon, Lewis Keseberg, three-year-old James Eddy, and four-year-old George Foster, Murphy's grandson. Those considered healthy enough to attempt the trip totaled seventeen—all were children except for three adults, Patrick and Margaret Breen and Elizabeth Graves; each woman carried her one-year-old baby.[79]

As the party headed over the pass and down the trail, the rescued were moving slower than Reed wanted. The cloud buildup was ominous. There was still no sign of Woodworth's rescue party. Reed sent three seasoned mountaineers ahead to their caches to bring food back and meet them on the trail with it. The men left, taking no food with them.[80]

A howling snowstorm hit, lasting for days. The men constructed a makeshift lean-to and battled to keep a fire going in the driving wind and snow, as they ran low on food. The third night of the storm, five-year-old

Isaac Donner died. Finally, on the afternoon of March 8, the storm broke. Their location would become known as Starved Camp.[81]

There was no sign of the three mountaineers or Woodworth's rescue party. Reed said they had to keep moving forward, but Elizabeth Graves and her children were too weak to continue. Patrick Breen said he would rather die in camp than on the trail. Reed told him he could not rely on the hope that Woodworth would arrive in time. Reed called the men together to witness Breen repeat he and his family would not continue on. Seven-year-old Mary Donner had severely burned a foot and could hardly walk so she stayed with the Breen and Graves families, thirteen people in all, as Reed and his two children, the three other rescuers, and Solomon Hook, fourteen-year-old son of Betsy Donner, made their way through the deep snow down the trail.[82]

Back at the Lake Camp, almost as soon as Reed and his party had left for the trek across the mountain pass, Charles Stone left and went to the Alder Creek Camp. Clark was gone, following a bear trail hoping to shoot the animal to add to their food supply. Stone met with Cady. They were both concerned about the scarcity of food and anxious at the approach of a major storm. Not waiting for Clark's return, they decided to leave immediately and join Reed's party. Tamsen Donner learned what they were planning. Concerned her three little girls might not survive another major storm, she pleaded with Stone and Cady to take the girls with them. She would pay them five hundred dollars to take six-year-old Frances, five-year-old Georgia, and four-year-old Eliza to their older half-sisters at Sutter's Fort. They agreed. Tamsen dressed the girls warmly and gave the men a few family keepsakes and silver spoons for the girls.[83]

They began following the trail back to Truckee Lake, but when they were out of sight of the Adler Creek Camp, the two men left the girls sitting on a blanket and walked a short distance away, where they stopped and held a long discussion. The girls were afraid they were being left behind. The men returned and took them to the Lake Camp, where they left them in the Murphy cabin. Stone and Cady most likely stayed in the Breen cabin as the snowstorm rolled in that caught the Reed party out in the open.[84]

After the storm abated on March 8, Stone and Cady left the Lake Camp and crossed over the pass without the children but with the items Tamsen Donner had given them. They made good time, passing but not stopping at Starved Camp and finally catching up with Reed's party. What was said between them was not recorded.[85]

William Eddy and William Foster, the male Forlorn Hope survivors, had recovered in California and were anxious about their families still in the mountains. They reached Johnson's Ranch, where on March 3 Glover's first relief party arrived escorting the refugees. Eddy learned his wife and baby daughter Margaret had died, but both Eddy and Foster were told they each had a son hopefully still alive in Murphy's cabin. Their hope was Woodworth had reached the Lake Camp by now.[86]

Eddy and Foster set out on the trail anticipating intercepting Woodworth's party on its return from the mountain camps. They were disheartened to find that Woodworth and his men were in Bear Valley and had not yet entered the mountains. The next morning Eddy, Foster, Woodworth, and five of his men set out to rescue the survivors. As they headed up the trail, they ran into the three mountaineers Reed had sent ahead for food. They had left food hanging from a tree for Reed and his party. That night after they made camp, Reed's people arrived and were fed. The next day they all went back to Woodworth's base camp.[87]

On March 11, Eddy and Foster led five of Woodworth's men to bring back any survivors from Starved Camp and retrieve the Eddy and Foster boys from the Lake Camp. On March 12, they reached Starved Camp to find the Breens and most of the children still alive. Elizabeth Graves, her five-year-old-son Franklin, and five-year-old Isaac Donner had died, and survivors had been living off their flesh.[88]

Three of the rescue party carried and guided the eleven survivors back down the trail while Eddy, Foster, Hiram Miller, and William Thompson raced east across the pass and reached the Lake Camp on the morning of March 13. They descended the steps through the snowpack and entered the Murphy cabin to find Levinah Murphy and her son Simon, Lewis Keseberg, the three Donner girls, and their mother Tamsen. To the horror of Eddy and Foster, their sons had died and had been eaten by Keseberg.

Georgia Donner said Mrs. Murphy accused Keseberg of strangling her grandson George Foster and then eating him.[89]

What was Tamsen Donner doing at the Lake Camp? Back at the Alder Creek Camp, Betsy Donner had died and now the only living people there were Betsy's four-year-old son Samuel, Tamsen, George, who was dying, Trudeau, and Clark.[90]

When the latest snowstorm had hit, Tamsen Donner had worried about the well-being and whereabouts of her three daughters. She had sent Clark to the Lake Camp to find out what he could about the children. He had returned to report that Stone and Cady had deserted the girls at the Murphy cabin and that "Kessburg [sic] was talking about killing here [sic] daughters to eat and that she had better go over to see to it." Leaving her ill husband in the care of Clark and Trudeau, Tamsen had rushed the seven miles to the Murphy cabin to ensure her daughters' safety.[91]

It was at that point the rescue party arrived. They promised they would see the Donner girls safely out of the mountains, and Tamsen returned to be with her husband. The rescuers had no additional food with them, but they did make the enfeebled Mrs. Murphy as comfortable as possible. It's a wonder they did not kill Keseberg then and there, but they let him alone.[92]

After a two-hour stay at the Lake Camp, the rescuers began their return with the three Donner girls and ten-year-old Simon Murphy. That evening, they made camp at the eastern foot of the pass. They were surprised when Clark and Trudeau joined them. Their surprise turned to disgust when they learned the two men had deserted the Donners. Clark had taken two guns and carried a forty-pound pack stuffed with Donner loot.[93]

The rescue parties all made it back to California without losing anyone. From March 23 to 28, another rescue expedition attempted to reach the remaining stranded people but failed to get through.[94]

A relief and salvage expedition was organized. The members received a daily wage and would get half of everything they salvaged. The mountaineer "Big" O'Fallon led the six-man expedition. One of the members was William Foster.[95]

They reached the Lake Camp on April 17, where they found butchered human remains. Following a fresh set of boot prints in the snow, they went to the Alder Creek Camp, where they found George Donner's body carefully wrapped in a sheet. However, someone had split open his skull and removed his brains as well as strips of flesh. The Adler Creek Camp appeared to have been ransacked. The Donners were known to be rich, having at least fifteen hundred dollars, but no money was found.[96]

Upon returning to the Lake Camp, they found Lewis Keseberg in one of the cabins, still alive. He had remained alive by eating human remains. He said Mrs. Murphy had died mid-March. After little Samuel and then George Donner had died, Tamsen Donner had planned to cross the pass and head to California. Keseberg said that when Tamsen arrived at the Lake Camp, she was so weakened she had died in the night. He then ate her. The men believed Keseberg had killed her and had been robbing the camps. Back at Sutter's Fort, Keseberg's wife had told the salvagers that they had little money. However, they found $225 in gold in Keseberg's waistband. O'Fallon wrapped a rope around Keseberg's throat and choked him until he revealed where he had buried an additional $273 belonging to the Donners. They left the camp on April 21, with Keseberg following along.[97]

In the end, thirty-six members of the Donner Party died in the camps or trying to escape, and forty-five survived.[98] Let's take a closer look at the survivors who did not resort to cannibalism, those who did, and those who have been identified as having eaten human flesh but may not have.

The First Groups Out

The men who left the Donner party early on did not resort to cannibalism. James Reed, William McCutchen, and Walter Herron are in this group.

There is no dispute that the two men and five women of the Forlorn Hope had to eat others to survive. This group included William Foster and William Eddy, who participated in later rescue and recovery efforts.

Aquilla Glover and Dan Tucker's rescue team brought out eighteen people from the mountain camps, none of whom had to resort to cannibalism.

Truckee Lake Camp

After Glover and Tucker's party had left the Truckee Lake Camp, Patrick Breen wrote an entry in his diary, "Fri 26th . . . hungry times in camp, plenty of hides but folks will not eat them we eat them with a tolerable good appetite. Thanks be to Almighty God. *Amen* Mrs Murphy said here yesterday that thought she would Commence on Milt. and eat him. I don't that she has done so yet, it is distressing."[99]

Note that Breen does not say Levinah Murphy had eaten anyone, only that she was *thinking* of eating Milt Elliott. Breen makes no further mention of Murphy possibly eating anyone, and three days later on Monday, March 1, the Reed rescue party arrived in the morning.

Milt Elliot had died February 9, 1847, in the Murphy cabin. Virginia Reed would write, "Milt Elliot died, our faithful friend who seemed so much like a brother. My mother [Margret Reed] and I dragged him out of the cabin and covered him up with snow."[100]

Jessy Quinn Thornton wrote the book *Oregon and California in 1848*. Much of it was based on interviews with William Eddy in late 1847.[101] Thornton wrote that after taking care of the children and adults in the Murphy cabin, Reed and the other rescuers saw "the mutilated body of a friend, having nearly all the flesh torn away, [it] was seen by the door— the head and face remaining entire. Half consumed limbs were concealed in trunks. Bones were scattered about. Human hair of different colors was seen in tufts about the fire-place." At the same time, Thornton stated that Murphy and Keseberg, the only adults in the cabin, were too weak to get out of bed to take care of themselves or the children.[102]

George R. Stewart's book *Ordeal by Hunger*, written in 1936 and revised in 1960, uses the same language as Thornton but elaborates by stating the mutilated body was "the faithful Milt."[103]

Charles F. McGlashan in his *History of the Donner Party*, published in 1880, tells about the cannibalism of the Forlorn Hope and other later incidents where survivors ate human flesh, but he does not mention any cannibalism at the Murphy cabin during Reed's visit. Elizabeth P. Donner Houghton, a Donner Party survivor who was four years old at the time of the ordeal, wrote *The Expedition of the Donner Party and Its Tragic Fate*, published in 1911. She makes no mention of cannibalism at the

Lake Camp during Reed's visit. Why doesn't either of these two authors mention the cannibalism? Because it did not happen.

A large part of Thornton's book was based on information Eddy told him, and some Donner Party survivors considered Eddy a liar.[104] Judge James F. Breen, one of the Breen children, would later write on June 8, 1889, "What [Thornton] wrote in that connection [Starved Camp] . . . was obtained from one Eddy—a member of the Donner Party—whose reliability will be better estimated when I tell you that his sobriquet in the train was 'Lying Eddy' and whose hostility to my mother was bitter and uncompromising because she had the courage in common with others to tell him how great a coward he was in the face of danger and privation, and how great a liar and hypocrite he was under all circumstances."[105]

Virginia Reed wrote to McGlashan in 1880, "So you received a letter from the son of W. H. Eddy, a physician! I did not think a son of William H. Eddy would have brains enough to be a professional man, but it is not always the smartest parents who raise the smartest children." She then continued concerning *Oregon and California in 1848*, "And about J. Quinton Thornton's version of Eddy's story, such a disconnected untruthful story. It sounds just like Eddy."[106]

In a letter to McGlashan, Billy Graves wrote that during the ordeal of the Forlorn Hope, his sisters Mary Graves and Sarah Fosdick told him later they worried about Eddy. They believed he wanted to get Mary away from the others and kill her for food.[107]

Eddy was not at the Lake Camp and had no direct knowledge of what was going on there. Breen's diary makes no further mention of cannibalism other than that Murphy was thinking of it. Even more significant, Reed kept a diary during his visit to the mountain camps and wrote about caring for the people at the Lake Camp, but he said nothing about a mutilated body at the Murphy cabin or any other cabin. In an April 1, 1871, lengthy article, "The Snow-Bound, Starved Emigrants of 1846" in the *Pacific Rural Press*, Reed talked about his visit to the Lake Camp and made no mention of cannibalism. In the same article, William McCutchen also told of his involvement with the Reed rescue party and made no mention of cannibalism at the Lake Camp.[108]

If Murphy and Keseberg, the only adults in the Murphy cabin, were so weakened and famished they could not get out of bed to care for the children and even themselves, how would they have had the energy to find Milt Elliott's body, dig it up, drag it to the door, butcher it, and cook it? I believe people in the Murphy cabin had not eaten human flesh at the time of Reed's visit.

Alder Creek Camp

As for the Alder Creek Camp, Patrick Breen, sitting in his cabin seven miles away at the Lake Camp, wrote in his diary on Friday, February 26, 1847, the same day he had written about Mrs. Murphy's talk about eating Milt, "The Donnos [Donners] told the California folks that they Commence to eat the dead people 4 days ago, if they did not succeed that day or next in finding their cattle then under ten or twelve feet of snow & did not know the spot or near it I suppose They have done so ere this time"[109]

Breen's diary entry is gossip passed on from the men of Glover's party. Breen had no idea if the Donners had started eating the dead or not.

Jessy Quinn Thornton wrote in *Oregon and California in 1848*, Volume 2, "When Mr. Reed arrived there, he found Messrs. Cady and Stone [it was actually Clark instead of Stone; Stone was left at the Lake Camp][110] who had been sent in advance with provisions to this camp. They informed him that when they arrived at the camp, Baptiste [Trudeau] had just left the camp of the widow of the late Jacob Donner, with the leg and thigh of Jacob Donner," which the George Donner family was going to use for food.[111]

Thornton continued, "The children were sitting upon a log, with their faces stained with blood, devouring the half-roasted liver and heart of the father." Thornton goes on to describe Reed's later visit to the interior of the Jacob Donner shelter, "Around the fire were hair, bones, skulls, and the fragments of half-consumed limbs." They later saw Jacob Donner's grave in the snow, which Thornton described: "His head was cut off, and was lying with face up, the snow and the cold having preserved all the features unaltered. His limbs and arms had been severed from the body which was cut open—the heart and the liver being taken out. Other graves were seen, but nothing remained in them but a few fragments."[112]

George R. Stewart in his book *Ordeal by Hunger* used the same language as Thornton in describing the scenes of cannibalism at the Alder Creek Camp.

Georgia Donner, daughter of George and Tamsen, was five at the time the Donners were snowbound at the Adler Creek Camp. In a letter she wrote to Charles McGlashan on June 15, 1879, she said she believed she and her sisters ate human flesh and she remembered her father turning away as they ate. Georgia wrote, "When I spoke of human flesh being used at both tents, I said it was prepared for the little ones in both tents. I did not mean to include the larger children (my half sisters) or the grown people, because I am not positive that they tasted of it.... Jacob Donner's wife came down the steps one day saying to mother, 'What do you think I cooked this morning?' Then answered the question herself, 'Shoemaker's arm.'"[113]

There is no evidence that any of Georgia's four sisters agreed with her. In fact, Elizabeth worked to refute that claim.[114] Georgia and her sisters grew up hearing and absorbing Donner Party stories. Did Georgia's memories become influenced by these stories? Although not directly referencing Georgia Donner, Kristin Johnson, who has studied the Donner Party for over twenty years, wrote in her *Unfortunate Immigrants*, "Certain survivors contributed information to early writers, whose works in turn influenced the later recollections of other participants. The motivations of the informants are also different—to inform, to shock, to justify—but all are to a degree self-serving."[115]

It's interesting to note that Thornton's grizzly imagery of children eating their father's organs, human remains strewn about the inside of the Jacob Donner shelter, and the butchered remains of Jacob Donner fit with the literature of the time. Shannon A. Novak writes in *Archeaology of Desperation*, "Graphic descriptions of murder, dismemberment, and mutilation were the fodder of nineteenth-century 'gothic' literature."[116]

I asked my doctor, Tom Huber, M.D., if a person who had been buried in the snow for a couple of months would be frozen solid all the way through, and if so, how hard would it be to remove the heart and liver to eat? He replied that yes, the body would be completely frozen. "A frozen carcass of any animal, including human, is extremely difficult to eat or dissect without power tools," he said. "Unless you are a wild carnivore—wolf, etc., with powerful jaws and sharp long canine teeth designed for just that purpose. Thawing the carcass first makes that easier but then rancid meat becomes another issue."

"When Reed's men got to Elder Creek Camp, the only adults were George, Tamsen, and Betsy Donner, as well as sixteen-year-old Jean Baptiste Trudeau," I said to Dr. Huber. "George and Betsy were both weak and bedridden, so maybe Tamsen and Trudeau could chop off legs and arms to cook. But to open a frozen body, extract the heart and liver from the mass of frozen tissue, and half-roast them for the kids to eat as they smeared their faces with blood, seems a little much to me."

"Yes, you're correct," Dr. Huber responded.

Charles McGlashan in *History of the Donner Party* does not mention any evidence of cannibalism at the Adler Creek Camp during Reed's visit. Elizabeth Donner Houghton's *The Expedition of the Donner Party and Its Tragic Fate* makes no mention of cannibalism at the Adler Creek Camp during Reed's visit. Why don't they write about the cannibalism? Because it did not happen.

When Reed visited the Alder Creek Camp, he made no mention of cannibalism in his journal. In the April 1, 1871, article, "The Snow-Bound, Starved Emigrants of 1846," in the *Pacific Rural Press*, Reed made no mention of cannibalism at the Alder Creek Camp, and in the same article, William McCutchen made no mention of cannibalism at the Alder Creek Camp.[117]

In 1884, William McCutchen brought Jean Baptiste Trudeau to meet Elizabeth Donner Houghton. Trudeau told her there had never been any cannibalism at the Alder Creek Camp. "The hair and bones found around the Donner fires were those of cattle," Trudeau said. "No human flesh was used by either Donner family. This I know, for I was there all winter and helped to get all the wood and food we had, after starvation threatened us. I was about sixteen years old at the time. Our four men died early in December and were buried in excavations in the side of the mountain. Their bodies were never disturbed. As the snows deepened to ten and twelve feet, we lost track of their location."[118]

It's interesting when referring to the burial of the four men that Trudeau used the phrase "buried in excavations in the side of the mountain." Maybe, they were not just buried in snow, but buried in the ground, which would have made it even harder to find the bodies once the snow began piling up.

Trudeau was later interviewed by a correspondent for the *St. Louis Republic*, and an account of the interview was printed in the October 11, 1891, edition of the *San Francisco Morning Call*, in which the correspondent wrote, "No human flesh was eaten in the camp where he was."[119]

Nicholas Clark, who with Charles Cady were the first members of Reed's rescue party to reach the Adler Creek Camp, disagreed with what Thornton wrote, saying he saw no signs of cannibalism at the Donner campsite. On November 16, 1879, Clark wrote to Charles McGlashan, "There was no human flesh eaten in the Donner Camp while I was there and nothing was tra[n]sacted there to reflect any dishonor upon the Donner children."[120]

Remember, Thornton's book *Oregon and California in 1848* was based upon interviews with William Eddy in late 1847 and that some Donner Party survivors considered him a liar. Eddy did not visit the Adler Creek Camp and had no direct knowledge of what was going on there.[121]

In referring to the cannibalism scenes at Alder Creek Camp that Thornton claimed Cady and Clark saw, Joseph King in his book *Winter of Entrapment* writes, "This is simply not true, which Stewart's own notes, ironically, make evident: 'The facts are plainly and circumstantially stated in Thornton,' he says. But Thornton does not state his sources, and neither Thornton nor Stewart had access to any written testimony of Cady and Clark in the matter. No such documents have been located."[122]

On April 4, 1879, Charles McGlashan interviewed Lewis Keseberg about what happened with the Donner Party and about his cannibalism. After George Donner's death, Tamsen Donner had made her way to the Lake Camp. Keseberg told McGlashan, "She said she was very hungry, but refused the only food I could offer. She had never eaten the loathsome flesh."[123]

In 2003 and 2004, an archeological study was conducted at Adler Creek at a site identified as one of the Donner brothers' shelters where a stone hearth had been uncovered. Bone fragments totaling 16,204 were recovered from the hearth area. They determined none of the bone fragments found were adult human. After analyzing over a hundred of these fragments, macroscopically and microscopically, no human tissue was found. The bones belonged to horses, cattle, deer, rodents, rabbits, and dogs.[124]

The researchers concluded, "The result of this study does not confirm or deny the practice of cannibalism at the site."[125] One theory on the absence of human bones is that the soil is so acidic, if the bones had not been cooked, then they would have deteriorated and vanished over the years; whereas, cooked bones would not break down as quickly. However, in 1984, Donald H. Hardesty conducted an archeological excavation of the Murphy cabin at the Lake Camp and found a few human bones mixed in with nonhuman bones, but they were so deteriorated, the researchers could not determine if the bones could show cannibalism.[126] For more detail on the methodology and results of the Adler Creek Camp investigation, read *An Archaeology of Desperation: Exploring the Donner Party's Adler Creek Camp*, edited by Kelly J. Dixon, Julie Schablitsky, and Shannon A. Novak.

No adults survived the ordeal at the Adler Creek Camp. Tamsen Donner had kept a diary, but unfortunately it has never been found.[127]

After reviewing the evidence and weighing the testimony of survivors and rescuers, there is not enough information to prove cannibalism occurred at the Adler Creek Camp.

Starved Camp

There is no dispute that people left by Reed at Starved Camp ate three bodies to remain alive. However, Eliza Farnham wrote in her book published in 1856, *California Indoors and Out*, that Margaret Breen told her that only seven-year-old Mary Donner and the remaining Foster children ate human flesh. Margaret said no one in the Breen family ate human flesh.[128]

The Last Survivor at the Mountain Camps

There is no contest that Lewis Keseberg ate human flesh. On April 4, 1879, Keseberg granted an interview with author Charles McGlashan. Keseberg admitted to McGlashan he had resorted to cannibalism to survive. He said Levinah Murphy died about a week after Foster and Eddy had left. "When my provisions gave out, I remained four days before I could taste human flesh," Keseberg said.[129]

When O'Fallon's rescue and salvage party reached the Adler Creek Camp, they found Tamsen Donner had wrapped George Donner's body in a white sheet. However, his skull had been split open to remove the brains as well as flesh had been cut and stripped away and placed in a kettle.[130] This was no doubt done by Keseberg when he visited the camp to search for the Donner family's money.

When O'Fallon's rescue and salvage party had arrived at the Lake Camp, and after that a party of Church of Latter Day Saints led eastward by elder Sam Brannan, and later a military expedition led eastward by General Stephen W. Kearny, they all saw not only evidence of bodies having been butchered but also body parts scattered about.[131]

In September 1847, emigrant Daniel Tyler recorded seeing "a skull covered with hair lying there, a mangled arm or leg yonder, with the bones broken as one would break a beef shank to obtain the marrow from it; a whole body in another place, covered in a blanket, and portions of the other bodies scattered around in different directions."[132]

Of course, for weeks Keseberg had lived off human bodies at the Lake Camp and briefly at the Alder Creek Camp, but the scattering of the remains was done by wild animals. Shannon A. Novak wrote in *An Archaeology of Desperation*, "The disarray of body parts and fractured bones that Tyler and others described are characteristic of carnivore scavenging."[133]

In the end, out of the eighty-one people who had been snowbound at the Lake Camp and Alder Creek Camp, thirty-six died in the camps or trying to escape. Forty-five people survived. Twenty-eight of the survivors were children under the age of fifteen. No more than half the survivors possibly had to eat human flesh to survive—depending on who you believe, eight to eleven were adults, the rest were children.[134]

CHAPTER 4

WHY DID JACK MCCALL KILL WILD BILL HICKOK?

JUST THE FACTS

In the public eye, James Butler Hickok, better known as Wild Bill, was a man larger than life. Being an expert shot, he has been called "Prince of the Pistoleers" and other such titles. After Colonel George Ward Nichols wrote an exaggerated yarn of Hickok's exploits in the February 1867 issue of *Harper's New Monthly Magazine*, Wild Bill became a national celebrity. His legend continued to grow even after his death with the publication of books such as J. W. Buel's *Heroes of the Plains* published in 1881.[1]

There were those who loved Wild Bill and those who hated him. During his short life, he held many jobs, including scout and law enforcement officer. He was a teller of tall tales and loved to gamble. He was kind but, if crossed, could be cold-hearted. He had a strong sense of justice. He constantly practiced firing his pistols and was considered an excellent shot. Nichols wrote in his *Harper's New Monthly Magazine* story that Wild Bill killed hundreds of men, while Hickok claimed he killed thirty-six. Wild Bill biographer Joseph Rosa documented Hickok killed seven men in gunfights. To reach his number of thirty-six men, Hickok may have included men he had killed during the Civil War and in Indian fights.[2]

James Butler Hickok was born on May 27, 1837, in Troy Grove, Illinois.[3] As a boy, he loved guns and hunting. Both of his parents were active in the Underground Railroad assisting slaves in their quest for freedom. Their example instilled a strong sense of justice in Hickok. When his father died, he and his brothers supported the family by farming, hunting, and odd jobs.[4]

By the mid-1850s, Hickok and older brother Lorenzo traveled to Kansas to homestead and make their fortunes. They farmed and worked at a variety of jobs. Lorenzo returned home to Illinois, but James stayed in Kansas. Tensions began heating up between proslavery and antislavery factions. Hickok joined the Free State Army, an antislavery group participating in actions against proslavery supporters.[5]

In 1857, Hickok met eleven-year-old William F. Cody, who would become a lifelong friend later known as Buffalo Bill. Cody said they both worked for Russell, Majors and Waddell, a freight company, hauling army supplies during the Mormon War. According to Cody, Hickok interceded when a bully was harassing him. Later, Mormon raiders captured their bull train and burned the wagons and freight.[6]

On March 22, 1858, Hickok was elected as a Monticello Township, Kansas, constable. From 1858 to 1861, he worked for the closely associated freighting companies Jones and Cartwright and Russell, Majors and Waddell. During the winter of 1860–1861, he was severely injured, some claimed in a bear attack. By the spring of 1861, he was working in Nebraska, at Russell, Majors and Waddell's Pony Express Rock Creek relay station, tending horses as his injuries healed. On July 12, he was involved in a fight at the Rock Creek Station that left David McCanles and two others dead. Hickok was later cleared of murder charges at a court hearing. George Nichols wrote an exaggerated account of the fight in his *Harper's New Monthly Magazine* story that propelled Hickok to national fame.[7]

During the Civil War, Hickok worked for the Union Army as a teamster, scout, and spy. It was during this time he earned the nickname "Wild Bill." In 1865, he was involved in a duel on the streets of Springfield, Missouri. He had a disagreement with a friend, Davis Tutt. They faced off in the street and Wild Bill won, shooting and killing Tutt.[8]

Wild Bill's reputation grew as he scouted for the army, guided famous individuals on hunting expeditions, acted as a law enforcement officer in Kansas cow towns, and was involved in gunfights, killing his opponents. When not working in law enforcement or scouting, Hickok earned a living by gambling.[9]

In September 1873, Hickok joined the Buffalo Bill Combination, a stage performance of the West that traveled from city to city in the East. Hickok did not like acting on stage in front of audiences, and in March 1874, he quit the performance in Rochester, New York. Hickok drifted from town to town throughout the West working at a variety of jobs, gambling, shooting exhibitions, and entertaining barroom listeners with tall tales, eventually winding up in Cheyenne, Wyoming.[10]

On March 5, 1876, Hickok married the traveling circus owner Agnes Lake in Cheyenne. Hickok and Lake had met in Abilene, Kansas, in 1871. Over the years they had occasionally spent time together and carried on an extensive correspondence.[11]

Back in July 1874, Lieutenant Colonel George Armstrong Custer had led a military expedition through the Black Hills of Dakota Territory. The 1868 Fort Laramie Treaty recognized the Black Hills as part of the Great Sioux Reservation, prohibiting white access; but General Phil Sheridan, whose official position was that the establishment of forts in and around the Black Hills might be a good idea, authorized Custer to lead an expedition to investigate potential fort locations. Shrouded in mystery, the Black Hills were relatively unexplored. Many hoped the expedition would confirm rumors of gold.[12]

On July 25, 1874, the expedition entered the Black Hills, and on August 2, while the troops camped along French Creek, two miners Custer had brought with him discovered gold flakes, enough to be considered profitable. Custer sent scout Lonesome Charley Reynolds with his report to Sheridan along with reporters' dispatches to Fort Laramie, Wyoming. Newspaper headlines were soon blaring the discovery of gold. The rush to the Black Hills was on. The army had its hands full intercepting prospectors, but by the fall of 1875, President Ulysses Grant quietly gave the directive that the army no longer evict whites from the Black Hills.[13]

By November 1875, prospectors had reached Whitewood Creek in the northern Black Hills. They found profitable deposits of placer gold, filed claims, and a new gold camp, Deadwood, mushroomed into existence. By the spring of 1876, Deadwood's population was booming with prospectors and those making a living off of prospectors. Deadwood was an illegal town. The Black Hills still belonged to the Lakota and everyone in town was an illegal trespasser. There was no government, and law enforcement did not exist. Each man was a law unto himself and carried weapons to protect himself and his gold. Saloons, dance halls, and establishments for every sort of entertainment flourished.[14]

There were four main trails to the Black Hills and Deadwood, and all had to cross the Great Sioux Reservation. The Lakota were angry with the invasion of their lands and would turn back or kill anyone they caught. The best way to get to Deadwood was with a large armed party.[15]

Wild Bill Hickok was seeking a new beginning. Maybe Deadwood was the place where he could make his fortune. He joined his friend Colorado Charlie Utter and four others interested in going to Deadwood and left Cheyenne about June 27, 1876, taking the Cheyenne–Deadwood Trail. Arriving at Fort Laramie in early July, the post's officer of the day told the six men they had better travel with a larger group or they stood a good chance of being attacked by Indians. They joined a waiting wagon train of thirty wagons and 130 people ready to head to the Black Hills. Before leaving, the officer of the day asked Wild Bill to take along a rowdy young woman who had been a disturbance at the fort. Hickok agreed, and Calamity Jane Canary accompanied them.[16]

Hickok and his friends reached Deadwood about July 12. Before entering town, they changed into buckskin clothing. Richard Hughes, who saw their cavalcade enter town, wrote, "Hickok had made a spectacular entry into Deadwood ... accompanied by ... 'Calamity Jane,' Charley and Steve Utter, brothers; and Dick Seymour, the last named as being known as 'Bloody Dick.'. . . The party . . . rode the entire length of Main Street, mounted on good horses and clad in complete suits of buckskin, every suit of which carried sufficient fringe to make a considerable buckskin rope."[17]

Hickok and his friends stopped at the Number 10 Saloon, owned by Carl Mann, who was good friends with him. Mann insisted Hickok make Number 10 Saloon his headquarters while he was in town. Hickok was much obliged, and it would be good business for Mann knowing people would want to come and see Wild Bill.[18]

Hickok and his friends set up camp on a level area under a grove of spruce and pine trees along Whitewood Creek. The first thing Wild Bill did each morning was conduct a little target practice with his pistols, take a shot of whiskey, and then eat breakfast. He tried his hand at placer mining but was more proficient at gambling and did quite well at that.[19]

Harry Young, one of the bartenders in the Number 10 Saloon, had known Wild Bill since Hayes City, Kansas. Young said Wild Bill maintained his cautious attitude while in a saloon. He poured his whiskey with his left hand, keeping his right hand free for any necessary gunplay. He always faced those drinking with him and he would not allow anyone to stand behind him. When playing cards, he always sat with his back to the wall.[20]

On the night of August 1, 1876, Wild Bill was in a poker game that included twenty-five-year-old Jack McCall, also known as Bill Sutherland. Late that night, bartender Harry Young's shift began. Gamblers kept their poke sacks of gold dust behind the bar for safe keeping. Young recalled that Wild Bill asked him how much gold dust McCall had in his sack. Young weighed the gold dust and called the amount to Hickok.

"You have overplayed yourself by ten dollars," Hickok said to McCall.

"All right, I will make it good next Saturday night," McCall replied as the game ended.

"I have not got money enough to buy my breakfast," McCall said. Hickok gave him seventy-five cents and told him to go eat and if he needed more later, he would help him. Hickok bought drinks for them and then McCall left.[21]

Early on the afternoon of August 2, Wild Bill Hickok and Colorado Charlie Utter walked into Number 10 Saloon. Carl Mann, a young gambler Charlie Rich, and riverboat captain William Massie, whom Hickok had beaten in cards the night before, were engaged in a poker game. Mann invited Hickok to join them. There was one open stool for Hickok. Rich had the stool with his back to the wall. Hickok asked him for it. Rich stood to give his seat to Hickok, but Massie made it clear he preferred Wild Bill sit across from him, stating, "No one is going to shoot you in the back." The others joined in good-naturedly telling Hickok the same thing.

"All right you old grouch," Hickok said pulling out the stool with his foot, "I will sit here."[22]

Hickok sat with Rich on his right, Mann to his left, and Massie across from him. He could keep an eye on the front door, but he could not see anyone coming in the back door. Charlie Utter pulled up a stool and sat behind Hickok.[23]

Jack McCall entered the front door of Number 10 Saloon and walked to the far end of the bar. It was around 3:00 p.m. Hickok was losing to Massie and called to Harry Young for fifty dollars of checks.

"Bill, I will go and get something to eat," Charlie Utter said, as he stood and walked out the door.[24]

Young brought over the fifty dollars of checks to the table. As he stood between Mann and Hickok, he laid them in front of Hickok, who looked up at him and said, "The old duffer [Massie] broke me on the hand." Young returned back behind the bar.[25]

Hickok was studying his cards. McCall acted quickly, moving along the bar until he was a few feet behind Hickok. McCall drew his pistol, pointed the muzzle at the back of Hickok's head, and pulled the trigger. The pistol fired, killing Hickok instantly.

"Damn you!" McCall shouted. "Take that!"

Hickok's body fell forward onto the table, then slumped to the floor. The bullet had passed through the base of Hickok's brain, out his right cheek between the jaws, and smashed into Massie's left wrist.[26]

As McCall backed toward the rear door, he pointed his pistol at a stunned Carl Mann saying, "Come on ye sons of bitches." Rich and Massie were running out the front door. Massie was shouting that Wild Bill had shot him, mistakenly believing that it was Hickok who had fired the shot. As George Shingle and Harry Young tried to run out the door, McCall swung the pistol in Shingle's direction and pulled the trigger— a misfire. He next pointed it at Harry Young and pulled the trigger— another misfire.[27]

Running out the back door, McCall approached a saddled horse at the hitching rail. He began to mount the horse, but the saddle swung under the horse's belly, throwing McCall to the ground. The cinch was loose, and McCall, being in a hurry, had failed to check it.[28]

A crowd gathered. Men were shouting, "Wild Bill is shot!" and "Wild Bill is dead!" The crowd pursued McCall down the street. White Eye Anderson was at a tailrace a short distance away. He drew his pistol and ran after McCall but could not get a clear shot as there were too many people in the way. He estimated there must have been fifty guns drawn in the crowd, but no one could shoot for fear of hitting others. McCall tried to shoot into the crowd several times, but his pistol did not fire. The caps were bad. McCall was cornered in a butcher shop and captured.[29]

"Bring a rope!" someone shouted. The mob was ready to hang McCall right then and there. They found a pine tree with a stout limb and then a rope. The hanging was interrupted when a Mexican on a galloping horse raced up Main Street, swinging the severed head of an Indian and shouting that Indians were attacking Crook City to the north. The mob forgot about McCall; some left to investigate the attack while others followed the Mexican with the severed head from saloon to saloon, congratulating him and enjoying alcoholic refreshments.[30]

Fortunately for McCall, cooler heads prevailed, believing there needed to be a trial. They hustled him off to a cabin, locked him inside, and posted a guard. Prominent citizens held a coroner's inquest and determined Hickok had been killed by a bullet fired by Jack McCall.[31]

That night, the citizens selected a judge, prosecutor, defense attorney, sheriff for the trial, a deputy, and twelve guards. The next day a jury was empaneled and the trial held at the Deadwood Theater. Witnesses were called, and when McCall was asked to defend himself, he said, "Well men, I have but few words to say. Wild Bill killed my brother, and I killed him. Wild Bill threatened to kill me if I crossed his path. I am not sorry for what I have done. I would do the same thing over again."[32]

Despite the testimonies of Carl Mann, Charlie Rich, and Harry Young that McCall had shot Hickok in the back of the head, the jury's verdict was not guilty. McCall was freed. However, Wild Bill's friends made it clear Deadwood was not a safe place for McCall and he soon left town.[33]

JACK MCCALL, HIRED ASSASSIN—BILL MARKLEY

Why did Jack McCall shoot Wild Bill Hickok? He told the Deadwood miners' court that Wild Bill had shot and killed his brother. That was a lie. He didn't have a brother.[34]

Was McCall angry Wild Bill had figured out he didn't have enough gold dust to cover his bets during their card game the night of August

1? Was it that Wild Bill stripped him of all his funds and then gave him money, making him a charity case? Or was there something more, something nefarious? Wild Bill's friends thought so.

Since Deadwood was located on the Great Sioux Reservation and the Dakota Territory government did not recognize it, Deadwood was an illegal town. There was no local government and no law enforcement. Hickok's friend White Eye Anderson and Leander Richardson, on-scene reporter for the Massachusetts *Springfield Republican*, both said several days before Hickok's death that a group of Deadwood business owners had approached him with the idea of hiring him as Deadwood's marshal. If Hickok was interested, they would call a miners' meeting and establish town rules for him to enforce. Hickok told them he would think about it and would let them know his decision later in the week.[35]

Some of the criminal element liked Deadwood just the way it was and did not want Wild Bill enforcing any new town ordinances. One of Hickok's old friends, California Joe Milner, and his son Charlie, had joined Hickok and were living in his camp. One day, the Milners, Colorado Charlie Utter, and Wild Bill left Deadwood on a hunting trip. On their return, some of Wild Bill's friends told him there was a plot to have him killed because he was being considered for Deadwood's marshal. Hickok laughed, saying, "There's no one here going to shoot me. I would not take the marshal's job."[36]

After Jack McCall murdered Wild Bill and the citizens of Deadwood decided to hold a trial, McCall's defense attorney concocted the story that Wild Bill had shot and killed McCall's brother. It was a good story. The jury believed the lie and acquitted McCall.[37]

At the trial's end, the prosecuting attorney, Colonel George May, announced he had learned two hundred ounces of gold dust had been given to members of the jury, and he declared he would pursue McCall until justice was done. White Eye Anderson later recalled that the jury was packed with McCall's friends, a rough crowd.[38]

The correspondent for the *Chicago Inter-Ocean* reported in the August 17, 1876, issue, "The prisoner was at once liberated, several of the model jurymen who had played their parts in this burlesque upon justice, and who had turned their bloodthirsty tiger loose on the community, indulged in a sickening cheer which grated harshly upon the ears of those who heard it. All lawabiding [sic] citizens feel that a terrible injustice has been done, and realize the fact that their only protection now is forming 'vigilantes.'"[39]

It was rumored that Tim Brady and Johnny Varnes, members of Deadwood's criminal element, had approached Jack McCall with the offer that if he would assassinate Wild Bill, they would pay him up front $25 in gold dust and an additional $175 after the murder was committed. White Eye Anderson later wrote that he heard McCall had been paid $1,000 to murder Wild Bill.[40]

Leander Richardson reported in the *Denver News,* later reprinted in St. Paul, Minnesota's *Pioneer Press* on September 8, 1876, "There were a dozen or more men in Deadwood who wanted to kill Wild Bill because he would not 'stand in' with them on any 'deadbeat' games, but not one man among them all dared to pick a quarrel with him. They were all waiting to get a chance to shoot him in the back. And it was this clique who got Sutherland [McCall] clear of the charge, whereupon he took the first opportunity of getting out of town."[41]

However, McCall did not leave Deadwood. He must have believed he was safe while he remained in town.[42]

The day Jack McCall murdered Wild Bill, California Joe Milner was out of town. He had ridden north to Crook City. While there, Milner's dog spooked one of his horses, which reacted by kicking out its hind legs, striking Milner in the side and severely injuring him. When Milner learned McCall had murdered Hickok, he vowed vengeance, but his injury was too severe to leave Crook City right away.[43]

California Joe was well enough to return to Deadwood on August 5. Colorado Charlie told him the particulars of Wild Bill's murder and that Jack McCall was still in town. The August 26, 1876, issue of the *Cheyenne Daily Leader* reported what happened next: "California Joe . . . walked down to McCall's cabin, and called him out asked him if he didn't think the air about there was rather light for him. McCall's cheeks blanched, and he feebly answered he thought it was. 'Well, I guess you had better take a walk then,' said Joe, and seating himself on the side of the hill he watched the retreating figure out of sight."[44]

After the trial, the court had appointed an escort to see McCall out of town, as it rightly believed Hickok's friends would seek revenge.[45] He must have quickly made use of the escort after his encounter with California Joe.

Once McCall left the relative safety of Deadwood, California Joe went after him, leaving town on August 6. Milner's search eventually led him to Laramie, Wyoming. McCall had been arrested there and was behind bars. Milner told the jailer he would save everyone the cost of a trial if he could have half a minute with McCall. The jailer refused to let him in.[46]

How was it that Jack McCall was behind bars? Others had vowed to bring McCall to justice, one of whom had been the prosecuting attorney at McCall's trial, Colonel George May. McCall wound up in Laramie, Wyoming, where he was not quiet about the murder of Wild Bill. He boasted about murdering Wild Bill to a reporter and confessed to him that Wild Bill did not kill his brother. George May located McCall in Laramie, notified authorities about McCall's murder of Hickok, and they issued a warrant for his arrest. On August 29, 1876, US Marshal St. Andre Durand Balcombe and May overheard McCall bragging about killing Hickok. Balcombe promptly arrested McCall.[47]

When taken before Judge Jacob Blair, McCall admitted to killing Hickok and admitted that Hickok had not killed his brother. The government did not recognize the Deadwood trial as a legal proceeding, as the miners' court was not sanctioned by Dakota Territory. McCall was sent to Yankton, the territorial capital for trial.[48]

McCall was indicted for the murder of Hickok on October 18, 1876. Realizing he was in a bad predicament, he tried to make a deal with the prosecution. He told them that gambler Johnny Varnes and Tim Brady had paid him to assassinate Wild Bill Hickok. The court sent a US deputy marshal and five-man posse to Deadwood to locate Varnes and Brady, but they had vanished.[49]

There is no information on Tim Brady, but there is on Johnny Varnes. It appears that he had had two run-ins with Wild Bill Hickok in the past. The following story appeared in the November 11, 1876, issue of Deadwood's *Black Hills Weekly Pioneer*:

Some time ago, Wild Bill and Varnes had a difficulty in Denver and the animosity between the two was augmented by a dispute over a game of poker at the "Senate" saloon in this city, a short time previous to the death of Wild Bill, at which time Wild Bill interfered in a dispute between Varnes and another man. Bill covered Varnes with his pistol and arrogated to himself the position of umpire, after which friends interfered and ended the difficulty.[50]

Wild Bill's brother, Lorenzo Hickok, attended McCall's trial and was allowed to visit McCall in his prison cell. McCall intimated that he had been paid to kill Wild Bill but would say nothing more about that or show remorse, to Lorenzo's disgust.[51]

A variety of sources claim there was a conspiracy to kill Wild Bill Hickok. The conspirators found their assassin in Jack McCall, whom they paid to kill Wild Bill. After the deed was done, they worked behind the scenes to ensure he would be let off and seen safely out of Deadwood. After that, McCall was on his own and soon received his just payment from the law. On March 1, 1877, Jack McCall was hanged by the neck until dead.

LIFE LOSER—KELLEN CUTSFORTH

Jack McCall murdered Wild Bill Hickok on August 2, 1876; there is no debate about this. What has come under debate in recent years were the intentions of McCall. Why did he kill the famous gunfighter? Was there a conspiracy afoot, or was McCall just looking for notoriety and vengeance for a perceived slight?

Jack McCall was supposedly born in the early 1850s in Jefferson County, Kentucky, or New Orleans, Louisiana. He eventually made his way West working on the Kansas–Nebraska border as a buffalo hunter.[52] By the time he murdered Wild Bill Hickok in 1876, he was not much more than a no-account drifter. Traveling under several aliases, McCall, at the time of the murder, went by the name Bill Sutherland.[53]

According to several sources, McCall also tried his hand at mining, which eventually led to him living in Deadwood and bunking in a miner's camp. While living under the Sutherland alias, McCall apparently acquired an amount of gold dust that he used as currency to gamble at the numerous saloons in town.[54]

When Wild Bill arrived in Deadwood, he took to playing cards in Nuttall & Mann's Number 10 Saloon. Not long after Hickok arrived in town, the gunfighter went to Nuttall's to have a game on August 1, 1876. McCall was drinking at the bar and saw Hickok sit down to play at a full table. Waiting his turn to try his hand at besting Hickok, McCall became increasingly drunk.[55]

When one of the players dropped out, McCall quickly took his place. At this point, McCall was absolutely soused from drinking away the afternoon and could hardly keep up with the hands being dealt. "Crooked Nose," a nickname McCall acquired, lost nearly every hand and was left penniless at the end of his run. It was reported that after discovering his hardship Wild Bill offered McCall some money to buy himself something to eat. Wild Bill also advised McCall to not play poker anymore until he could pay his debts. Crooked Nose took Hickok's cash but apparently left feeling insulted and embarrassed. The following day, McCall would walk into the same saloon and shoot Wild Bill in the back of the head, killing him.[56]

After McCall shot Hickok in Nuttall & Mann's, he was quickly captured after botching an escape attempt, falling from a stolen horse whose saddle had been loosened. He was brought to trial in front of a quickly cobbled together miners' court full of his friends. In his own defense McCall said, "Well men, I have but few words to say. Wild Bill killed my brother and I killed him. Wild Bill threatened to kill me if I crossed his path. I am not sorry for what I have done. I would do the same thing over again."[57] This had been proven to be an absolute lie, and most historians believe he employed this ruse to gain sympathy with the jury. After a short deliberation, McCall was found "not guilty."

Following the trial, McCall hung around Deadwood for a few days, but he soon realized he was not the most popular man amongst Wild Bill's friends and confidants. Deciding to leave town, McCall headed for Wyoming Territory. Crooked Nose left feeling he had escaped justice. However, it was later revealed that the Deadwood trial had no legal basis, as the miners' court was not sanctioned by Dakota Territory. So, the decision handed down by the jury that sweltering August was made void. This meant McCall could now be retried for the murder of Hickok without the threat of double jeopardy.

At this point, it is interesting to note, a town existing on the outskirts of the law like Deadwood, which was not recognized by the Dakota Territory government since it was located on the Great Sioux Reservation, was essentially illegal. Because of this nebulous status, many of Deadwood's residents felt they were not subject to the normal laws and regulations of the United States. So, situations like those between McCall and Hickok were often solved with revolvers.[58]

Lesser notables than Wild Bill were shot down in Deadwood's muddy streets and there was usually no accompanying trial, with most murderers escaping justice.[59] Men killed one another in the boomtown over whiskey, women, and gambling debts. Petty grievances or presumed slights turned into full-blown shootouts, and men pulled their shooting irons just to cut each other down. This really lies at the heart of this situation. Jack McCall had been publicly embarrassed at the poker table by Wild Bill, and then his ego was irreparably bruised by the old lawman when he offered to give McCall money for a meal. The drifter was clearly angered by his public shaming.

Though he had the opportunity to slink away, and most likely live out his life, McCall could not keep his mouth shut. He blabbed about the murder while living in Julesburg, Colorado, and again got slack-jawed while he resided in Laramie in Wyoming Territory. He even gave interviews about the murder to the local newspapers. The crowing about his dastardly deed eventually caught up with him, and he was arrested for the murder of Hickok after apparently admitting the killing to Judge Jacob B. Blair.[60]

McCall was eventually transferred to Yankton, Dakota Territory, for a legitimately recognized trial. From the onset of the proceedings, McCall realized he was not going to be acquitted. Fearing conviction, he and his cellmate attempted a joint jailbreak by attacking their jailer. The two nearly sprang from the jail scot-free when they were detained by the arrival of a US marshal.[61]

After McCall's recapture, his trial resumed. Knowing his goose was cooked, Crooked Nose tried to broker a deal with the prosecution. He told the territorial lawyers a bewildering conspiracy theory wherein Deadwood resident John Varnes had hired him to shoot Wild Bill in the back because of a perceived slight Hickok supposedly inflicted on Varnes years earlier in Denver.[62] This concocted conspiracy, though followed by many newspapers, was nothing more than a desperate attempt by a desperate man to save his neck from stretching on the gallows pole. McCall was a murderer who was going to face the ultimate justice and wanted to escape any way he could think of.

Prosecutors were having none of McCall's garbage. Following through on a threat, the prosecution continued the court proceedings. Carl Mann, one of the prosecution's witnesses, stated that McCall had lost an amount of gold dust to Hickok in a previous poker game before he gunned down the famous lawman. Jack even admitted to having lost the precious dust to Hickok in an interview in the *Laramie Daily Leader* newspaper.[63] This was reason enough for a coward like McCall to kill Wild Bill.

McCall was nothing more than a damn bum who had lost money to Hickok in a game of chance, and it hurt his fool pride. Fueled by booze and anger at having been schooled at the poker table, Crooked Nose walked up like a rotten coward and shot one of the Old West's most famous gunfighters in the back of the head.

There is no conspiracy here. There is no outside influence guiding the actions of a hired sole assassin looking to settle a score. There is only a sad no-account of a man whose life was already spiraling downward. He was looking to mend his wounded pride and score an ounce of notoriety in the process.

Crooked Nose Jack McCall was a lousy coward who, after shooting one of the Old West's greatest gunfighters in the back of the head, blathered on about it like he had accomplished some great deed. In the end, he received precisely what he deserved when he was found guilty of Hickok's murder and was strung up by his neck on March 1, 1877. McCall acted alone and deserved to die alone.

CHAPTER 5

DID GENERAL GEORGE CROOK DOOM CUSTER AND THE SEVENTH CAVALRY?

JUST THE FACTS

During the spring of 1876, US military officials began a campaign to force Lakota, Cheyenne, and Arapahoe Indians to their federally designated agencies. In June of that year, following these plans, Brigadier General George Crook led a column of soldiers attempting to converge with two other columns in southern Montana Territory to confront a multitude of hostile Indians amassing in the area.

Crook's thirteen-hundred-man Yellowstone and Big Horn Expedition made the arduous march north from Fort Fetterman in Wyoming Territory. The idea was for them to eventually join both Colonel John Gibbon's five-hundred-man Montana column making the trek east from Fort Ellis in Montana Territory and Brigadier General Alfred Terry's thousand-man Dakota column marching west from Fort Abraham Lincoln in Dakota Territory. These three columns, each capable of independent action, were to pursue the hostile Indian bands, destroy their resistance, and force the survivors back to their agencies.[1]

Terry's column included the entire twelve companies of the Seventh Cavalry under the command of Lieutenant Colonel George Armstrong Custer. All three of these armies planned to converge on the valley of the Big Horn River in Montana Territory with hope that one of the commands would drive the massing multi-tribal Indian forces toward the other two. This, however, never came to fruition. George Crook encountered a host of Lakota and Cheyenne warriors led by the famous leaders Crazy Horse, Sitting Bull, and several other chieftains in a fight that became known as the Battle of the Rosebud. [2]

On June 17, 1876, General Crook's column came to grief against a larger than expected force of Lakota and Cheyenne warriors at the Battle of the Rosebud, taking place along Rosebud Creek in Montana Territory. Ranging over three miles of territory, the battle consisted of disconnected actions, charges, and countercharges by Crook and Crazy Horse.[3] Many scholars believe that this was one of the only times Indian armies fought similarly like American and European armies.

Crook's allied Crow warriors had told scout Frank Grouard that Sitting Bull's large camp was on the Rosebud. Crook prepared to lead most of his men from his Goose Creek camp to the Rosebud for an attack on the Lakota village.[4]

Crook believed, much like his fellow officers, that the Lakotas would flee once they were confronted by a large army. There was some merit to this way of thinking as this had been the case in several previous engagements and was standard Army doctrine. Crook's Indian scouts, however, suspected the Lakota warriors were led by Crazy Horse and would not run at the sight of their enemy.[5]

Early on the morning of June 17, Crook's contingent of 1,300 men (which included 262 Crow and Shoshone Indian scouts) stopped in the valley of Rosebud Creek to allow their horses to recuperate and for the rear of the column to catch up. As they dismounted, Crook's men were caught completely off guard by a multitude of Lakota and Cheyenne warriors. Historians estimate 500 to 1,000 warriors were involved in the battle.[6] From the onset, Crook realized he was in for a major fight.[7]

Crook's army, assisted by his Crow and Shoshone scouts, quickly mounted a defensive attack by fighting and retreating against the Lakota warriors that kept them at bay. Because of this initial action, Crook was able to position his troops defensively and meet the Indians' multiple assaults, eventually mounting charges of his own. The Indians' disconnected attack and retreat style of fighting continued for several hours, taking a toll on both sides. Toward the end of the battle, Crook had sent officer Anson Mills and a group of soldiers to look for a village he believed to be in the area. When Mills was recalled to the battlefield, they arrived at the Lakota's rear making them believe reinforcements had arrived and the Lakota then withdrew from the field. They had fought Crook's army to a standstill.[8]

At the conclusion of the battle, Crook counted ten killed and another twenty wounded. After assessing his losses, Crook decided to regroup and return to his camp on Goose Creek near the future site of Sheridan, Wyoming. His decision to wait for reinforcements meant Crook would not converge with the other two columns near the Big Horn River. Estimates of Lakota and Cheyenne dead range from thirteen to thirty-six and possibly one hundred wounded. On June 25, eight days after the Rosebud battle, the Battle of the Little Big Horn would take place, where a combined force of Lakota, Cheyenne, and Arapahoe Indians would crush Lieutenant Colonel George Custer's command and send him into the annals of history. Crook, however, would play no part in the infamous battle and would spend the following seven weeks after the Rosebud waiting for reinforcements.[9]

A LEADER'S FAILURE—KELLEN CUTSFORTH

Much has been written about the decisions made, and not made, leading up to the vast military failure known as the Battle of the Little Big Horn. During this most famous fight, George Armstrong Custer and his immediate Seventh Cavalry command perished while attempting to subdue a massive, combined force of Lakota, Cheyenne, and Arapahoe Indians in southern Montana Territory.

The three-pronged approach employed by Generals Terry and Crook and Colonel Gibbon to engage their Indian opponents was, in theory, a good one. Leading up to the Great Sioux War of 1876, nearly every large-scale battle the US military won against the plains tribes ended when the Indians were confronted with that type of opponent. Normally, when caught by surprise, the Lakotas ran instead of engaging a superior opponent. This was usually for self-preservation and to allow their warriors the ability to protect escaping elders, women, and children.

In a fight, Lakota tactics usually consisted of ambushes and strategic hit-and-run techniques. So, when Crook encountered Crazy Horse at the headwaters of Rosebud Creek, it is little surprise he was unprepared for a pitched battle. Crook's Crow and Shoshone scouts' early engagement of the large Lakota force was truly a life-saving action, buying the American troops time to find their footing.[10] As the fiercest fighting commenced, Crazy Horse's warriors met Crook's every charge with charges of their own.[11]

The battle, by all accounts, was grueling and bloody, with fighting lasting over six hours. There were several engagements between cavalry troops and infantrymen, with the Lakota and Cheyenne warriors ranging over the countryside. Crook's second in command Lieutenant Colonel William B. Royal's cavalry unit was put in grave danger by Lakota and Cheyenne warriors in a separate engagement but were assisted by the Shoshone and Crow scouts. In other conflicts on the battlefield, Crook's troops were able to gain ground and drive the Indian onslaught back, but they did not do enough damage to dissuade the Lakotas' attacks for sustained periods. Because of this, Crook was unable to control the field for any amount of time.[12]

Crook, having learned from catastrophes like the destruction of William J. Fetterman's entire command in a skillful ambush at the hands of Crazy Horse in 1866, tried to not allow parts of his command to be drawn too thin by engaging in skirmishes where they could be cut off from the rest of his main battalion. Crook was fortunate that he had resourceful Shoshone and Crow scouts who held off the early onslaught of Lakota and Cheyenne charges. With the strategic deployment of his troops across the battlefield, Crook eventually caused Crazy Horse to withdraw his warriors when the Lakota leader realized the battle would not end decisively.

Though Crazy Horse abandoned the field first, Crook and his troops were left the worse for wear, however. Including deaths among his Crow and Shoshone scouts, Crook counted ten casualties and around twenty wounded. The number of dead and wounded damaged Crook as well. His troops had also used up a quarter of their ammunition holding off the onrushing Indians. The greatest detriment to Crook's cause, however, was the fact that many of his remaining Crow and Shoshone scouts abandoned his command, returning to their families. Some have speculated that these scouts left believing the Sioux were going to attack their homes. Lacking effective guides, Crook was forced to return to his camp on Goose Creek and wait for reinforcements.[13]

The jury is not out on any of this. There is no controversy. Crook's command was dismayed by their encounter with Crazy Horse's contingent and their allies abandoning them. The Battle of the Rosebud was a particularly brutal and bloody affair. The Indians themselves incurred numerous injuries and casualties attempting to attack Crook's troops and sap their supplies. During this epic engagement, Crook surely made tactical mistakes, but returning to his camp to wait for reinforcements was not one of them.

During the battle, Crook incorrectly believed that the Lakota warriors were attacking so ferociously because they were defending a large nearby village. Normally, Indians would fiercely engage a large military force to allow their people to escape the fight. In fact, there was no village close by, but it was much farther away. This mistaken assumption led Crook to command Captains Anson Mills and Henry Noyes to withdraw from the field and begin a fruitless search for a phantom village. This decision nearly led to the destruction of Lieutenant Colonel William B. Royall's six companies of cavalry.[14]

As the engagement progressed, Royall's troops pursued the Indians who initially attacked Crook's position. Before they realized it, the cavalry was drawn into a brutal firefight with surging Sioux and Cheyenne warriors. Crook stated that he ordered Royall to withdraw from the field on multiple occasions after realizing the dire situation. Royall denied he received such orders. But the incoming volleys he received from the Indians' rifles were too intense. It was not until the arrival of the Crow and Shoshone scouts that he was able to repel the Lakota attack.[15]

In support of the Crow and Shoshone scouts, Crook sent two additional infantry units to lay long-range suppressing fire on the aggressive Indians swarming Royall's cavalry. This combination of scouts and infantry allowed Royall to slowly withdraw from the fierce fighting and dig into a defensive position. Retreating at a snail's pace, partly because of rough terrain, Royall was able to join Crook's main force while Mills's cavalry units eventually arrived from their futile search for the Indian village. Mills's arrival caused Crazy Horse to reassess the situation, thinking reinforcements had arrived, and abandon the field.[16]

Crook claimed victory at this point because he was left occupying the battlefield, but the severe damage to his army was already dealt. In fact, if one makes an honest assessment of the Rosebud battle, it is obvious Crook had absolutely no choice but to return to his camp on Goose Creek near the future site of Sheridan, Wyoming, and wait for reinforcements.

Crook was not an incompetent soldier. The mistakes he made during the Rosebud, especially sending troops to root out a believed nearby Indian village, were thought-out educated guesses. Up to that point, military encounters with plains tribes met with a ferocious counteroffensive normally was an indication that a large village was nearby.

Unfortunately for Crook, there was no village to draw the Lakota warriors toward. Crazy Horse played a master strategic stroke by instructing his warriors to engage Crook's column, much like a European or American army would do, in a constant attack, which split up his forces and gave the Indians the best chance for victory. They inflicted casualties on Crook's cavalry, exhausted some of his supplies, and, most importantly, caused his Crow and Shoshone scouts to abandon him.

Eight days following the Rosebud fight, the infamous Battle of the Little Big Horn took place. On June 25 and June 26, General George Armstrong Custer and his immediate Seventh Cavalry command would locate and engage a combined force of eighteen hundred to two thousand Lakota, Cheyenne, and Arapahoe Indians. In what was to be a surprise assault, Custer, who believed his troops had been discovered by the Lakota, decided to attack the village immediately to prevent the village's inhabitants from scattering.[17]

During the ensuing battle along the Little Big Horn River, Custer and five companies were overwhelmed in the ravines and on the hills and eventually engulfed by a massive combination of Indian warrior bands. The Seventh Cavalry lost 268 out of 660 men, including scouts and civilians. Custer, along with 210 men under his immediate command, died that day.[18]

Before knowing he was going to encounter a massive hostile enemy, Custer decided to split his twelve companies into four battalions. This crucial decision ultimately led to the death of nearly 300 men under Custer's command and his historic and infamous defeat.[19] General Crook played no role in the outcome of the Battle of the Little Big Horn for good reason. After the Battle of the Rosebud, he had no choice but to return to the camp at Goose Creek for supplies and to tend to his dead and wounded.

It can be debated whether Crook had to wait the seven weeks he eventually did at the Goose Creek camp for reinforcements. In retrospect, that was perhaps a little too much time. What is not debatable, however, is that he could have somehow had time to reequip his troops, march them back into Indian territory, find a hostile village without adequate scouts, and be able to save Custer and prevent the greatest military disaster in the history of the United States, when he had no idea where Custer was. With the condition his army was in after tangling with Crazy Horse, it simply was not possible. End of story.

CROOK'S DITHERING WAS CUSTER'S DOOM—BILL MARKLEY

There is no doubt General George Crook's inaction doomed Lieutenant Colonel George Armstrong Custer and members of the Seventh Cavalry on June 25, 1876. Let's examine the evidence for this, day by day, starting with the aftermath of the Battle of the Rosebud on June 17, up to the Battle of the Little Big Horn on June 25. What actions did Crook and his Yellowstone and Big Horn Expedition take? What were General Alfred Terry and his Dakota Column, which included Lieutenant Colonel George Armstrong Custer's Seventh Cavalry, and Colonel John Gibbon, who was leading his Montana Column, doing? What actions did the Indians in Sitting Bull's village take?

Saturday, June 17, 1876

At the end of the day, General George Crook and his thirteen-hundred-man Yellowstone and Big Horn Expedition held the field of battle at the headwaters of the Rosebud Creek, and Crook would declare it a victory. His troops had two days of rations left. They had carried a hundred thousand rounds of ammunition, expending twenty-five thousand rounds. Ten of Crook's men had been killed and more than twenty wounded, a few of whom were not expected to live. They found thirteen Indian bodies and 150 dead horses on the field. There was no telling how many dead and wounded the Indians had carried off.[20]

That evening, Crook planned to pursue the Lakotas and Cheyennes and attack their village the next day. However, his Crow and Shoshone allies refused to go with him, declaring they had plenty of scalps. The Crows also recognized some of their horses being ridden by Lakota warriors and were concerned the Lakotas might have attacked their villages in their absence. Both the Crow and Shoshone warriors planned to break off fighting and ride back to their villages. Apparently, they did not like Crook's style of fighting. The Crows called him "Squaw Chief." Realizing he was losing 250 allied warriors, Crook had a change of heart and decided that instead of advancing he would escort the wounded back to his base camp where he would resupply.[21]

The troops were concerned about Crook's actions. Sergeant George Howard of the Second Cavalry wrote in his journal that night, "The Fighting was so poorly conducted that the Enemy came in our rear and stole everything left back where we were when the fighting commenced. The soldiers have lost all confidence in General Crook."[22]

Led by the Lakota leaders Sitting Bull and Crazy Horse, as well as Cheyenne leaders, the warriors who fought against the troops that day knew they had won a great victory. They left the battlefield not because they were defeated but because they were hungry, their horses were tired, and they were concerned the Crows and Shoshones might try to raid their village.[23]

Sitting Bull's village was encamped on Reno Creek, a tributary of the Little Big Horn River, roughly twenty-four miles northwest of the battlefield. When the warriors returned, the people wanted to hold a victory celebration. However, they would have to wait and hold it at a new camp, since families were mourning at this campsite for loved ones who had been killed in the fight. They planned to move to a new location the next day.[24]

General Alfred Terry, leading the thousand-man Dakota Column, which included Lieutenant Colonel George Armstrong Custer and his Seventh Cavalry, had left Fort Abraham Lincoln on May 17, 1876. Marching west, the column reached the mouth of the Powder River on the Yellowstone River by June 8, where the riverboat *Far West* was moored, having brought troops and supplies up the river. On June 9, the *Far West* conveyed Terry upriver to confer with Colonel John Gibbon, who had been leading the five-hundred-man Montana Column eastward along the Yellowstone. Gibbon told Terry that on May 26, a detachment led by Lieutenant James Bradley had ridden eighteen miles up Rosebud Creek where he had seen a large Indian camp off in the distance. Gibbon had not acted on that information. Neither Terry nor Gibbon had any knowledge as to General Crook's whereabouts.[25]

On June 10, Terry sent Major Marcus Reno, with six companies of the Seventh Cavalry and a Gatling gun, on reconnaissance south along the Powder River. Terry's orders stated for Reno to head upriver as far as the Little Powder River, then turn west to the Tongue River, and descend north to the Yellowstone where Terry would be waiting for him. Reno went beyond the bounds of his orders, riding farther west into the Rosebud watershed, where on June 17 he found evidence of a large Indian trail heading south, upstream, as well as large, abandoned campsites. Reno's scouts followed the Indian trail nineteen miles upriver and returned to Reno, reporting fresh abandoned campsites. Reno was low on provisions, the horses and mules were tired, and the scouts were concerned the Lakotas and Cheyennes would defeat them if attacked, so Reno turned back, heading downstream, north to the Yellowstone.[26]

Sunday, June 18, 1876

Early in the morning, Crook turned his back on advancing toward Sitting Bull's village and began his return to his Goose Creek camp. Small parties of Lakota and Cheyenne warriors watched from Camel-Back Ridge, as the thirteen-hundred-man Yellowstone and Big Horn Expedition left the field of battle.[27]

After traveling twenty miles from the battlefield, Crook made camp at 2:00 p.m., to alleviate the suffering of the wounded.[28]

That night, Sergeant Howard wrote in his journal, "Another disastrous retreat with nothing accomplished." By mentioning "another disastrous retreat," Howard was referring to Crook's troops attacking a Cheyenne village they thought was Crazy Horse's Oglala Lakotas back on March 17, 1876, along the Powder River. Although Crook did not lead the attack, he was ultimately responsible. His troops, under the command of Colonel Joseph Reynolds, burned down the village and killed two Indians. Reynolds destroyed food, buffalo robes, and furs that could have been used by the troops. When the Cheyennes counterattacked, Reynolds panicked and retreated in haste, leaving three bodies behind. Possibly one man was wounded but still alive and then killed. The warriors soon recaptured their horses the troops had taken. Reynolds chose not to go after them. Crook returned to Fort Fetterman without further pursuing the Indians. On his return, he filed charges against Reynolds, who filed charges against two of his subordinates. Reynolds was convicted of "conduct to the prejudice of good order and military discipline" and suspended from service for a year. His subordinates were convicted of similar charges. Crook's Yellowstone and Big Horn Expedition did not return to the field until May 29.[29]

During the night of June 18, the Crow warriors left Crook, vowing they would return in fifteen days to continue the fight against the Lakotas and Cheyennes.[30]

Earlier that morning, Sitting Bull's village broke camp and followed present-day Reno Creek downstream to the river valley they called Greasy Grass, known to the whites as the Little Big Horn. At their new camp, the people celebrated their victory. Festivities would last for six days and nights with singing, dancing, and feasting. Adding to their happiness, scouts returned from the battlefield to report that the soldiers were returning to their camp on Goose Creek.[31]

From June 18 to June 25, Sitting Bull's camp would double in size. People who had wintered over at the agencies were arriving—some to hunt and others to fight if need be. An estimated one thousand lodges housed possibly seven thousand people. Numbers of warriors ranged up to eighteen hundred, but no one took a head count.[32]

Meanwhile, Reno's Seventh Cavalry contingent reached the mouth of the Rosebud on the Yellowstone and rode a mile downstream, where they camped across from Gibbon's Montana Column. Terry with his Dakota Column and the *Far West* were stationed downriver at the mouth of the Tongue on the Yellowstone.[33]

Monday, June 19, 1876

At noon, Crook's men arrived at their base camp on the south fork of Goose Creek. Since the horses and mules had eaten most of the grass in the immediate area, the men moved camp two and a half miles upstream later that day.[34]

Crook prepared a telegram to be sent to General Phil Sheridan, commander of the Division of the Missouri, informing him of the battle. Crook explained that he had been attacked by a large force of Indians and was able to repulse them. He returned to Goose Creek to care for the wounded and to send for reinforcements. Crook prepared a second telegram to be sent to Lieutenant Colonel Robert Williams, assistant adjutant general at the Omaha department headquarters, stating that he needed five companies of infantry to be sent to him. That evening, the civilian courier Ben Arnold, carrying Crook's telegrams and the five newspaper reporters' dispatches, rode out alone for Fort Fetterman, reaching the fort on June 22, where the telegrams were sent and the public learned of the fight on the Rosebud.[35]

The people at Sitting Bull's camp feasted and celebrated as new groups continued to join them.

Up on the Yellowstone River, Reno marched his troops downriver toward Terry's Dakota Column and late in the day camped eight miles above Terry's position. He sent a dispatch to Terry stating that he had been to the Rosebud and would report on his findings to him the next morning. Angry that Reno had disobeyed orders, Terry sent back a message telling him to remain in place and the Dakota Column and the *Far West* would come to him the next day.[36]

Tuesday, June 20, 1876

General Crook had the camp moved another seven miles upstream on the South Fork of Goose Creek, where there was abundant grass and wood. The men named it Camp Cloud Peak. Crook spent his time writing a detailed report on the battle to be sent to Sheridan. Three Shoshones rode west to report to their people about their fight with the Lakotas and Cheyennes.[37]

At Sitting Bull's camp, new people arrived as the festivities continued.

General Terry moved up the Yellowstone and met with Reno and Custer aboard the *Far West*. Although Terry was angry with Reno's disobedience of orders, Reno did supply new information on movements and the whereabouts of the Indians.[38]

Wednesday, June 21, 1876

General Crook sent the wounded under escort on a 169-mile journey back to Fort Fetterman. Along with the wounded, Crook also sent Quartermaster Captain John Furey to bring back more supplies. An additional person, who had sneaked along with the expedition and was now being returned, was Martha Canary—better known as Calamity Jane.[39]

That same day, most of the Shoshones left for their villages to celebrate, promising they would return. Ten Shoshones remained with Crook. Five had been wounded and five remained to care for them. Crook still had his three original scouts: Frank Grouard, Louis Richard, and Baptiste Pourier.[40]

Life in Sitting Bull's camp continued as in previous days with more people arriving and feasting, dancing, and visiting.

General Terry met with Custer, Gibbon, and Major James Brisbin at about 2:00 p.m. aboard the *Far West*, now located on the Yellowstone two miles downriver from the mouth of the Rosebud. The officers believed Sitting Bull's village was located at the headwaters of Rosebud Creek, Big Horn River, or Little Big Horn River. Terry's plan was to split his forces, sending Custer with the Seventh Cavalry south up the Rosebud to its headwaters. From there they were to ride west to the Little Big Horn and then downriver from there. At the same time Gibbon's Montana Column was already marching up the Yellowstone to the mouth of the Big Horn River. From there they would head up the Big Horn to the Little Big Horn, where they could block any Indians Custer might push their way. Since Gibbon's infantry was slower moving than cavalry, Terry estimated they would not arrive at the Little Big Horn until Monday, June 26, and wanted Custer to give them time to get into position. Custer's Seventh Cavalry was to leave the next morning.[41]

Thursday, June 22, 1876

General Crook left camp on an expedition into the Big Horn Mountains—a hunting and fishing expedition. For six weeks, Crook did not advance but waited for reinforcements and resupply. To pass the time, he and his men went hunting and fishing. Soldiers played baseball and panned the streams looking for gold. Crook himself shot plenty of game, and one day he caught seventy trout.[42]

General Crook's aide-de-camp Lieutenant John Bourke later wrote, "My note-books about this time seem to be almost the chronicle of a sporting club, so filled are they with the numbers of trout brought by different fishermen into camp." Later he added, "General Crook started out to catch a mess [of trout] but met with poor luck. He saw bear tracks and followed them, bringing in a good-sized 'cinnamon,' so it was agreed not to refer to his small number of trout. Buffalo and elk meat were both plenty, and with the trout kept the men well fed."[43]

Life continued peacefully at Sitting Bull's camp. New people continued to arrive. Men went out on hunts. Socializing and festivities continued.

At noon, Lieutenant Colonel Custer led approximately 660 men of the Seventh Cavalry and scouts south along Rosebud Creek. At 4:00 p.m., Custer called a halt. The men were having problems with the pack train mules. The column had advanced twelve miles, and Custer decided to make camp for the night. The *Far West*, carrying General Terry and his officers, had left after 3:00 p.m. steaming up the Yellowstone River toward the mouth of the Big Horn River, where Terry would lead the combined Dakota and Montana Columns up the Big Horn and hopefully trap the Indians between Custer, Crook, and his own troops.[44]

Friday, June 23, 1876

General Crook and the members of his Yellowstone and Big Horn Expedition continued to relax—fishing, hunting, playing games, bathing, and exploring.

People continued to arrive at Sitting Bull's camp. The large concentration of people was exhausting the resources of the immediate area, and they needed to move. Scouts reported large antelope herds to the north and west. The camp leaders determined that everyone had obtained enough buffalo meat so they would now hunt antelope. Plans were made to move the camp the next day.[45]

Lieutenant Colonel Custer's men broke camp at 5:00 a.m. and followed the Rosebud upstream. They came upon the remains of several large campsites. The pack train mules continued to cause problems and lag behind the rest of the column. At 4:30 p.m., after traveling thirty-three miles, Custer called a halt for the day to allow the mules to catch up. The last did not reach camp until almost sundown.[46]

General Terry, aboard the *Far West*, continued to proceed up the Yellowstone. At 8:40 p.m., the *Far West* was moored along the riverbank for the night. They were about fifteen miles from the mouth of the Big Horn River.[47]

Saturday, June 24, 1876

General Crook and his men continued to relax along Goose Creek at the foot of the Big Horn Mountains.

Sitting Bull's camp was on the move. The entire village traveled north, downriver eight miles, and established camp along the flood plain on the west bank of the Little Big Horn River. Groves of cottonwood trees lined the river. Ravines intersected a series of bluffs rising from the river's east bank. The village was immense, stretching three miles along the river with Sitting Bull's Hunkpapas at the upstream end and the Cheyennes at the downstream end with the rest of the Lakota bands in middle positions.[48]

Lieutenant Colonel Custer and the Seventh Cavalry broke camp and continued riding upstream along the Rosebud. They came upon multiple abandoned village sites and multiple trails. The farther upstream they rode the larger the trails became and the fresher the campsites. When they reached a location that was an easy crossing into the Tullock Creek watershed to the west, scout George Herendeen approached Custer and asked leave to go to General Terry's column. Terry had instructed Custer to search the headwaters of Tullock Creek and then send Herendeen down Tullock Creek, a tributary of the Big Horn River, to report to Terry who planned to be on the Big Horn River. Custer decided not to reconnoiter Tullock Creek and did not send Herendeen but continued to follow the large Indian trail up the Rosebud. After riding twenty-five miles, Custer called a halt at 7:45 p.m. They camped on a flat area along the Rosebud.[49]

The *Far West* had reached the mouth of the Big Horn River at 5:00 a.m. and began ferrying troops across to the far side, finishing by 4:00 p.m. An hour later, General Terry's column, consisting of about four hundred men, began marching up the Big Horn River. After a four-mile march, they reached the mouth of Tullock Creek and headed up that waterway, marching an hour before making camp for the night. Terry was expecting the arrival of scout George Herendeen to communicate Custer's findings. There was no sign of Herendeen, so Terry sent Crow scouts up the creek to look for Herendeen, Custer, or Sitting Bull's village. After riding between fifteen and twenty miles, the scouts returned to say they saw no signs of any of them.[50]

Sunday, June 25, 1876

It was another day like all the others at Camp Cloud Peak on Goose Creek. General Crook was away from camp on a hunt in the Big Horn Mountains. After fulfilling their daily military obligations, men took care of personal concerns, relaxed, hunted, and fished. Reuben Davenport, reporter for the *New York Herald*, wrote, "Idleness in camp is the most irksome experience in the world." Joe Wasson with the *Daily Alta California* wrote, "With the single interval of the big skirmish on Rosebud Creek, June 17. . . . Crook's campaign has been thus far little else than a picnic excursion. . . . During this tedious interval, various attempts were made to break the monotony. Books were almost unknown in camp, and the newspapers were invariably from twenty days old to one month. Cards became stale amusement."[51]

Officers were getting on each other's nerves. Reporting for the *Chicago Times*, John Finerty wrote, "The monotony of camp, despite the beauty of the surroundings, became more intolerable than ever. Officers, who, in time of excitement, would take no notice of trifles, became irritable and exercised their authority over their subordinates in a decidedly martinetish manner. This, in a matter of course, produced friction and occasional sulking."[52]

Captain Anson Mills and two soldiers rode into the foothills of the Big Horn Mountains to find a stream to fish. Later in the day, they returned with one hundred trout. They said they had seen dense smoke far to the northwest. Finerty wrote, "All agreed, that it must be a prairie fire or something of the kind."[53]

Frank Grouard said he was on a scout, riding in the mountains when he saw the smoke. It was not a prairie fire but smoke signals from the Indians indicating they were battling soldiers. Grouard rode back to camp and told this to the officers, but they did not believe him.[54]

Seventy-five miles to the north of Camp Cloud Peak, life was peaceful in Sitting Bull's camp. The day began like any other day in the massive camp along the Little Big Horn River. By midday, the temperature was getting hot as people went about their business. Boys took horses to the river to water while other children played and swam. Some people were sleeping late after the previous night's victory dance. Some women were dismantling their lodges as the plan was to continue heading downriver to hunt antelope. Women were outside the village digging wild turnips when a mounted warrior raced toward them shouting that soldiers were coming. Looking east, they saw a cloud of dust raised by cavalry. The women ran to camp sounding the alarm, surprising the people[55]

Earlier that morning, Lieutenant Colonel Custer's scouts reported a large Indian village was fifteen miles away on the Little Big Horn River. Custer planned to hit the village in a morning attack on June 26, but he changed his plans, deciding to attack that day after receiving information that Indians had discovered their whereabouts and most likely would warn the village.[56]

Custer and his men crossed from the Rosebud watershed into the Little Big Horn watershed and proceeded down Reno Creek. The pack mules were slowing the advance, so Custer left Company B and a few men from each of the other companies to guard the pack train while the rest of the troops moved out rapidly. Custer divided his men again, sending Captain Fredrick Benteen with three companies to reconnoiter the Little Big Horn bluffs off to the left. Custer told Benteen if he saw Indians, he was to attack; if he did not see anything, he was to rejoin Custer as quickly as possible. Custer assigned Major Reno three companies to form the left battalion and ride on the left bank of Reno Creek, and Custer commanded the right battalion consisting of five companies that rode on the right bank of the creek.[57]

Reports came in from the scouts that Indians were fleeing downstream. Custer ordered Reno to pursue them. Custer would support Reno as Custer continued down the right side of Reno Creek and up into the bluffs. Reno crossed the Little Big Horn River and followed the Indians toward the village. As the Indians reached the edge of the village, they stopped running and stood their ground. Reno ordered his men into line of battle, then shouted "Charge!" and the battalion advanced at a gallop.[58]

That day, the warriors from Sitting Bull's village routed Reno's troops, annihilated Custer's immediate command, and had the survivors pinned down on what later would be named Reno Hill. Altogether, Custer would lose 268 out of 660 men.[59]

By the end of the second day of fighting, Monday, June 26, the Lakota and Cheyenne warriors withdrew from their positions. The Seventh Cavalry survivors on Reno Hill watched as the massive Lakota and Cheyenne village broke camp and leisurely moved south toward the Big Horn Mountains. General Terry's column would not arrive at the battlefield until Tuesday morning, June 27.[60]

On July 10, General Crook was out hunting in the Big Horn Mountains when Louis Richard and Ben Arnold arrived at Camp Cloud Peak with dispatches from General Sheridan informing Crook of Custer's demise. A detachment was sent out and found Crook eighteen miles away. When Crook entered camp later that day, he and his hunting party were hauling the meat from fourteen elk they had shot. After being resupplied and reinforced, General Crook finally felt comfortable enough to pursue the Lakotas and Cheyennes on August 5, 1876.[61]

Reviewing General Crook's actions, it's plain to see he did absolutely nothing to pursue the Lakota and Cheyenne warriors or try to determine the location of their village. He still had plenty of food and ammunition at his Goose Creek base camp. His inaction doomed Custer and a large number of the men of the Seventh Cavalry. Let's examine what he might have done differently.

Instead of having each man take four days of rations with him, he could have taken pack mules with sufficient provisions for a longer period of time. That way, the men could have remained in the field after the battle of the Rosebud. He could have sent the wounded back with a strong escort and still had plenty of men in the field.

Even with two days of provisions, he could have followed the Lakota and Cheyenne warriors' trail down the Rosebud and on to Reno Creek, where he could have attacked Sitting Bull's village. As another alternative, he could have remained at the Rosebud battlefield and sent for more provisions from his camp on Goose Creek and then advanced.

In his book *Rosebud, June 17, 1876*, Paul Hedren considered what might have happened if Crook had attacked Sitting Bull's camp: "Here Crook would have been taking the fight straight to Sitting Bull. Win, lose, or draw, the disruption would have been catastrophic. In some likelihood, the village could not have remained cohesive."[62]

Even if Crook had not advanced farther, just remaining at the Rosebud battlefield would have been a concern for the people of Sitting Bull's village.

On Crook's return to his base camp at Goose Creek, he could have sent the wounded back to Fort Fetterman and then advanced north or sent out strong patrols to keep the Lakotas and Cheyennes watchful of his movements. Even a slow advance would have been a concern to the Indians, and they might have been driven toward Terry and Gibbon's columns, or they might have scattered.

Paul Hedren writes that after Crook returned to his Goose Creek camp and sent the wounded on their way to Fort Fetterman, he could have resupplied his troops and set out to follow the Lakota and Cheyenne warriors by June 21. Two days later, his Yellowstone and Big Horn Expedition could have been back on the Rosebud, following it downstream with the possibility of running into Custer's scouts who were ranging ahead of the Seventh Cavalry on June 24. A combination of Crook and Custer attacking Sitting Bull's village could have led to a completely different outcome.[63]

The Hunkpapa warrior Rain in the Face said in a 1905 interview that had Crook "pushed on and connected with the Long-Haired Chief [it] would have saved Custer and perhaps won the day."[64]

Any offensive action or even a show of force by Crook's Yellowstone and Big Horn Expedition could have changed the dynamics of the size and location of Sitting Bull's camp. There may not have even been a battle at the Little Big Horn had Crook taken military action instead of establishing a "sporting club" in the Big Horn Mountains.

CHAPTER 6

DID ROBERT FORD KILL JESSE JAMES?

JUST THE FACTS

Frank and Jesse James top the list of best known and most successful American outlaws. Both James boys were born in Clay County, Missouri—Alexander Franklin on January 10, 1843, and Jesse Woodson on September 5, 1847. During the Civil War, they fought as Confederate sympathizer guerrillas called bushwhackers. After the war, they used their combat and evasive skills to enter the world of banditry.[1]

On February 13, 1866, in broad daylight, a gang robbed sixty thousand dollars from the Clay County Savings Association in Liberty, Missouri, not far from the James boys home. The money was never recovered, and no one ever stood trial for the robbery. Many suspected the James boys were involved. The robbery went down in history as the first peacetime, daytime bank robbery in the United States.[2]

The James boys eventually teamed up robbing banks with their friends the Younger brothers—Cole, John, Jim, and Bob. In 1873, the James–Younger Gang upped their game robbing trains.[3]

The James boys and Younger brothers knew who their friends were and who could be trusted. They had an extensive network of former Confederate and bushwhacker supporters. In 1907, William Allan Pinkerton of Pinkerton's National Detective Agency would say, "As a rule the James and Younger brothers and their associates, after each crime, would return to their home, Clay County, Mo., where they were virtually immune from arrest, either through fear of them by the respectable element or through the friendly aid they received from their admirers."[4]

During the Civil War, they had learned the art of disguise to the point of fooling Union troops and supporters into thinking they were Yankees. Frank and Jesse created aliases and new identities for themselves, fitting into communities and acting as model citizens. For years, Jesse and Frank eluded law enforcement and private detective agencies. Jesse successfully used the aliases John Davis Howard and Thomas Howard until the end of his life, and Frank went by B. J. Woodson.[5]

There are few photographs of Jesse after the Civil War, which makes sense. If you are an intelligent and successful criminal, you're not going to want your likeness to be made public for people to recognize you.

After the James–Younger Gang's botched raid on a bank in North-field, Minnesota, on September 7, 1876, where the Younger brothers were captured, the James boys went to ground and weren't heard from for several years.

Frank and Jesse were leading separate lives in Tennessee but remained in close contact. In 1879, Jesse recruited a new gang without Frank. The James Gang began its new crime wave, robbing the Chicago and Alton Railroad train at Glendale, Missouri, on October 8, 1879.[6]

On the night of September 7, 1881, five years to the day of the North-field, Minnesota, raid, the James Gang, this time including Frank James and a new member Charlie Ford, robbed the east-west running Chicago and Alton Railroad train at Rocky Cut, Missouri.[7]

The gang split up after the robbery. Frank took his family and moved to Lynchburg, Virginia, where he went by the alias James Warren. Jesse and his family had been living in Kansas City, Missouri, but on November 5, 1881, they moved to St. Joseph, Missouri. Charlie Ford went along to help with the move and stayed from time to time with the James family. Jesse continued to use his alias Thomas Howard.[8]

Trouble was brewing with other James Gang members. Dick Liddil and Wood Hite had been feuding over women and the distribution of loot from the Rocky Cut robbery. On December 4, 1881, they were both at the Harbison place, a James Gang refuge. The farm was the home of the Ford family and both Charlie Ford and his brother Bob were there. They were all at the breakfast table in the small dining room. Liddil and Hite were sitting across from each other. Hite accused Liddil of taking a hundred dollars that was not his. Liddil called him a liar. They drew their revolvers and began shooting at each other. Liddil fired five shots to Hite's four. Hite was hit in the right arm and Liddil was hit in the right thigh. Bob Ford drew his revolver, aimed at Hite, and shot him in the head. Hite died twenty minutes later.[9]

Wood Hite was Jesse's cousin. The gang members were afraid if Jesse found out they had killed Hite they would be on his hit list, so they buried Hite's body in a remote area. Charlie returned to Jesse's home, never saying anything about Hite's death. Liddil left and went into hiding; Jesse suspected Liddil had turned against him but didn't know why.[10]

On Christmas Eve 1881, Jesse moved his family, along with Charlie, to 1318 Lafayette Street situated on a high hill with an excellent view of the surroundings.[11]

Dick Liddil worried that Jesse would learn of his involvement in killing Hite and hoped he could make a deal with the state. Martha Bolton, the Ford brothers' sister, met with Missouri governor Thomas Crittenden on Liddil's behalf. Crittenden promised that if Liddil surrendered to Clay County Sheriff James Timberlake and testified against the James boys, he would not be prosecuted. Bolton also told the governor that her brother, Bob Ford, wanted to cooperate in the matter of Jesse James as long as he was assured the governor would protect him.[12]

On January 13, 1882, Governor Crittenden met with Bob Ford and agreed that if Ford took care of Jesse James, he would give Ford a pardon and the reward money. Crittenden later said he had told Ford that Jesse needed to be brought in alive. Ford later remembered the governor saying he wanted Jesse dead or alive. Governor Crittenden told Ford to work with Sheriff Timberlake and Kansas City Police Commissioner Captain Henry Craig.[13]

On January 24, 1882, Dick Liddil surrendered to Sheriff Timberlake and told everything he knew about the James Gang. Liddil's arrest was kept secret to prevent Frank and Jesse from learning.[14]

During March, Jesse took Charlie Ford on a tour of Kansas towns, looking for a good bank to rob. Jesse asked Charlie if he knew someone reliable to join the gang. Charlie recommended his brother Bob. They rode to Harbison place, where they recruited Bob.[15]

From that time on, both Ford brothers lived in Jesse's St. Joseph home. They kept in contact with state authorities and notified them of Jesse's address, but no one made a move to arrest him. The brothers decided to kill Jesse, but they had to wait for the right time. Jesse and his wife Zee treated the Fords as part of the family. They slept in the James house, ate their food, and played with their two little children.[16]

Dick Liddil's disappearance was a concern to Jesse. He asked Bob what had become of him since Liddil had been living at the Ford home at the Harbison place. Bob replied that Jesse knew as much as he did. Sheriff Timberlake had told Bob not to say anything to Jesse about Liddil's surrender and to try to keep newspapers away from Jesse. Reporters were hearing rumors of Liddil's surrender, and the news was bound to leak. Then on March 31, 1882, state officials put out a press release that Dick Liddil had surrendered. However, Jesse was still unaware.[17]

Jesse decided to rob the bank in Platte City, Missouri. They would leave for Platte City the night of April 3 and rob the bank the next morning.[18]

It was Monday morning, April 3, 1882, and Zee was preparing breakfast in the kitchen. Bob Ford entered the front room with the latest newspapers and gave Jesse the *St. Louis Republican*. As they looked through the papers, Bob saw in large print on the front page of the *Kansas City Times* the announcement of Dick Liddil's surrender. Bob tried to hide the paper, but Jesse saw it and took it into the kitchen. As Bob followed, he made sure his revolver was in position on his belt near his right hand.[19]

Charlie Ford and the two James children were already seated at the kitchen table as Bob sat down across from Jesse. Jesse spread the newspaper on the table, exclaiming, "Hello, here! Surrender of Dick Liddil!" Jesse looked across the table at Bob.

"Young man," Jesse said, "I thought you told me you didn't know anything about Dick."

"I didn't."

Jesse glared at Bob and said, "Well it's very strange. He surrendered three weeks ago, and you were right here in the neighborhood. It looks fishy to me."[20]

Bob walked out of the kitchen into the front room. Jesse followed, saying, "Well, it's all right anyway, Bob."

Bob believed Jesse was on to him but would not kill him in front of his wife and children; he would probably do that when they were out of town.[21]

After breakfast, Jesse and the Ford brothers went to the stable to feed and curry the horses. The day was becoming hot. When they returned to the house, Jesse commented he was hot and left the front room door open to let in a cool breeze. Removing his coat, he laid it on a bed in the room. Not wanting people passing by the open front door to see him wearing guns, Jesse took off his gun belt and guns and laid them on the bed. Charlie left Jesse and Bob in the front room and walked into the kitchen, joining Zee and the children.[22]

Jesse looked at a picture of a horse hanging on a front room wall. He was thinking of either rehanging it, adjusting it, or dusting the frame as he placed a straight back chair under the picture and stood on it to reach the picture. Jesse was unarmed with his back to Bob—vulnerable. Bob pulled his Smith & Wesson .44 New Model No. 3 revolver, a gift from Jesse, and aimed it at the back of Jesse's head. As Bob cocked the revolver's hammer, Jesse's head began to turn. Bob pulled the trigger, firing a bullet into the back of Jesse's head. He fell lifeless to the floor. Charlie and Zee ran into the room. Early accounts say Charlie was in the kitchen. Later accounts had him in the front room with Bob, maybe so Charlie could share in the reward.[23]

Zee knelt by Jesse's head, trying to wipe away the blood.

"It was an accident!" Bob said.

"Yes, an accident on purpose," Zee said. "You traitor. Bob Ford, traitor! Traitor!"[24]

IMPOSTERS GALORE—BILL MARKLEY

Bob and Charlie Ford ran from the James home yelling to a passerby to inform the police that they had killed Jesse James. The brothers raced to a telegraph station where they sent messages of Jesse's death to Missouri governor Thomas Crittenden, Clay County sheriff James Timberlake, and Kansas City police commissioner Captain Henry Craig. They found St. Joseph marshal Enos Craig and informed him they had killed Jesse James. Craig arrested them and placed them in jail.[25]

Jesse's body was taken to Buchanan County Coroner Dr. James Heddens's establishment, where reporters examined the body, finding two bullet wound scars on the right side of his chest, the tip of the left-hand middle finger missing, as well as other distinguishing marks confirming the body was Jesse James. Crowds of people showed up to view the corpse of the famous outlaw. Four doctors performed the autopsy. They surgically removed part of Jesse's skull to examine the bullet damage to his brain. The bullet was removed from Jesse's head and Dr. Heddens kept it. The bullet remained in the Heddens family for many years.[26]

The coroner impaneled six citizens for the inquest. It began at 3:00 p.m. the same day as Jesse's murder and lasted into the next day. A large crowd listened to the witnesses who were there to testify as to the identity of the body. Jesse's wife Zee James and the murderers Bob and Charlie Ford testified the body was Jesse James. Jesse's mother Zerelda Samuel arrived early the next morning and testified at the inquest. When she was asked if the body was her son Jesse, she responded, "Would to God that it were not!" and bitterly denounced the Ford brothers. William H. Wallace, prosecuting attorney for Jackson County, who had sworn to bring the James Gang to justice, arrived. He brought along Clay County farmer William Clay; former bushwhackers who rode with Jesse James, Harrison Trow and James Wilkerson; and Mattie Collins, wife or mistress of Dick Liddil. They all identified the body as belonging to Jesse James, to Wallace's satisfaction. Additional bushwhackers and friends testified that the body belonged to Jesse James.[27]

Kansas City Police Commissioner Captain Henry Craig testified, "The body corresponds with the description of Jesse James. I know the Fords. Bob Ford assisted Sheriff Timberlake and myself. He was not commissioned. Robert Ford acted through our instructions, and Charles was not acting under our instructions."[28]

Clay County Sheriff James Timberlake testified concerning Jesse, "We were personally acquainted. I saw him last in 1870. I knew his face. He had part of a finger shot off. I told Ford to get his brother to assist him."[29]

James Gang member Dick Liddil, who had surrendered and had agreed to testify against the James boys, was brought in and testified, "I have seen the body and recognize it as the body of Jesse James. I have no doubt of it."[30]

When Zerelda saw Liddil at the inquest, she pointed a finger at him and said, "Traitor, traitor, traitor! God will send vengeance on you for this; you are the cause of all this. Oh, you villain; I would rather be in my boy's place than in yours!"[31]

Governor Crittenden asked Dr. George W. James, no relation to Jesse, to identify the body. Dr. James had treated Jesse after he had accidently shot off the tip of his finger. Dr. James said, "Yes, it was Jesse, all right. The finger I attended was easy to identify."[32]

The coroner's jury's verdict was, "We the jury find that the deceased is Jesse James, and that he came to his death by a shot from a pistol in the hands of Robert Ford." Zee James swore out a warrant for the arrest of the Ford brothers in the murder of her husband Jesse James. They were arrested and kept in the St. Joseph jail.[33]

Jesse's body was photographed. The newspapers said there were scars from two old wounds on his chest and the tip of the middle finger of his left hand was missing, all identifying marks that the body was indeed Jesse James. The body was viewed by many people who knew Jesse James, and no one said it was not him.[34]

The Hannibal & St. Joseph Railroad provided a special train to take Jesse's body and the funeral party to Kearney, Missouri. When they reached town, Zerelda said to Sheriff Timberlake, "Oh, Mr. Timberlake, my son has gone to God, but his friends still live and will have revenge on those who murdered him for money." A viewing of his body was held at the Kearney Hotel. Hundreds of people, many of them friends and family, passed by the casket and viewed Jesse's body, paying their last respects. It was the largest number of people in Kearney up to that time.[35]

On April 6, 1882, Jesse's funeral service was held at the Mt. Olivet Baptist Church. An estimated two thousand people attended Jesse's funeral, friend and foe alike, including Captain Henry Craig and Sheriff James Timberlake, who was a pallbearer. After the service, the funeral procession went to the Samuel farm, where a deep grave had been dug under a large coffee bean tree in the yard near the house. Jesse's body was buried at 5:00 p.m. that evening.[36]

A grand jury indicted Bob and Charlie Ford for the murder of Jesse James. On April 17, they pled guilty and were sentenced to be hanged, but that afternoon, Governor Crittenden gave them a full and unconditional pardon.[37]

Zee James had been in poor health and on November 13, 1900, she died. Before dying, she requested that Jesse's body be disinterred and reburied alongside hers in Kearney's Mount Olivet Cemetery. In 1902, her wishes were fulfilled, and his body now lies alongside hers.[38]

Jesse James was dead and buried, but years later impostors would emerge, claiming to be him.

In January 1932, John James arrived in Excelsior Springs near Frank and Jesse James's family farm in Missouri. John James revealed he was actually Jesse James and had returned to visit his old haunts. He stated the man the Ford brothers killed in Jesse James's home in St. Joseph was a man named Charlie Bigelow. Some prominent residents believed him, and the national news media began proclaiming that Jesse James was alive and well.[39]

Jesse James's son, Jesse Jr., and his wife Stella were living in California at the time. Jesse Jr. was disturbed by John James's claim but was unwell and not able leave home. Stella traveled to Missouri to investigate John James.[40]

When questioned, John James could not remember Jesse's half-brother Archie's name or which of Zerelda's arms had been mangled in the 1875 Pinkerton bomb attack on her home. When Stella met with John James, she brought along a pair of Jesse's boots as well as Frank Milburn, who had made them for Jesse. Jesse had small feet, size six and a half. Stella asked John James to try them on, but he could not—his feet were too big for the boots.[41]

Stella learned that John James was on parole from Menard Penitentiary in Illinois, where he had served time for killing a man. She found John James's sister, Dr. Bessie James Garver, who wrote an affidavit stating his name was William John James and that he was mentally unbalanced and a potential threat to society. Undeterred, John James continued to proclaim he was Jesse James and appeared across the country in shows and circuses as Jesse James.[42]

It's not known how many men claimed to be Jesse James, but Jesse Jr. said he knew of twenty-six Jesse James claimants. One claimant named J. Frank Dalton revealed himself on national radio in May 1948.[43]

Dalton was from Lawton, Oklahoma, and the day after the radio show, the local newspapers picked up on the story as thirty thousand curiosity seekers descended upon the town. Over the years, Dalton had claimed many things. Among them: he served in the Confederate Army; he was a Texas Ranger, and a Chief of Police of Alpine, Texas; he served in the US Cavalry from 1866 to 1868 at Fort Harker, Kansas; and he was a US deputy marshal serving under Judge Isaac Parker, the hanging judge, at Fort Smith, Arkansas. There was a Frank Dalton working at Fort Smith as a US deputy marshal, but he was killed November 30, 1887. Dalton said he piloted an airplane at age sixty-nine in World War I. None of these claims were true.[44]

Dalton's story was similar to John James's tale and used material from it. He said a man named Charlie Bigelow had been shot and killed while he, Dalton, hid in a nearby stable. The James family was upset with this latest imposter and refused to talk with him.[45]

During the Civil War, Jesse had been wounded twice in the same lung. Skeptics wanted Dalton to have an X-ray taken of his chest to show evidence of those wounds. He refused. Dalton also bore no scars on his skin from where the bullets should have entered. Dalton explained their absence, saying that he had had skin grafts done on the scars in the 1890s, but medical professionals said that type of procedure was not done during that time period.[46]

Jesse James was missing the tip of his middle finger on his left hand. J. Frank Dalton had a compete middle finger on his left hand.[47]

Analysis of Jesse James handwriting compared to J. Frank Dalton's handwriting do not match.[48]

In 1948, Dalton began earning a living at carnivals and fairs, proclaiming he was Jesse James. He appeared on stage with "Colonel" James Russell Davis, who claimed he was Cole Younger, as well as with William Henry "Brushy Bill" Roberts, who claimed he was Billy the Kid. On January 13, 1950, all three claimants appeared on NBC's national *We the People* radio and television show.[49]

On September 6, 1952, over a year after J. Frank Dalton's death, the *St. Louis Post-Dispatch* published a letter from Stella James, the widow of Jesse James's son. In the letter she stated that J. Frank Dalton was not Jesse James. Stella said Orvus Lee Howk, who was Frank Dalton's promoter, admitted to her that Dalton was using the same information that had been used by the imposter John James back in 1932, claiming Bob Ford had shot Charlie Bigelow. Howk offered to pay the James family fifty thousand dollars if they would say Dalton was Jesse James. They refused.[50]

Toward the end of the letter Stella James wrote, "I want to assure you that if Jesse James had lived these many years he would have cared for his son and family and not have been exploited over the country for a few dollars that would be made from such an exploitation."[51]

On July 17, 1995, Jesse James's remains were exhumed for DNA testing against James family descendants' DNA. Ironically, the exhumation was guarded by the Pinkertons, who had hounded the James boys when they were alive. Not only were human bones and teeth found in Jesse James's second grave, but also a .36 caliber bullet in the area of the right rib cage. In addition, a .38 caliber bullet had earlier been found in the original grave at the Samuel farm. Jesse had been shot in the chest twice during the Civil War.[52]

Professor James Starrs led a forensic team that analyzed the remains found in Jesse James's grave. On February 23, 1996, Starrs held a press conference at the Forty-eighth Annual Meeting of the American Academy of Forensic Sciences in Nashville, Tennessee. After conducting DNA tests and reviewing artifacts found with the human remains, Professor Starrs stated, "I feel a reasonable degree of scientific certainty that we have the remains of Jesse James."[53]

If the Ford brothers' murder of Jesse James was a hoax, there would have been lots of people involved. It's human nature to have to tell someone a secret. News of the hoax would have gotten out. No one keeps a secret. Jesse James still lies moldering in his Kearney, Missouri, Mount Olivet Cemetery grave.

YET SHALL HE LIVE—KELLEN CUTSFORTH

History states that on April 3, 1882, after eating breakfast, the bandit Jesse James walked into the living room of his home in St. Joseph, Missouri. He was joined by two compatriots, Charlie and Robert Ford. While in the living room, Jesse took off his revolvers, laid them on a bed, then climbed on to a chair to dust a picture hanging on the wall.[54]

While Jesse was cleaning the picture, Robert Ford crept up behind him, drew his .44 caliber revolver, and fired a single shot into the back of the notorious outlaw's head. The Fords then ran from the scene, pled guilty to the murder, and were sentenced to be hanged. However, they eventually received a full pardon from Missouri governor Crittenden exonerating them. Many believe Governor Crittenden and the Ford boys conspired together to murder Jesse.[55]

Following these events, Robert Ford never denied his part in the slaying of Jesse and even went on to star in a popular traveling stage show about the murder of the bandit.[56] In 1892, Ford would be gunned down himself inside a tent saloon he operated in the small town of Creede, Colorado.[57] This moment supposedly marks the end of Jesse James's tale. However, there are those who would disagree.

Since the supposed death of Jesse James, some twenty-six men have been documented as impersonating the infamous outlaw. At one point, Jesse was apparently witnessed attending his sister's funeral in Wichita Falls, Texas, in 1889. Jesse and his brother Frank were also seen in 1906 at the Dallas County Fair. The desperado duo was apparently very congenial with everyone and spent a long time at the event in conversation with friends.[58]

With several sightings by people who knew the James boys, is it impossible to think that Jesse escaped death's icy clutches, at least for a time? It is not so far-fetched to believe the Jameses cooked up a plot to dupe authorities into believing Jesse was dead so he could live out the rest of his days anonymously. Of the twenty-six men documented to have claimed to be Jesse James, a man named John Frank Dalton, perhaps, has the most convincing claim. In Dalton's case, he said there were two sets of Jesse Jameses, a pair in Missouri and another set in Kentucky. He said that George James married Matilda Dalton, the sister of Lewis Dalton, who founded the infamous Dalton Gang. This pair of brothers was Jesse Woodson James and Sylvester Franklin James [59]

Dalton went on to state the second set of Jameses in Missouri were born to Reverend Robert James and Zerelda Cole. These brothers were Jesse Robert James and Alexander Franklin James. According to Dalton, both sets of men were cousins and guerrilla fighters during the Civil War. Afterward, they all joined outlaw gangs, robbing banks and trains together. As the years went by, the outlaws got married and the bounties on these men's heads for their deaths or capture increased to the point that all the men wanted to drop their desperado ways. So, the James boys hatched a plan to fake Jesse's death.[60]

At the same time the James relatives were hatching their plot, a man named Charlie Bigelow was masquerading around Missouri as Jesse James. Framing Jesse and his gang for the crime, Bigelow robbed several stores, banks, and trains in the state. Angered by his actions, both sets of Jameses caught up to Bigelow and killed him. They took his corpse to a home in St. Joseph, Missouri, where Jesse Robert James was living, and placed his body on the floor.[61]

The James boys then called in their family friend Robert Ford, desperate for money. They hired him to fire a bullet into the wall and then run out of the home to take credit for cutting down the country's most famous outlaw, Jesse James. Jesse's mother, wife, Missouri governor Thomas Crittenden, and most of their closest friends were all in on the conspiracy and corroborated Ford's claim of killing Jesse. They all agreed to not reveal the truth until one of the collaborators reached the age of one hundred.[62]

After this cover-up, Jesse Robert James, the Missourian Jesse, traveled south with his family and lived out the rest of his life in Pensacola, Florida, under the alias George Hines. Jesse Woodson James, the Kentuckian Jesse, left for South America. After living there for several years, he decided to return to the United States, coming back to Gladewater, Texas. While there, he lived under the alias John Franklin Dalton. He often went by J. Frank Dalton, later revealing that the "J" stood for Jesse, Frank for his brother Frank, and Dalton, his mother's maiden name. When he reached one hundred, he revealed to the world he was the real Jesse James.[63]

There are several facts that give credence to Dalton's claim. After he divulged his secret, Dalton went on a two-year speaking tour. He revealed he knew dates, names, places, and other facts historically verified about Jesse James's history. There were also numerous men, almost too many to count, who stated in 1892 they saw Jesse James after his supposed death.[64]

Continuing along these lines, the imposter Charlie Bigelow, who was killed by the James brothers, appears on census records in 1880 and is not found on any other historic records. In 1978, the supposed corpse in Jesse's grave was exhumed, and the bullet lodged in the ribcage was found to be a .38 caliber. Robert Ford was photographed with a .44 caliber, the self-admitted murder weapon.[65]

When J. Frank Dalton unmasked himself in 1948, he was said to be around one hundred years old. On April 24 of that same year, he signed an affidavit in front of a notary public in Lawton, Oklahoma. Almost a month later, on May 19, the affidavit was reprinted in full in the *Lawton Constitution* newspaper:

> *KNOW ALL MEN BY THESE PRESENTS: That I, J. Frank Dalton, being of sound mind and body, wish to state that I am the son of Robert James, a Baptist minister, and Zerelda Cole, and that I was born at Centerville, Missouri, on September 5, 1847. The town of Centerville was later changed to Kearney, Missouri, same being located and situated in the present County of Clay, the State of Missouri. I have used many different names and aliases over many years, but my real name is and always has been JESSE WOODSON JAMES. My full brother was ALEXANDER FRANK JAMES, four years older than myself. We were members of QUANTRILL'S MISSOURI IRREGULARS that fought through the Civil War on the side of the Confederacy, later we became outlaws or bandits who operated over a wide area of several states. IN WITNESS WHEREOF, I hereunto set my hand and seal this the 24th day of April, 1948.[66]*

After his confession, Dalton conducted an interview with journalist Robert C. Ruark. Some of the contents of this interview ended up in three separate articles that ran in newspapers all over the country. Within these confessions, Dalton first told the story of killing Charlie Bigelow and faking his own death. Dalton would live until 1951, dying at the age of one hundred three.

Following Dalton's death, much controversy swirled around his claim to being the actual Jesse James, so much so that in July 1995 Professor James Starrs and Professor David B. Weaver exhumed the purported corpse of Jesse James from Mount Olivet Cemetery in Kearney, Missouri. After exhumation, they performed a DNA test on the remains.[67] The DNA comparison was done using what is referred to as mitochondrial DNA (mtDNA), which deals with mitochondria inherited from one's mother. Supposedly, Starrs and Weaver used mtDNA taken from living descendants through his sister Susan to compare with Jesse's.[68]

After receiving the test's results, Starrs concluded there were three possibilities: "one: the exhumed remains were Jesse's, two: the remains are not Jesse's but from a maternal relative, or three: the remains are from an unrelated individual who has the exact same mtDNA."[69] These results have, of course, been challenged.

Critics of the results have noted that the DNA samples used in the test did not actually come from the exhumed "Jesse" remains. It has also been noted by the same critics that the origins of the DNA compared with the descendants' mtDNA could not be precisely determined. Because of this, detractors believe the results in the report unreliable and, therefore, false.[70]

The claim of J. Frank Dalton does have some holes in it, to be sure, but the fact that a DNA test could not definitively settle the death of Jesse James is interesting and lends credence to Dalton's claim. It is also interesting that Dalton waited until he was one hundred one years old to make his claim. At that advanced age, he did not have a lot of time to enjoy any fame or notoriety. Dalton had to know that there would be no book deal or film contract to cash in on, so making his claim did not really benefit him in any way other than associating himself with a well-known character in American history.

With little to gain from his unmasking, what would the point be for Dalton to reveal his identity as Jesse James? This question really muddies the waters when it comes to Jesse and his death. It is completely reasonable to believe that an outlaw looking to reform and avoid his unscrupulous past would attempt to form a new identity when the opportunity presented itself. The history of the Old West is full of hundreds of these types of characters. Many criminals and wanted men from the east made their ways west. While there, they created aliases and new backgrounds to hide their less than savory past. Is it so hard to believe that Jesse James would attempt the same thing?

Being a famous criminal, the idea that Jesse would fake his death is also not that far-fetched. He was the type of celebrity that people would miss, and the type authorities would continue to pursue. In death, no one would look for him, and no one would question what happened to him. If he could pull it off, Jesse would live out the rest of his days in relative peace and quiet.

Whether J. Frank Dalton's tale was true remains to be determined. What is a fact, however, is there are still two graves marked for Jesse Woodson James: one in Kearney, Missouri, and one in Gladewater, Texas.[71] Both still claim to be the final resting place of one of America's most notorious outlaws. With little definitive evidence pointing to an ultimate answer, it is not hard to fathom that the man who was buried in 1882 in the earth of the Show-Me state was not the real Jesse James.

CHAPTER 7

SITTING BULL'S TWO GRAVES

JUST THE FACTS

During the early morning hours of December 15, 1890, the great Hunkpapa Lakota leader and holy man Sitting Bull was roused from his bed by armed Indian police pounding on his cabin door at his home along the Grand River on the Standing Rock Indian Reservation in South Dakota. Thirty-nine policemen and four volunteers, all Lakota Indians, had come to arrest the old man and escort him from his home into a bitter, early morning cold. Their mission was to take him to the Standing Rock Agency, North Dakota, thirty miles to the north.[1]

Sitting Bull's arrest that frigid December morning stemmed from his involvement in the Ghost Dance movement. The Ghost Dance was initiated by a Paiute Indian named Wovoka and spread among many tribes. This religious leader, whom some called the messiah, taught that if the native peoples danced and chanted hard enough, God would remove the white people from the earth, renewing it, returning the buffalo, and reviving deceased relatives. When the Ghost Dance came to the Lakotas, they learned from the Arapahos to make Ghost Shirts that were supposedly impervious to bullets. Many of the dancers were outfitted in these.[2]

In the fall of 1889, Lakota tribes had sent a delegation to see the messiah for themselves and report back. The delegation included a Miniconjou named Kicking Bear from the Cheyenne River Reservation. Having no interest at the time, the Hunkpapas sent no one.[3]

By the summer of 1890, the Ghost Dance had spread throughout all the Lakota reservations except for Standing Rock. The dancers believed the new world would be coming in the spring of 1891. In the meantime, they would keep dancing into the fall and throughout the winter until it happened.[4]

Many of them related that while dancing and falling into trances they saw the new world to come and were visited by their dead loved ones. The white people in surrounding areas did not understand the Ghost Dance and were becoming nervous, thinking the Lakotas were planning a breakout.[5]

Many people were participating in the Ghost Dance on the Cheyenne River Reservation to the south of Standing Rock.[6] Sitting Bull wanted to find out more about this new movement. He asked Standing Rock agent James McLaughlin several times for permission to go to the Cheyenne River Reservation to investigate, but McLaughlin refused to let him travel. Sitting Bull found another way to view the new movement. If he could not go to see the Ghost Dance, he would bring it to the Grand River. He invited Kicking Bear to come and explain the Ghost Dance. Kicking Bear, along with a few followers, arrived on October 9, 1890. He addressed a large Hunkpapa crowd, explaining his journey west to visit the prophet, telling about what he had seen and experienced, and relating the prophecies of things to come. Kicking Bear's revelations inspired the people. Sitting Bull gave the go-ahead to hold the dance.[7]

Kicking Bear instructed and led the Ghost Dance. Many people, including Sitting Bull, danced. He hoped that during the dance he would see one of his daughters who had recently died, but it did not happen. He did not experience anything. However, others did, talking about seeing the new world to come as well as their dead loved ones. Sitting Bull listened to them, allowed the dances to continue, and even sponsored dances; however, he remained skeptical.[8]

Sitting Bull's involvement with the Ghost Dance increased Agent James McLaughlin's wariness of him. The two had engaged in a struggle for leadership of the Hunkpapa people and shared a dislike for each other ever since Sitting Bull's arrival at Standing Rock on May 10, 1883.[9] As white settlers and newspapers in North and South Dakota became alarmed about the Ghost Dance, the commissioner of Indian Affairs asked McLaughlin for a list of troublemakers. On November 20, 1890, he complied, including Sitting Bull on the list.[10]

In early December, Ghost Dance leaders from other reservations planned to travel to the South Dakota Badlands on the Pine Ridge Reservation. One of them had had a revelation that the messiah was going to visit the dancers there, and the leaders were headed there to see him. They invited Sitting Bull to attend.[11]

Sitting Bull was in no hurry to go. He spent days mulling over the invitation. On December 11, McLaughlin sent Sitting Bull a letter ordering him to send the Ghost Dancers home.[12] That night, Sitting Bull held a council meeting in his home with the Silent Eaters, a warrior society whose mission was to look after the people. They discussed what to do about McLaughlin's letter and if Sitting Bull should go to see the messiah in the Badlands. They all agreed he should go. Sitting Bull dictated a response letter to McLaughlin. It was written respectfully and stated that the Hunkpapas were just trying to find the good road to follow. Sitting Bull said he wanted to go to the Badlands to investigate whether the Ghost Dance was true or not. The letter ended requesting permission to leave, "So I want to let you know this. I want answer back soon."[13]

However, it was too late; the wheels were in motion to arrest Sitting Bull. On December 10, 1890, with the support of President Benjamin Harrison, General Nelson A. Miles had sent a telegram to Brigadier General Thomas Ruger, commander of the Department of Dakota, ordering him to "secure the person of Sitting Bull."[14] On December 12, Ruger, in turn, sent a telegram to the Fort Yates commander, Colonel William Drum, ordering him to arrest Sitting Bull.[15]

Drum showed the message to McLaughlin. McLaughlin believed the message gave enough wiggle room to use his Indian police to make the arrest on behalf of the army. The army could follow along and remain in the background to step in if the Indian police needed assistance. Drum agreed with his plan. McLaughlin was confident his Indian police could make the arrest.[16]

At 6:00 p.m., on December 12, Bull Ghost, one of Sitting Bull's trusted men, delivered Sitting Bull's message requesting permission to travel to the Pine Ridge Agency to Agent McLaughlin.[17] Believing

Sitting Bull was about to flee the Standing Rock Reservation, McLaughlin ordered the Indian police to arrest him.[18]

On Saturday, December 13, McLaughlin gave Bull Ghost a letter for Sitting Bull, which he delivered to him later that day. McLaughlin wrote that Sitting Bull needed to send the Ghost Dancers home and that he was not approving Sitting Bull's request to travel to Pine Ridge, saying, "Therefore, my friend, listen to this advice, do not attempt to visit any other agency at present."[19]

On the morning of December 15, 1890, the Indian police escorted Sitting Bull out of his home. Turning, Sitting Bull sang a song of farewell to his family. Lieutenant Bull Head, the Indian police leader, held Sitting Bull's right arm, Sergeant Shave Head, another Indian police officer, held his left arm. Sergeant Red Tomahawk walked behind Sitting Bull, pointing a revolver at his back. Other Indian policemen were at the nearby corral attempting to catch Sitting Bull's horse and saddle it.[20]

A crowd of Sitting Bull's supporters had gathered around the Indian police. They began shouting and hurling insults at the police as they screamed at them to let their leader go. Many of Sitting Bull's followers began yelling, "You will not take our Chief!" This ruckus caused Sitting Bull to pull back from his captors.[21]

As Sitting Bull struggled, the policemen tightened their grip, and Red Tomahawk pushed the chieftain from behind toward his waiting horse, telling him, "You are arrested. You can either walk or ride. If you fight, you shall be killed here." Hearing this, many in the crowd erupted with anger and began calling more aggressively for Sitting Bull's release.[22]

Raising his Winchester, Catch-the-Bear, Sitting Bull's supporter and enemy of Lieutenant Bull Head, blasted Bull Head in the right side. As Bull Head fell, he shot Sitting Bull in the chest. Red Tomahawk reacted by firing his gun into the back of Sitting Bull's head. As he crumpled to the ground dead, all hell broke loose. The police and Sitting Bull supporters exchanged gunfire in an intense battle lasting several minutes.[23]

As each side shot at the other from defensive positions, Captain Edmond Fechet led a detachment of US Cavalry to a ridge overlooking Sitting Bull's settlement. Fechet ordered a Hotchkiss gun unlimbered and then fired shells at Sitting Bull's followers in the trees along the river and on a hilltop, driving them away. The cavalry then descended to the settlement to assist the Indian police.[24]

One of the Indian policemen killed in the fight was Strong Arm. His brother, Holy Medicine, lived nearby and soon arrived after the fighting was over. In his grief and anger over his brother being killed, Holy Medicine picked up a neck yoke and smashed Sitting Bull's face. First Sergeant James Hanaghan quickly placed a guard over Sitting Bull's body so there would be no further mutilation.[25]

When the smoke cleared, seven Sitting Bull supporters lay dead. The tribal police counted four casualties, and Lieutenant Bull Head and Sergeant Shave Head would die later. Sitting Bull's corpse was thrown onto a wagon with the four dead police officers placed on top of him. Then a caravan of corpses, including the Lakota leader, headed toward Fort Yates in North Dakota. Two weeks later, the massacre at Wounded Knee would take place.[26]

INVASION OF THE BODY SNATCHERS—KELLEN CUTSFORTH

After Sitting Bull's death, his body was taken to Fort Yates, North Dakota, and buried in the far corner of the post cemetery.[27] When the Sioux medicine man was alive, no state in the Union, including the one he was buried in, wanted to claim him. In the years following his death, however, the holy man's bones have become a source of contention amongst those living in the Dakotas.

Much like Buffalo Bill Cody's gravesite in Golden, Colorado, the spot where Sitting Bull's remains truly lay have come under considerable dispute over the years. Two states, North Dakota and South Dakota, claim to be the final resting place of the Lakota leader. For folks in Fort Yates, however, the arc of history is on their side.

It is an indisputable fact that when Sitting Bull was murdered on December 15, 1890, his remains were taken to Fort Yates, North Dakota. The Lakota leader's body was then buried in the fort's military cemetery. During the burial, there was no formal service for Sitting Bull as four military prisoners dug the grave and covered the coffin with soil. This process was overseen by Indian agent James McLaughlin and three military officers.[28] There is no debate about these circumstances. Where the controversy surrounding the burial of Sitting Bull comes into play starts in a little hamlet called Mobridge, fifty-five miles south of Fort Yates in the neighboring state of South Dakota.

Mobridge is a classic, small western town with a population of about thirty-five hundred people located in Walworth County, South Dakota. The land the town sits on was at one time heavily occupied by Lakota Sioux Indians. Many Lakotas still live in the area because of its proximity to the Standing Rock Reservation. Founded in 1906, Mobridge was named for its railroad designation, a contracted form of "Missouri Bridge" after the original railroad bridge over the Missouri River.[29]

Coincidentally, the bridge over the Missouri River that Mobridge was named for was eventually demolished in the 1960s. The US Army Corps of Engineers replaced it with a higher elevated bridge after the construction of the Oahe Dam in 1962.[30]

However, in 1953, while the original bridge was still standing, a group of Mobridge businessmen, including Julius Skaug, George Walters, Dan Heupel, Ray Miles, and their leader Walter Tuntland, formed a group they referred to as the "Dakota Memorial Association." The intent of this group was to extricate Sitting Bull's corpse and bring his remains to Mobridge, which claims to be close to the great medicine man's birthplace.[31] When the federal government ceased all operations at Fort Yates in 1903, all the military graves were removed and reburied, while Sitting Bull's was left behind. This fact led directly to Sitting Bull's grave being neglected and left in a state of disrepair for decades.[32]

Apparently Tuntland and his cohorts received the blessing of Sitting Bull's relatives to go forward with their grave robbing plan. These relatives included Clarence Grey Eagle, Sitting Bull's nephew. Grey Eagle had taken issue with the deteriorating condition of the Lakota holy man's gravesite and the state of North Dakota's reluctance to improve it. Eventually, Grey Eagle convinced Sitting Bull's three living granddaughters, Angelique Spotted Horse LaPointe, Nancy Kicking Bear, and Sarah Little Spotted Horse, to allow him to act on their behalf. After receiving their approval, Grey Eagle began working with the Dakota Memorial Association men to disinter Sitting Bull.[33]

The Dakota Memorial Association's members concocted two plans to extract Sitting Bull's bones from Fort Yates. One involved the use of a small plane to land in the vicinity of the gravesite, extract the body, and carry the corpse to Mobridge. Though this plot is entirely ludicrous, the only reason the conspirators did not follow through with it was because of a forecast of inclement weather. The second plan involved two automobiles, both loaded down with identical wooden boxes. One coffin acted as a decoy to distract the North Dakotan authorities, while the other was to contain Sitting Bull's actual remains and head directly back to Mobridge for reburial.[34]

During a snowstorm on the evening of April 8, 1953, the South Dakotan conspirators descended upon Fort Yates. Using a tow truck, these men removed the concrete slab and then four men dug by hand, snatched the bones they found, and hightailed it across the Dakota state line. When Walter Tuntland and his associates arrived in Mobridge, they encased the bones they stole in a steel vault, embedded it in a twenty-ton block of concrete, then buried the whole lot in a bluff overlooking the Missouri River.[35]

In addition to the sunken vault, the people in Mobridge erected a historical marker and concrete steps leading up to the grave, which overlooks a small bluff. Impressively, Walter Tuntland asked Korczak Ziolkowski, the visionary behind the massive Crazy Horse Mountain Monument located in South Dakota's Black Hills, to design a bust of Sitting Bull that would act as a grave marker.[36]

Ziolkowski used a piece of granite from the Crazy Horse monument to sculpt a seven-ton concrete bust in the likeness of the medicine man to set atop a pedestal overlooking the Missouri River.[37] Unbeknownst to the Dakota Memorial Association's members and the people of Mobridge, however, the grave they robbed that night in 1953 was not Sitting Bull's.

It has always been the official stance of the North Dakota Board of Tourism that Sitting Bull's final resting place is still in Fort Yates. In a way, they are right. In 1890 when Sitting Bull was going to be buried, a coffin was constructed to house his corpse. According to direct testimony at the time from the head Fort Yates carpenter, J. F. Waggoner, who helped construct the coffin, soldiers poured quicklime into the box with the holy man's remains right before he was laid to rest.[38]

Waggoner stated that the quicklime was used to dissolve Sitting Bull's body and return it to the earth as quickly as possible. After the holy man was laid to rest in a bath of quicklime, his flesh and bones mostly dissolved.[39] Afterward, an anonymous pioneer and his horse who died at Fort Yates were supposedly buried above Sitting Bull's grave. At some point, a thin layer of concrete was laid above the grave and a large boulder placed on the surface as a marker.[40] It is important to note that at this time Sitting Bull was not as revered as he is today. The quick disposal of his body, along with a dose of quicklime, makes the most sense, and an eyewitness in Waggoner, with absolutely no reason to lie, proves this.

When the Dakota Memorial Association eventually descended upon the gravesite in 1953, quicklime and the passage of time had dissolved all that was left of the great Lakota leader's remains. The bones removed that day were not Sitting Bull's but belonged to someone else. Grey Eagle and his relatives were right to give Sitting Bull respect with a proper burial, but they were just six decades too late.

PAYING PROPER RESPECT: SITTING BULL'S REBURIAL
—BILL MARKLEY

Clarence Grey Eagle, Sitting Bull's sixteen-year-old nephew, watched as the Standing Rock Indian police threw the body of his uncle into a wagon and laid four of their own dead over him on a frigid December 15, 1890, morning. The police and US Cavalry escorted the bodies from Sitting Bull's home on the Grand River north across the new border dividing the states of South Dakota and North Dakota to Fort Yates.[41] Controversy over the treatment of Sitting Bull's remains has continued into the twenty-first century.

Soldiers wrapped Sitting Bull's body in a blanket and canvas, then placed it in a wooden coffin. Four military prisoners dug a grave in the fort's cemetery, lowered Sitting Bull's coffin into the hole, and covered it over as Standing Rock Indian agent James McLaughlin and three army officers watched. There was no memorial service. Grey Eagle said one of Sitting Bull's wives sat at his grave attempting to mourn, "but she was chased away because her mourning was too noisy."[42]

Private J. F. Waggoner said that since he was a carpenter, he was detailed to make Sitting Bull's casket in the Fort Yates carpenter shop. When the casket was finished, Waggoner and others took it to the fort's death house where they wrapped Sitting Bull's body in blankets, then canvas and placed the body in the casket without nailing down the lid and drove it in a wagon out to the gravesite. After the casket was lowered into the grave, Waggoner climbed down and removed the lid, then climbed back out. Waggoner said, "Acting under instructions, Johnnie Hughes poured five gallons of muriatic acid and I another five gallons of chloride of lime into the casket. When this was done, I got down into the grave again, put the lid in position, got out, and then filled up the grave."[43]

There is no corroboration of Waggoner's story. However, let's suppose his story is true; if so, quicklime which is a strong base when combined with muriatic acid, also known as hydrochloric acid, a strong acid, will neutralize each other forming water and the salt, calcium chloride. Combining an acid and base would not have much effect breaking down the wood casket, canvas covering, blankets, clothing, and body.[44]

However, another man claimed he built Sitting Bull's casket and refuted other claimants. Edward Forte, former First Sergeant Company D, Seventh Cavalry, was a civilian carpenter at Fort Yates at the time of Sitting Bull's death. Forte wrote, "The body of Sitting Bull was buried in the military grounds in a pine coffin made by me. I being the agency carpenter. I made the coffin, regardless of what anybody else says about it."

Forte continued, "I not only made the coffin, I still have the Henry Disston hand saw with which the work was done. I refer you to James Yellow Fat and George Pleets, who were apprentices in the carpenter shop at the time."[45]

Another rumor emerged right after Sitting Bull's burial. The allegation was Sitting Bull's body had not been buried but had been dissected. On December 20, 1890, the *Bismarck Daily Tribune* headlined on its front page "Where's Bull's Body?" followed by a string of subheadings, "It is said the box he was buried in was 'very light,'" "And there is belief that Sitting Bull's body is still 'out of ground,'" "The last seen of the remains they were in the hospital dissecting room," and "Perhaps the government's museum is to be graced with the chieftain's skeleton." The text went on to say, "Editor Hickle, who is direct from Fort Yates, says it is believed by many at the fort and agency that the remains of Sitting Bull were not in the box; that the box was handled as if it was light and that a guard was put around the grave just as a blind—to thwart any suspicion. It is possible that the body of Sitting Bull is to be dissected in the interest of medical science and the skeleton be placed in the national war museum. The utmost secrecy prevails at Fort Yates regarding the movements of the military and Indian authorities on all matters relating to the Indians and no one except the highest officials know what is to be done until the time of its doing.

There is also another theory advanced regarding the burial of Sitting Bull, and that is that his body was not buried where generally supposed for fear that it might be stolen. However, all these opinions are only conjectures."[46]

The December 20, 1890 issue of the *Chicago Tribune* had a similar report, "It is learned tonight from a gentleman just in from the Standing Rock Agency that Sitting Bull's body, when brought in from Grand River, was taken to the military hospital to be dissected. ... It is an open secret that really the box did not contain the remains and that the guard was put on the grave as a blind. It is believed that Sitting Bull's body is now in the dissecting room, and that in time the skeleton will turn up either in the Government museum or some other place."[47]

On December 27, 1890, Thomas Bland, founder of the National Indian Defense Association, sent a letter to the Commissioner of Indian Affairs wanting the government to investigate the rumors of the dissection of Sitting Bull's body and the sale of his bones and skin for a thousand dollars, and, if true, to punish those involved.[48]

The commissioner wanted answers. On January 23, 1891, H. M. Deeble, Acting Assistant Surgeon at Fort Yates, responded, "I received the body of Sitting Bull about 4:30 p.m. on the 16th day of December, 1890, and it was in my custody until it was buried on the 17th. During that time, it was not mutilated or disfigured in any manner. I saw the body sewed up in a canvas, put in a coffin and the lid screwed down and afterwards buried in the northwest corner of the post cemetery in a grave about eight feet deep, in the presence of Capt. A. R. Chapin, assistant surgeon, U.S.A., Lt. P. G. Wood, 12th Infantry, Post Quartermaster, and myself."[49]

The commander of Fort Yates, Lieutenant Colonel W. F. Drum, endorsed Deeble's report, "The grave does not appear to have been disturbed."[50]

Indian Agent James McLaughlin sent Deeble's response with Drum's endorsement to the Commissioner of Indian Affairs with his own report on January 27, "I saw Sitting Bull's remains upon arrival at the Agency, and was present in the afternoon of December 17, 1890, in the Military Cemetery and saw his grave, which had been partly filled in with soil before I got there, and I feel confident that he was neither dissected nor scalped before burial and also quite confident that his grave has not been disturbed since."[51]

The army abandoned Fort Yates in 1903. The bodies of military personnel were removed and Sitting Bull's remains were the only ones left in the cemetery.[52]

Several years after the fort's closure, two youths dug into Sitting Bull's grave. Frank Fisk said James Davies and he were attending a dance in the Standing Rock Agency hall one October night when they slipped away from the festivities. Borrowing a pick and shovel, they walked to Sitting Bull's gravesite and dug down until they reached the decaying coffin. They broke through the wood and rotting canvas and each took a bone. Fisk took a humerus (upper limb) bone and Davies took a rib. They filled in the hole and smoothed over the soil before returning to the dance.[53]

In 1933, Fisk decided to tell the story of digging into Sitting Bull's grave. He claimed that, several years after taking Sitting Bull's bone, he went back to the grave and reburied it. However, Roy Johnson, staff writer for the *Fargo Forum*, wrote in the newspaper's April 11, 1953, edition that Fisk had shown him the bone in 1949.[54]

By the 1930s, a thin slab of concrete had been poured over Sitting Bull's grave, a wire fence and iron railing built to surround it, and a stone marker placed on top.[55]

A sign was later erected along a dirt road one hundred yards from the grave with an arrow pointing to the grave. Written on the sign was:

GRAVE
SITTING BULL
SIOUX MEDICINE MAN
AND LEADER OF
THE MESSIAH CRAZE
DIED DEC. 15, 1890[56]

Over the years, Sitting Bull's gravesite deteriorated. The wire fence vanished, the iron railing broke, and the concrete chipped. No one tended the grave. Sitting Bull's nephew, Clarence Grey Eagle, brooded on the disrespect shown his uncle. He had petitioned North Dakota state officials to do something about the poor condition of the grave. They promised to do something if the federal government would appropriate the funds. That did not happen, and nothing was done.[57]

Grey Eagle worked with Walter Tuntland, president of the Mobridge Chamber of Commerce, and a few other men from Mobridge, South Dakota, to develop a proper resting place at a new location for Sitting Bull. The town of Mobridge is located on the east bank of the Missouri River across from the Standing Rock Sioux Tribe Reservation. Their plan was to move Sitting Bull's remains from Fort Yates to a new burial site with a proper monument still within the reservation boundaries, across the Missouri River from Mobridge. There he could be honored properly. Mobridge businessmen also saw this as not only a way to honor Sitting Bull but also an opportunity to bring visitors to the Mobridge area.[58]

Three of Sitting Bull's granddaughters gave Grey Eagle the power of attorney to disinter Sitting Bull's remains and move them to the new location. Tuntland visited Korczak Ziolkowski, who was carving a mountain monument to Crazy Horse in the Black Hills. Tuntland asked him to carve a bust of Sitting Bull to be placed over the new gravesite, and Ziolkowski agreed, selecting a piece of granite from the Crazy Horse monument to carve the bust.[59]

In 1953, Grey Eagle met with North Dakota state officials who told him he could not disinter Sitting Bull from North Dakota and move him to South Dakota. News of North Dakota's refusal sparked a newspaper war between the two states. Even Montana newspapers jumped into the fray, stating that Sitting Bull should be buried at the Little Big Horn battlefield. Of course, that would be beneficial to the Crow tribe, traditional enemies of the Lakotas, since the Little Big Horn battlefield is within the boundaries of the Crow Reservation.[60]

On March 21, 1953, the Standing Rock Tribal Council passed two resolutions stating that Sitting Bull's next of kin had the right to rebury Sitting Bull's remains wherever they wanted as long as it was on the reservation. Standing Rock Tribal Chairman David Blackhoop stated, "North Dakota officials had no right to thwart the wishes of Sitting Bull's next of kin in this matter. The council demands that Indian rights be recognized, and it vigorously protests the arbitrary action of the North Dakota authorities."[61]

Grey Eagle and his team were undaunted. Realizing that North Dakota had no authority over Standing Rock Reservation lands, they contacted the US Department of the Interior for permission to move Sitting Bull's remains. On April 7, 1953, the Department of the Interior sent a letter stating that it would not interfere with the disinterment and reburial of Sitting Bull, that it was strictly a matter for the next of kin to approve.[62]

Grey Eagle and his team needed to move fast, before North Dakota tried to block Sitting Bull's removal. On the night of April 8, 1953, Grey Eagle and Mobridge citizens, including Al Miles, a mortician registered in both South Dakota and North Dakota, drove through a snowstorm to Fort Yates. There they met Standing Rock superintendent Charles Spencer, and with his help, they removed the concrete slab using a tow truck. They dug by hand through the soil until they reached what was left of the rotted wood coffin and Sitting Bull's bones.

As Grey Eagle watched, they carefully removed large bones and sifted the soil to recover small bones. They also found a small piece of leather and a button. When they came upon Sitting Bull's skull, they gently extracted it. It was in bad shape, with the back of the skull damaged. Grey Eagle took the skull and cradled it in his hands. After more digging and sifting, Miles examined the bones and said he was confident that they had everything they were going to find. One humerus bone was missing. Grey Eagle said he was satisfied, and they refilled the hole. Placing the remains in a bone box, they returned to South Dakota, making sure they traveled on reservation land.[63]

They had a grave waiting for Sitting Bull's remains on a western bluff overlooking the Missouri River. As Grey Eagle watched, the men placed the bone box inside a steel vault, lowered it into the grave, and poured twenty tons of concrete overtop it.[64]

North Dakotans were outraged. "South Dakota Ghouls Steal Sitting Bull's Bones," headlined the *Bismarck Tribune*.[65]

"I was tired of the white man's red tape and delays," Grey Eagle responded in the *Rapid City Journal's* April 8, 1953, edition. "North Dakota had done nothing to honor our great leader and they were trying to keep his own people from obtaining a memorial for him. So we went and got him."[66]

On April 11, 1953, after more than sixty-two years, a memorial service was held for Sitting Bull, attended by Grey Eagle, Sitting Bull's three granddaughters, and a crowd of several hundred Lakotas and whites. On September 2, Ziolkowski's bust of Sitting Bull was dedicated at the site with Sitting Bull's relatives and an estimated crowd of five thousand Indians and whites in attendance.[67] Sitting Bull, the great Lakota leader, was finally given the respect he deserved.

CHAPTER 8

THE LOST DUTCHMAN MINE

JUST THE FACTS

Located in what is today the state of Arizona, the Superstition Mountains stand out against the arid desert landscape like monstrous jagged and craggy peaks. Formed twenty-five million years ago from a mass of cooling molten lava and rock, the mountain range was originally called Crooked Top Mountain by the indigenous Indian population because of the mountain's sharp and misshapen points. When Spanish conquistadors first saw the mountains in the sixteenth century, they referred to Superstition Mountain itself as "Sierra de la Espuma," or Mountain of Foam, because of the swath of white limestone highlighting the top of the mountain. It was not until Americans settled in the area that the mass of ash- and basalt-composed rocks became known as the Superstition Mountains. No exact reason for the mountain's name has ever been officially determined.[1]

Just to the east of the Superstition Mountains, deposits of gold, silver, and copper ore were discovered in several rock outcroppings. The presence of these precious minerals brought a hoard of American miners to the area. Eventually, towns and settlements sprang up around this vast mineral belt and gave birth to famous mines like the Silver King. On the western edge of the Superstitions, however, the town of Goldfield caused one of the biggest stirs.[2]

Goldfield sprang to life in 1893 when a vein of gold was discovered in the area the previous year. The boomtown flourished for five years but soon went bust when the ore grade dropped and the veins ran dry.[3] This golden discovery, however, helped to bolster one of the greatest legends in American history, the Lost Dutchman Mine.

Several years before the founding of Goldfield, tales of the Lost Dutchman Mine circulated throughout the West. Originally believed to have been discovered by German immigrant Jacob Waltz and possibly another immigrant named Jacob Weiser, the Lost Dutchman is believed to contain a "mother lode" of gold ore. In this period, before German unification, the slang term "Dutch" was used for people from both the Netherlands and Germany.

In truth, there are multiple versions of tales relating to the Lost Dutchman Mine. Many of those tales revolve around Jacob Waltz. Waltz immigrated to the United States from Germany somewhere around 1848. According to historic records, he was most likely born in Wurttemberg in 1810.[4] Waltz apparently relocated to Arizona in the 1860s, living there until the end of his days.[5]

In 1868, Jacob Waltz homesteaded 160 acres of farmland outside of Phoenix. Twenty years later in 1891, a devastating flood wiped out Waltz's farm. Jacob fell ill shortly afterward, contracting pneumonia during the flooding. During his illness, Waltz was nursed by a woman named Julia Thomas, an acquaintance of his living in the area. Jacob eventually died from the illness on October 25, 1891.[6]

On his deathbed, Waltz supposedly told Thomas about the location of an alleged secret gold mine. It is also believed that Waltz provided Julia with a crudely hand-drawn map of the mine's location in the Superstition Mountains. As early as September 1, 1892, local newspapers reported that Thomas and several compatriots were attempting to unearth the location of the lost mine. They were unsuccessful in discovering the gold mine and resorted to attempting to sell copies of the sketched map.[7] Waltz was buried in Phoenix at what is today the Pioneer and Military Memorial Park. His gravestone notes his birthdate to be 1808.[8]

Following the decades since Julia Thomas first circulated the legends of Jacob Waltz's Lost Dutchman Mine, thousands (if not millions) of adventurers have trekked into the Superstition Mountains searching for untold riches. Many of these fortune seekers are usually aware of some version of Waltz's hidden gold mine narrative and have an idea about how to locate the mine. Incredibly, some of these treasure hunters have even died or disappeared while pursuing the hidden gold. Searchers with varying skill sets and intellects have attempted to discover the mine, including former Arizona attorney general Robert K. Corbin.[9] At an expanse of 320 acres, Lost Dutchman State Park, located just outside of the Superstition Mountains, is named for Jacob Waltz's legendary mine. To this day, no gold has ever been found in the range.

FOOL'S GOLD—KELLEN CUTSFORTH

All societies have their legends and tall tales. Some of these stories are as old as time and revolve around cataclysmic supernatural events or creation theories. Others lean toward the more contemporary, chronicling mysterious lands full of vast wealth and incredible riches. Like the myth of King Solomon's Mines or Captain Kidd's infamous buried treasure, the Lost Dutchman Mine stands out as the pinnacle of American legend.

Perhaps the most famous hidden treasure in American history, the Lost Dutchman Mine is shrouded in mystery, with countless tales on where the treasure is located and what it contains. In all, it is believed there are some sixty-two variations of the Lost Dutchman tale. Most versions contain subtle differences, while others are stark in contrast. One of the more famous stories contains a legend within a legend.

That account revolves around the tale of what has become known as the "Peralta Massacre," a quite dubious myth. The story details a band of Apache Indians, in 1848, falling upon the members of a mining party who had been sent into the Superstition Mountains to transport gold to northern Mexico from a mine owned by the wealthy Mexican Peralta family. Following the massacre, and believing all the expedition members were dead, the Apaches buried the already extracted gold and collapsed the entrance to the mine. However, the story survives because apparently one or two of the Peralta family members, depending upon the version one is given, survived and went on to propagate the tale of hidden gold.[10]

Over the years, a portion of the Peralta Massacre legend has been woven into the fabric of Jacob Waltz's Lost Dutchman folktale. Though there are variations of the story, the gist of the account details Waltz and a prospecting partner named Jacob Weiser mining in the Superstitions. While treasure hunting, they rescued a member of the doomed Peralta family whom they found wounded and lying amongst the rocks. For their bravery, this surviving Peralta member rewarded Waltz and Weiser by telling them the location of the hidden bonanza. Then, after many years of living life as a rancher and farmer, Waltz divulged the location of the mine and corresponding hidden cache of gold to Julia Thomas in a sort of deathbed confession.[11]

Now, to muddy the waters even further, sometime in the mid- to late 1950s an Oregon man named "Jack" who was vacationing with his wife in Arizona stopped along the roadside near Apache Junction to get a better look at the Superstition Mountains. While surveying the range, Jack discovered what have become known as the "Peralta Stones." These are a supposed map containing the location of the Lost Dutchman Mine.[12] In reality, the "map" consists of three sandstone tablets and a separate heart-shaped red quartzite stone that fits neatly into one of the slabs.

The first of these stones contains an image of a priest blessing the Peralta Stones in the left corner with words carved in broken Spanish, reading, "This path is dangerous. I go 18 places. Look for the heart." On the flipside of the stone, there is a horse carving surrounded by more broken Spanish, reading, "I pasture north to the river. The horse of the Holy Faith."[13] The second Peralta Stone features several carved wavy lines and Xs. Following the main continuous wavy line, one finds 18 holes; according to legend, this is referenced as "18 places" on the first Peralta Stone. On the flipside of the second stone, there is the word "Don" lightly etched on the slab's surface.

The third and final Peralta Stone contains the carving of a Christian cross on one side. On the other are several carved wavy lines and markings similar to those on the second slab. In the middle of this third stone is a heart-shaped indentation. At the center of the indentation are the numbers "1-8-4-7," which many believe is either a date or a numbered location. There is also a separate quartzite heart cut precisely to fit into this indentation. The heart has markings and an arrow on it that points to a specific marking. On the left-hand portion of the stone is a carved dagger.[14] According to Dutchman enthusiasts, with all these stones combined, one is supposed to be able to decipher the location of the hidden Peralta gold mine.

Complicating matters even more, a US Cavalry officer in the 1890s named William Edwards was apparently present when the supposed remains of the slaughtered Peralta family members were discovered in the Superstitions. When first uncovered, the bones were originally believed to be those of Indians left behind after an intertribal battle. However, Edwards identified a gold tooth in one of the skulls (which was common amongst the Mexican aristocracy). Believing these were the bones of the massacred Peraltas, Edwards set out on a separate expedition to discover the hidden treasure. While on this self-assigned mission, he supposedly discovered more human remains leading up to a Superstition canyon. Edwards and his son eventually spent most of their lives searching for the buried bonanza.[15]

If readers are confused by this mishmash of information, secret maps, and barely coherent stories, they are not alone. Attempting to decipher these clues and wade through the nonsense contained in the litany of Lost Dutchman stories is almost an insurmountable task. Aside from the fact that none of these tales ever produced an ounce of gold, or any other precious metal for that matter, they are also supported by absolutely zero verified evidence.

To find the truth about the Dutchman's gold, one must dig deep into the legend's lore and separate fact from fiction. It is true that Jacob Waltz was a real man and that the people with the Peralta surname owned an extensive gold mine. Pedro de Peralta was the Spanish governor of New Mexico, and a man named Miguel Peralta and his family owned and operated a mine in the 1860s. However, this successful mine was located near Valencia, California, nowhere near Arizona, let alone the Superstition Mountains.[16]

It is believed by many Dutchman historians that the Peraltas of California and former governor of New Mexico were melded into one family and eventually incorporated into the Dutchman narrative to give it more validity. Though Jacob Waltz was a real man, many historians believe his supposed partner, Jacob Weiser, never existed and that Waltz, over many years of Dutchman propaganda, was morphed into two men.[17]

According to historic records, Jacob Waltz pursued prospecting and mining but ultimately proved unsuccessful at these ventures. Before his death, Waltz homesteaded about 160 acres of farmland outside Phoenix. He contracted pneumonia from intense flooding in 1891 and ultimately succumbed to the disease that same year.[18] After Waltz related this tale of hidden gold to his nurse Julia Thomas in 1891, there has been an onrush of treasure seekers heading to the Superstition Mountains for over 130 years. What seems even more bizarre than Waltz's tale of hidden gold is that the German never hauled the supposed vast treasure from the Superstitions himself but instead waited until his dying day to make a deathbed confession about its location.

In the book *Sterling Legend: The Facts Behind the Lost Dutchman Mine*, Estee Conatser relates the story of a man named Jacob Walzer selling $250,000 in gold to the US Mint sometime in the 1880s.[19] Many Dutchman apologists believe that Walzer is Jacob Waltz, and they point to this story as proof of the Dutchman's riches. However, this report is supported by no primary evidence. In fact, there is also no historic documentation for a Waltz, Walzer, or Weiser ever having a mining claim in or around the Superstition Mountains.

When it comes to the Peralta Stones, they are regarded by most experts as complete fabrications. Ethnohistorian and associate of the Southwestern Research Center at Arizona State Museum Father Charles Polzer performed a painstaking examination of the stones. He is considered an expert in the field. When reviewing the slabs, Father Polzer discovered that the stones were nowhere near one hundred years of age and noted that the Spanish on the stones was an illiterate form of the language and not colonial Spanish. However, perhaps the biggest discrepancy Polzer found with the tablets was with the carvings themselves. The Jesuit priest noted that the carvings were made with modern tools and not implements from the nineteenth century.[20]

Furthermore, geologists who have studied the igneous rocks of the Superstition Mountains have concluded that the chances of any gold being found in the range are slim to none. Aside from this fact, there are also several stories of at least four separate "Lost Dutchman" gold mines throughout the West. Supposedly, there is one in Colorado, one in

California, and two more in Arizona (outside the Superstitions). Much of the lore revolving around these Dutchman mines has also found its way into the tales of Jacob Waltz's Superstition gold.[21]

Realistically, the mine that Jacob Waltz described to Julia Thomas on his dying day was most likely the Bulldog Gold Mine located near Goldfield, Arizona. His description is nearly identical to that of the Bulldog. By 1893, two years after Waltz's death, the Bulldog was all but played out.[22] Interestingly, the story of the Dutchman only exists because of a man named Adolph Ruth. An amateur adventurer, Ruth disappeared in 1931 while looking for the mine. Six months after his disappearance, his skull was discovered with two bullet holes in it. The story caused quite a stir and made national news, with people treating it as a murder for a treasure map.[23] From that time forward, it has been estimated by park officials that around eight thousand people a year come to the Superstition Mountains searching for the Lost Dutchman Mine.[24]

Unfortunately for those souls who travel to the Superstition Mountains in search of renowned riches, they will come away sorely disappointed. The Lost Dutchman Mine does not exist, nor did it ever exist. There is no hidden cache of Peralta gold waiting to be unearthed by a lucky adventurer. The Superstition Mountains of Arizona hold only folly for those who venture into them, for the only gold "that's in them thar hills" is of the fool's variety.

THE STUFF THAT DREAMS ARE MADE OF—BILL MARKLEY

Well, if I knew where the Lost Dutchman Mine was, I do not think I would be writing about it. That being said, over the years many people have searched Arizona's Superstition Mountains for the Dutchman's legendary mine and its golden rewards.

The Superstition Mountains are a forty-mile drive east from downtown Phoenix, Arizona, the fifth largest city in the United States with a population over 1.7 million people, not counting its outlying areas. You would think with that large a population in close proximity to the Superstitions people would have located the mine by now. However, the mountains are a maze of torturous canyons cutting their way through jagged peaks. Most people stick to established trails since it's easy to get disoriented. If visitors are not properly prepared, which includes having plenty of water, they can get into serious trouble, in some cases leading to death. So, grab your canteen and let's investigate the search for treasure in the Superstition Mountains and see if we can't ferret out its possibilities.

Starting thirty-five million years ago and lasting over a period of twenty million years, violent, volcanic activity created the Superstition Mountains, releasing an estimated twenty-five hundred cubic miles of uplifted ash and lava.[25] Erosional processes have been continuously at work on the volcanic rock, leaving behind the harder material in the form of craggy peaks such as the famous Weaver's Needle. Sheer cliffs and narrow twisting canyons make traveling difficult through the Superstitions.

The three major rock types are found in the Superstitions: sedimentary, metamorphic, and igneous, which is the most common. Along the Apache Trail, Highway 88, is the old mining town of Goldfield in the foothills of the Superstition Mountains. This area, known as the Superstition Mining District, is composed of granitic igneous rock that was mineralized, meaning that quartz and minerals such as gold accumulated in veins in this formation.[26]

Today, much of the Superstition Mountains are part of the Superstition Wilderness Area covering 160,200 acres or 250 square miles in the Tonto National Forest.[27]

The first known people to have lived in the area were the Hohokams, two thousand years ago, but they later disappeared. There are many petroglyphs carved into the rocks of the Superstitions, but no one knows how old they are or who made them. The Pima and Maricopa Indians were living in the area by the 1400s, but they would not enter the Superstition Mountains. Yavapai Apaches later lived in what is now the Superstition Wilderness Area. Some writers claim the Apaches would not set foot on Superstition Mountain itself, holding that it was the home of the Thunder God. Anyone who intruded was cursed and would die.[28]

The Spanish sent expeditions through what would become Arizona and in the late 1600s began to establish missions, colonize, and prospect for mineral resources. Spanish prospectors stayed away from the Superstition Mountain area until the early 1800s.[29]

By 1821, Mexico which included modern-day Arizona, had achieved its independence from Spain. During this period, the first major lost mine story took place in the area of the Superstition Mountains. The story has many variations. Here is one that is plausible.

In the 1840s, well-to-do Mexican silver mine owner Don Miguel Peralta from Arizpe, Sonora, sent his three sons Pedro, Manuel, and Ramon along with some of his employees on a gold prospecting expedition to what is now Arizona. Panning for gold along the Salt River, they found color (gold flakes), and following upriver they hit pay dirt (a large amount of gold flakes and nuggets in the sediment) at what would later be known as Mormon Flat. There they established a placer mining operation.[30]

While some of the men continued to placer mine, others searched the foothills for the sources of the gold flakes and nuggets. After several days exploring, the men found a rich gold-bearing outcrop. The brothers and their men returned to Mexico to report their findings to their father. Peralta sent the brothers back to the mine site with more men and mining equipment.[31]

They continued the placer mining operations and began mining the gold-bearing outcrop while others continued discovering more gold-bearing sites, totaling eight. In order to crush the ore into a smaller, more manageable size, the men built an arrastra, a simple device used to grind ore into finer particles.[32]

They soon discovered that they had accumulated more gold than their pack mules could carry, so they cached the surplus gold. Pedro created a map showing the locations of the eight mines, making copies for his brothers as well. Don Miguel Peralta was in poor health and died soon after the brothers' return. The brothers were preoccupied with family business and had returned to Arizpe with enough gold to live comfortably.[33]

In 1846, disputes between Mexico and the United States flared into open warfare. American troops were winning and had taken over New Mexico Territory, which included Arizona. The Peralta brothers were concerned that if the United States gained possession of New Mexico, their access to their gold mines would be cut off. They made the decision to return to the mines one last time to recover as much gold as they could. Manuel, who was recently married, stayed behind, and a cousin named

Gonzales took his place. They took one hundred employees and almost two hundred pack animals.[34]

They began working the eight mines and continued the placer operation. Without warning, Apaches attacked a small group of the miners in what they had named Canyon Fresco. Everyone in the group but Gonzales was killed. Not bothering to recover the initial stash of gold from the first mining expedition, the rest of the men quickly loaded the pack animals with all the gold they had recently mined and started their return to Mexico. They reached the western end of the Superstition Mountains when the Apaches attacked again. After a three-day battle, every Mexican was killed except Gonzales, who was able to escape and make his way back to Mexico.[35]

The Apaches hid the gold ore and concealed the entrances to all but one mine located high on a mountain wall. The Apaches thought it was in such an out-of-the-way place that no one would ever find it. Manuel was the only surviving brother, and he still had his map to the eight gold mines. So goes the Peralta story.[36]

Peralta is a common last name among people living in Mexico, the Southwest, and California. There is no information linking the Peraltas of Arizpe, Sonora, who mined in the Superstition Mountain area, to Pedro de Peralta, who was the Spanish governor of New Mexico from 1610 to 1613. There is no information linking the Peraltas of Arizpe to Miguel Peralta, who operated a mine in the 1860s near Valencia, California, and who was later associated with the disputed Peralta Spanish Land Grant in Arizona.[37]

In 1848, Mexico and the United States signed the Treaty of Guadalupe Hidalgo, in which New Mexico, including Arizona and the Superstition Mountains, became a territory of the United States. Americans now began to enter Arizona, but most everyone stayed out of the Superstition Mountains' rough country.

If one man's story is tied to the Superstition Mountains, it belongs to Jacob Waltz, known as the Dutchman. There is so much legend encrusted onto the man, it's hard to flesh out the truth. So here is the story of Jacob Waltz and his fabled Lost Dutchman Mine with hopefully most of the dross removed.

After roaming the West for years, Jacob Waltz settled in the Phoenix, Arizona, area in 1868, homesteading 160 acres north of the Salt River. By 1872, he was tired of farming and set off on solitary prospecting expeditions in the direction of the Superstition Mountains.[38]

Over the years, Waltz found plenty of gold to live a moderately well-off life. Tax records for 1875 show he paid tax on $250 of personal property, which was a lot at the time. On August 8, 1878, Waltz and Andrew Starar, an old friend, signed an agreement whereby Waltz turned over his land and all his property to Starar and paid Starar an additional $50. In return, Starar agreed to take care of Waltz for the rest of his life.[39]

Waltz never filed any mining claims from the 1870s through to the end of his life in 1891, but he always had gold, selling ore in the Florence area and paying for items with gold imbedded in white quartz.[40]

Waltz was well known during his time in Arizona and was given the nickname "the Dutchman." When he frequented saloons, people would question him about his gold mine. He would spin tall tales about his mine and its location, such as, "From the tunnel of my mine I can see the Military Trail below, but from the Military Trail you cannot see the entrance to my mine."[41] He often said his gold was from a quartz vein eighteen inches thick. Think about it: He did not have a claim on his mine. Why would he tell anyone the truth about his mine and where it was located?

He usually left town heading toward the Superstition Mountains. People attempted to follow him, but he always lost them. Since the 1890s, people have believed that Waltz had a partner, Jacob Wiser, who in some stories was killed by Indians and in other stories was murdered by Waltz himself. However, to date, no historical records on Jacob Wiser have been found.[42]

How did Waltz get his gold ore? There are four major theories, each with its own variations, and they can each have Wiser involved—or not. The first theory is that Waltz acquired a Peralta map and found the mines, or that he came upon Mexican miners who might have been Peraltas, killed them, and took possession of the mine. P. C. Bicknell wrote in the January 13, 1895, edition of the *San Francisco Chronicle* that Waltz met members of the Peralta family in Sonora and they sold him a copy of their map. The second theory is that he high graded, that is stole, gold ore from the Vulture Mine near Wickenburg, Arizona, but there is no information that he worked at that mine or lived in that area. The third theory is that he found old Mexican arrastras or gold-bearing outcrops in what would become the Superstition Mining District. Gold would not be officially discovered in this area until 1893, a year and a half after Waltz's death. The fourth theory is that he found a treasure cache in the Superstition Mountains hidden by the Peraltas, Apaches, Jesuits (another legend), or others. There are proponents and opponents to all these theories. Take your pick.[43]

Waltz was living on his old homestead along the Salt River that he had turned over to Andrew Starar. In 1886, Starar failed to pay the taxes on the Waltz homestead, Waltz was evicted, and he moved into a small adobe building behind the home of Julia Thomas.[44]

Julia Thomas, whose maiden name was Corn, was born in Louisiana in 1862 to German immigrants. In 1883, she married Emil Thomas in Colorado City, Texas. The Thomases moved to Phoenix, where they opened a confectionary business. On March 23, 1890, Emil abandoned Julia and moved to Centralia, Washington. Julia, along with Rhinehart Petrasch, who as a young boy had immigrated with his family from Germany, were close friends to Waltz and each other.[45]

In February 1891, there was major flooding along the Salt River. Apparently, Waltz had to climb a tree to escape the floodwaters and was stranded there for several days and nights. There are several stories as to who rescued Waltz. One of the more popular is that Julia Thomas sent Rhinehart to look for Waltz, who found him in the tree, and took him to Thomas's house. There were at least three other men who claimed to be rescuers.[46]

Waltz developed pneumonia after being stranded in the flood, and Julia cared for him. It was said that he paid her in gold ore for taking care of him. He never fully recovered from his bout with pneumonia and in October 1891 he took a turn for the worst. On October 25, he died and was buried the next day in the Maricopa County Cemetery.[47]

Rhinehart and Julia stayed by Waltz's side as he was dying. Waltz talked about his mine. Rhinehart and Julia drank as Waltz gave them directions to find the mine. Julia attempted to draw a map based on what

Waltz was telling her. However, according to Hermann Petrasch, Rhinehart's brother, the two of them drank a little too much and got some of Waltz's directions wrong.[48]

After Waltz died, they went through his possessions. Under his bed they found a candle box holding high-grade gold ore that proved to be of bonanza quality.[49]

Julia and the Petrasch brothers agreed to search for Waltz's mine. Julia put all of her resources into the venture buying supplies. On August 11, 1892, the three of them headed off in a wagon to the Superstition Mountains. They spent three and a half weeks searching the area near Weaver's Needle and the west side of Bluff Springs Mountain. It was extremely hot, they ran low on water, and the animals were stressed, so they gave up without finding Waltz's gold mine. Julia had risked everything and was now practically destitute. Hermann Petrasch was so angry with Rhinehart and Julia for getting drunk while listening to Walz's instructions and getting them garbled that he never spoke to either of them again.[50]

For the rest of their lives, the two Petrasch brothers continued the search for Waltz's mine—separately. Julia married Albert Schaffer in 1893. Albert encouraged Julia to produce copies of her map and sell them. They did well, selling the maps ranging from three to ten dollars.[51]

On March 10, 2020, I was visiting the Superstition Mountain Lost Dutchman Museum outside Apache Junction, Arizona, where I met Jim Swanson, coauthor of *Superstition Mountain: A Ride Through Time*. Jim showed me an exhibit that had color photographs of a matchbox made of thin sections of gold-bearing quartz. Jim said that after Julia Thomas's failed attempt to find the Lost Dutchman Mine, she had a little bit of Waltz's ore left and had it made into a matchbox. Jim has seen the matchbox, but for obvious reasons the owner chooses to remain anonymous.[52]

Another exhibit of interest in the Superstition Mountain Lost Dutchman Museum is Jacob Waltz's mining tools. The exhibit information board states that when Waltz was living at Julia Thomas's house, he told her and "Rhiney" (Rhinehart) that he would take them out to his mine in the fall. Rhinehart said he knew where he could get some tools and Waltz said that would not be necessary because he had cached his tools near one of his camps. Waltz mentioned he had broken one of his hammer handles and had repaired it with tree pitch and wrapped it with rawhide. He also wrapped the handle with calico for a better grip.[53]

In the 1920s, two men found Jacob Waltz's tools under a natural rock overhang on Peter's Mesa. A five-pound hammer was one of the items found. Its handle had been repaired with tree pitch and wrapped in rawhide. The men said calico had been wrapped around the handle, but it disintegrated when touched.[54]

As mentioned earlier, in 1893, gold was discovered in what would become the Superstition Mining District in the foothills of the Superstition Mountains and the town of Goldfield would come into existence. Mammoth, the Black Queen, the Black King, Mother Hubbard, and Tom Thumb were all big gold-producing mines.[55]

People continue to search the Superstition Mountains for the Lost Dutchman Mine. Some get into trouble and wind up dead. One of the more infamous incidents was the mysterious death of Adolph Ruth.

Adolph Ruth's son Erwin was in Mexico during the years 1913 and 1914 during the Mexican Revolution working as a US Department of Agriculture inspector or on the medical staff of General Venustiano Carranza. One of Erwin's friends, Juan Gonzales, was being held as a political prisoner. Erwin was able to win Gonzales's release. Gonzales, who was a Peralta descendent, was so grateful that he gave Erwin some old documents that included the Peralta Superstition Mountain mine map.[56]

Having no interest in the map, Erwin gave it to his father, Adolph, who was an avid lost mine and treasure hunter. As happens with many of us, life issues, including work, get in the way of following our dreams and this happened to Adolph, but in 1931 he was ready for his trek into the Superstition Mountains to follow the map to the Peralta mines. Ruth, who was living in Washington, DC, traveled to Phoenix, Arizona, arriving May 13, 1931. Ruth, now in his sixties, had never been to the Superstitions before. He was excited about the Peralta map and would talk with anyone who would listen about the map and the mines it led to.[57]

Ruth went to William "Tex" Barkley's ranch near the Superstitions and tried to convince Barkley to immediately go with him into the Superstitions. Barkley agreed to go with Ruth but said he first had business to attend to in Phoenix. Ruth wouldn't wait for him. Unbeknownst to Barkley, on June 13, two cowboys with the last names of Purnell and Keenan escorted Ruth to Willow Springs in West Boulder Canyon, where Ruth set up his base camp. When he was situated, the cowboys left him by himself. On June 18, prospector Glen Ward ran into Ruth and talked with him for several hours.[58]

When Barkley returned to his ranch, he learned that Ruth was off in the Superstitions by himself. Worried about Ruth, Barkley rode into the Superstitions to check on him. When he reached the camp on June 20, there was no sign of Ruth and it appeared he had been gone from camp for twenty-four hours.[59]

Barkley rode back to his ranch and contacted the sheriffs of Pinal and Maricopa Counties. Search parties combed the area of Ruth's disappearance. After forty-five days, they ended the official search, finding no trace of Ruth.[60]

In December 1931, the Archeological Commission of Phoenix and the *Arizona Republic* were conducting an expedition into the Superstition Mountains to study ancient Indian ruins. On December 11, they reached a flat area east of Needle Canyon and north of Bluff Spring Mountain, when Music, a black and tan hound dog, found a human skull under a palo verde tree. The skull had two holes in it. They sent it to Doctor Ales Hrdlicka, one of the leading anthropologists, in Washington, DC. Comparing the skull to Ruth's photographs, Hrdlicka concluded that it belonged to Ruth. He wrote in his report, "Holes in the skull, one about two inches in diameter on the left side and a much larger one on the right side, indicate a strong probability that the man was shot to death by a high-powered gun and that the bullet passed somewhat downwardly from the left. I have examined skulls with bullet holes found on battlefields."[61]

Tex Barkley continued to look for Ruth. On January 8, 1932, Barkley and Maricopa County Deputy Sheriff Jeff Adams found the rest of Ruth's remains three quarters of a mile from the skull. In Ruth's clothing they found his watch, a hand-drawn map, and a cryptic note ending with Julius Caesar's quote *"Veni, Vidi, Vici"* ("I came, I saw, I conquered"). The official ruling was that Ruth died of natural causes. The Peralta Superstition

Mountains mine map was not found in Ruth's camp nor on his body. Erwin Ruth believed his father had been murdered for the map.[62]

There are hundreds of theories as to where the Lost Dutchman Mine and other treasures of the Superstition Mountains are and a preponderance of maps to their locations. Since the early 1920s more than 170 individuals have claimed they found the Lost Dutchman Mine.[63]

What clues did Jacob Waltz leave to his mine? The clues may be real or may be made up to throw people off. According to the Superstition Mountain Lost Dutchman Museum, Waltz left the following clues:

No miner will find my mine. To find my mine you must pass a cow barn. From my mine you can see the military trail, but from the military trail you can not see my mine. The rays of the setting sun shine into the entrance of my mine. There is a trick in the trail to my mine. My mine is located in a north-trending canyon. There is a rock face on the trail to my mine.[64]

One final clue possibly could be investigated. Julia Thomas's golden matchbox could be the key to finding where Waltz obtained his gold. If the matchbox could be analyzed to determine what ore body it originated from, then possibly it could be compared to known deposits in the area to see if Waltz had obtained his ore from one of the known existing sources.

I asked Brennan Jordan, Associate Professor of Sustainability and Environment at the University of South Dakota, about this possibility. "It certainly seems like some kind of geochemical provenance ("fingerprinting") analysis would have potential," he said. "Adequately non-destructive analytical approaches do exist (though that depends on how much damage the specimen can bear). Like all provenance analysis approaches, this would depend upon there already being a fairly comprehensive library of distinct compositions to compare analyses to. However, I do not readily find that this kind of thing has been done in the US and worry that the 'library' necessary to pursue the approach may not exist. A specimen like the matchbox has some distinct characteristics which could be helpful, in that the texture of the ore is preserved, rather than just a refined gold product. A geologist with extensive knowledge of western US gold deposits might be able to narrow down possible areas on this basis."

There you have it—the basics to the treasures of the Superstition Mountains. If you do go on a search for the Lost Dutchman Mine or any of the other fabled treasures in and around the Superstition Mountains, there are things you need to know and do. Do not put your faith in any maps. Remember that Julia Thomas and Rhinehart Petrasch, the closest folks to the Old Dutchman, got it wrong from him, even if he did tell the truth. If someone wants to sell you exclusive maps or information to any mine or treasure locations, do not buy it. If the information is real, why don't they act on it themselves?

Remember, the Superstition Mountains are in the desert. If you are going to tromp around in the wilderness, know your physical limits. Learn how much water you will need to take for the duration of your trip. You need to have previous experience in desert camping. Know your desert flora and fauna—most everything wants to stick or bite you. Many people have died in the Superstition Mountains—take care of yourself.

Most important—if you want to prospect for minerals, mine for gold including panning, metal detect, or uncover a treasure trove, you must first get permission from the property owner, whether a private entity, county, state, or federal government. If you plan to do any of this in the Superstition Wilderness Area, you need to have a permit approved prior to any action. Contact the Tonto National Forest for permit information.[65]

Maybe it's best to end with Walter Brennan's "Dutchman's Gold":

> In the Arizona desert
> Stands a giant of earth and stone
> Mighty superstition mountain
> With its mystery and its gold.
>
> A miner, out prospecting
> Found his fortune and his fame
> Found the gold of superstition
> Just plain Dutchman was his name.

Oh, the Dutchman was a gambler
And a party was his fun
But he kept his precious secret
Never trusting anyone.

And in death, he still is laughing
For the grave his secret holds
And the mighty superstition
Keeps the Dutchman's yellow gold.[66]

CHAPTER 9

WAS TOM HORN GUILTY OR INNOCENT?

JUST THE FACTS

It was early morning on Thursday, July 18, 1901, at the Kels Nickell homestead in the Iron Mountain country of southeast Wyoming, about forty miles northwest of Cheyenne. Nickell had learned his sheepherder, John Scroder, would be quitting at the end of the month. Tuesday night of that week, Scroder had bedded down in his wagon when his dog started barking. Scroder heard a person prowling around on foot. The person did not identify himself and that scared Scroder.[1]

Nickell needed someone to care for his three thousand head of sheep. The day before, a man passing through had stopped, looking for work. Nickell told the man he had nothing for him. That was before he knew Scroder was quitting. Nickell had seen the man head down the road toward Iron Mountain Depot. Thursday morning Nickell told his fourteen-year-old son Willie to go after the man and see if he wanted a job herding sheep.[2]

Ranchers considered this part of the Iron Mountain range cattle country. It was an unwritten law that sheep country was farther to the south. Nickell had broken the unwritten law and his neighbors did not like it.[3]

Forty-six-year-old Kels Nickell, originally from Kentucky, had been a cavalryman on General George Crook's expedition against the Lakotas and Cheyennes in 1876. By 1891, Kels and his wife Mary had nine children.[4]

Nickell had a hair-trigger temper and most of the time he was at odds with neighbors. In March 1890, while looking for stray cattle, Henry Curtis and Ernest Addington had entered through an open gate onto Nickell's property. Nickell caught up with them and accused them of opening the gate and leaving it open. Nickell cursed them, and the two sides started shooting at each other, long distance. That July, Nickell got into a dispute with rancher John Coble and another man. Nickell drew a knife, stabbing Coble in the abdomen. It was a serious wound. Fortunately, Coble survived.[5]

However, Nickell's biggest feud was with his neighbors living a mile south of his property—Jim and Dora Miller and their nine children. The feuding was so bad it made the newspapers. The June 23, 1900, issue of the *Wyoming Tribune* headlined, "Feud between the Nickell-Miller Faction Again Re-opened." The article covered how Kels Nickell was accusing the older Miller boys, Gus and Victor, of "mutilating" his fence. The article further told of Kels Nickell and Jim Miller shooting pistols at each other. In one instance, Jim Miller had chased Willie Nickell with his shotgun and "snapped it at him."[6]

By August 1890, the older males in each family never went anywhere unless they were armed. Tragedy struck the Miller family on August 21. Jim drove his spring wagon out to a field to cut hay. Fourteen-year-old Frank and nine-year-old Maude went with him. The children were playing in the wagon when Miller's shotgun accidently fired, shooting Frank in the head, killing him, and severely wounding Maude in the face. Miller blamed Nickell for Frank's death; because of Nickell's actions Miller felt he needed to have the shotgun on hand.[7]

Four months later, Miller and Nickell ran into each other in a Cheyenne restaurant. Miller pulled a knife and Nickell pulled a gun. Miller stabbed Nickell in the shoulder, but Nickell never shot his pistol. It continued—Nickell had Miller arrested twice. A judge imposed peace bonds on both men. If they broke the peace, they forfeited their bonds.[8]

It was before 7:00 a.m. on July 18, 1901, when Kels Nickell along with Mary's brother William Mahoney, who was living with the Nickells, and John Apperson, a Cheyenne surveyor, headed northeast about a mile from the house to conduct a survey. Shortly after they left, Willie saddled his father's horse to ride out to find the man looking for work.[9]

When Willie reached the wire gate about three-fourths of a mile west from the Nickell's house, he dismounted, opened the gate, and led the horse through. Two rifle shots rang out. A pause, and then a third shot was fired. Two bullets hit Willie. One bullet struck him a few inches below his left armpit exiting out his sternum; the second bullet struck him just below the first wound, passed through his aorta and intestines, and exited above his right hip. Willie ran about twenty yards toward home, collapsed on his face, and died.[10]

The killer walked up to Willie's body, flipped him over on his back and pulled his shirt out to look at the bullet holes. He put a small rock under his head and left.[11]

Kels Nickell and the other two men heard the shots but thought it was someone hunting. When Willie did not return home that evening, no one worried much; they thought he was probably spending the night at Iron Mountain Depot.[12]

The next morning, ten-year-old Freddie Nickell was sent out to the gate to do a chore and found Willie's body. Crying, he rode back home. Mary was standing at the front door and asked him, "What is the matter?"

"Willie is murdered," he said.

When the family reached Willie's body, they found he was lying on his back in the road with his head pointed toward the house and his hands at his sides. His shirt was pulled out in the front and a two-inch diameter rock was under his head. There were no other rocks of that size in the immediate area. A trail of blood led back to the gatepost. Apperson believed the killer had turned Willie's body over onto his back because when they examined the body, they found a pool of blood about three feet away and sand and gravel were on Willie's face and the front of his clothing.[13]

Of course, Nickell's first thought was that the Millers were involved with the murder of Willie. A coroner's inquest began at the Nickell ranch on Saturday, July 20. After the initial questioning, Coroner Thomas Murray, the sheriff, members of the jury, and those staying at the Nickell ranch searched the crime scene for spent cartridges, tracks, or any other evidence. Cattle had walked through the area, so most tracks were obliter-ated. They found one boot print near the gate, and behind some nearby rocks they found what might have been the imprint of the butt of a gun in loose sand. An autopsy was performed on Willie's body in Cheyenne on Sunday, July 21, and the inquest resumed in town on Monday, July 22, 1901, continuing into early August.[14]

The assassination of Willie Nickell was first degree murder, which carried the death penalty. Members of both families, their friends, and neighbors were questioned during the coroner's inquest. People suspected someone in the Miller family had killed Willie. On July 22, Laramie County attorney Walter Stoll questioned Kels Nickell.[15]

Stoll: Do you suspect anybody of killing the boy [Willie]?
Nickell: I do.
Stoll: Who is it, or do you suspect it?
Nickell: I suspect the Millers.
Stoll: Who does that include?
Nickell: That includes Jim Miller, Gussie Miller, and Victor Miller.

Then through continued questions and answers Nickell told his side of the confrontations with the Millers.[16]

Stoll: Did you have a talk with Tom Horn here in Cheyenne about his coming to that locality?
Nickell: Yes, sir.
Stoll: What was your talk with him?[17]

Nickell proceeded to tell of his encounter with a well-known stock detective named Tom Horn back in May at Kerrigan's saloon in Chey-enne. The gist of the long testimony was that Horn wanted to let Nickell know that he believed Nickell was a man of his word and he also wanted to let him know that he was not out to kill him.

Nickell: He [Horn] said, "I will tell you, Tom Horn [referring to him-self] may be a damned son of a bitch, but he says you have proved to be a man of your word. You heard I was going to kill you when you got in with the sheep." I said, "I have heard a whole lot." "Now," he says, "I will tell you, the damned son of a bitch the other day made the expression that Nickell was after his sheep and would soon be in here with them; he wouldn't last long because Tom Horn was going to kill him as soon as he got in here." He said, "That son of a bitch don't know Tom Horn." I said, "Who was that." He said, "It was Miller's oldest boy." He said, "Those fellows making talk like that are more in danger of Tom Horn than anybody in the country."[18]

Nickell continued his testimony, saying that Horn told him that his employers John Coble (whom Nickell had knifed back in July 1890) and the Two Bar outfit had no animosity toward him for bringing in sheep. Stoll asked about an earlier encounter that Nickell had had with Tom Horn outside the courthouse in Cheyenne. Nickell admitted he threatened Horn that if he ever caught him off the road passing through his property, he would shoot him. Horn replied if he were ever on the Nickell property, he would stick to the road.[19]

Stoll: Do you know if Horn was in that vicinity anywhere this last week?
Nickell: I do not.
Stoll: Have you heard that he was?
Nickell: Willie Edwards told me Saturday night that Horn had been seen around there, somewheres Wednesday.
Stoll: Willie Edwards is who?
Nickell: He is the son of Charles Edwards.
Stoll: Do you know whether Tom Horn told Miller that your sheep had been in his pasture?
Nickell: I do not know.
Stoll: Did you hear that he told him that?
Nickell: Never before this.
Stoll: Whose horse was Willie riding when he was killed that morning?
Nickell: Mine.

The testimony revolved around the significant differences between Kels Nickell's horse and Willie's.[20]

Stoll returned to Nickell's conversation with Horn in Kerrigan's saloon and wanted to know if they had more conversations. Nickell replied that they did, but they never repeated the conversations at the courthouse or the saloon.[21]

Later, Stoll questioned nineteen-year-old Gus Miller, Jim Miller's oldest son. He led Gus through the troubles between the two families and his involvement in them. Gus maintained that he and his brother Victor were on good terms with Willie Nickell. Stoll had Gus tell of his and his brother's whereabouts during the time of Willie's murder.[22]

Stoll asked about what weapons the Miller family owned. Gus said he owned a .30-40 Winchester and that Victor had a .30-30 rifle that their father would borrow from time to time. They went through the characteristics of the weapons and the ammunition used.[23]

Stoll continued questioning Gus on the family members' whereabouts before and after the murder. Next, Stoll began asking about visitors to the Miller place working through each day, and Gus answering that no one had visited. Then—

Stoll: [Was anybody in the locality] On Thursday?
Gus: No, I don't know of anybody.
Stoll: Or on Friday—was anybody there on Tuesday?
Gus: Yes.
Stoll: Who?
Gus: Tom Horn left there Tuesday morning.
Stoll: Left where?
Gus: Our place.
Stoll: How did he come to your place?
Gus: He stayed there all day Tuesday; he left there Wednesday morning about 10 o'clock.
Stoll: How did he come to your place?
Gus: He came there on horseback in the evening.
Stoll: What did he come for?
Gus: I don't know what he came for, just visiting I guess.

Stoll: What did he have with him in the shape of firearms?
Gus: He had a thirty thirty rifle.
Stoll: Same kind as yours?
Gus: It shoots the same size as my brother Victor's.
Stoll: The same kind of bullets?
Gus: Yes, sir.[24]

Stoll continued to question Gus on his activities and whereabouts around the time of the murder. Stoll then changed his line of questioning in reference to Kels Nickell's earlier statement that Horn had told him in Kerrigan's saloon in Cheyenne that Gus Miller had said Horn was out to kill him.

Stoll: Did you ever make a statement to anyone that as soon as Nickell brought his sheep into the country Tom Horn intended to kill him?
Gus: No, sir.[25]

Stoll pursued this line of questioning, but Gus maintained he never said such a thing to anyone.[26]

After finishing his questioning of Gus Miller, Stoll continued to call additional people to question into the next day, July 23. Those questioned included Glendolene Kimmell. Twenty-two-year-old Kimmell was from Hannibal, Missouri, and in mid-January 1901 she had arrived in Wyoming. When Stoll questioned her, she said she had started teaching at the Miller-Nickell school two weeks earlier and was boarding with the Miller family.[27]

Tom Horn had ridden up to the Miller ranch house on Monday evening, July 15, 1901. He stayed there all day Tuesday, and left Wednesday morning, July 17, riding south toward Iron Mountain. While at the Miller ranch, he spent the nights in a tent with Gus and Victor. By remarks Horn made to Gus, he had been watching him closely from a hilltop on the evening of either Friday, July 12 or Saturday, July 13. Gus overheard Horn tell Glenolene Kimmell that he was a cattle detective.[28]

Tuesday morning, Horn went fishing with Jim Miller. They also did some target practice, shooting at tin cans and at a buzzard that they missed. In his testimony, Jim Miller said he didn't think Horn was a good shot. About 4:00 in the afternoon, Horn rode up to an area the Millers called their tree claim. When Horn returned less than an hour later, he told the Millers that Nickell's sheep were up there.[29]

Tom Horn spent lots of time with Glendolene Kimmell; sometimes it was just the two of them. When Stoll asked her to describe Horn, she said he had "excellent features" and was well spoken using the best English. The last time Kimmell saw Horn was when she left for school Wednesday morning; when she returned to the Miller home, Horn had left.[30]

At the conclusion of the coroner's initial inquest on July 23, the *Cheyenne Daily Leader* stated, "Up to the present date not a single definite clue has been obtained that might lead to the apprehension of the murderer."[31] There had been lots of mention of the stock detective Tom Horn. Who was he?

Tom Horn was born November 21, 1860, in Scotland County, Missouri. His parents were Ohioans but had to flee the state due to shady land transactions on their part and their failure to pay debts. The Horns were a religious family, but Tom's father was hard on him. Young Tom would take every chance he got to get away from his father and hunt in the woods with the family dog Shedrick. One day, Tom had an altercation with some immigrants passing through and they shot and killed Shedrick. Tom later wrote, "I believe that was the first and only real sorrow of my life."[32]

When Tom was fourteen, he and his father got into a fight. His father beat him severely with a single harness trace. After a week's recovery in bed, Tom left home for good, heading west.[33]

By Christmas 1874, Horn had reached Santa Fe, New Mexico, where he got a job driving stagecoach from Santa Fe to Prescott, Arizona. He was a fast learner and quickly picked up speaking Spanish.[34]

In July 1876, Al Sieber, Chief of Scouts at San Carlos Apache Agency in Arizona, hired Horn as an interpreter to translate Spanish. Horn was involved in the pursuit of Geronimo and other Chiricahuas into Mexico until Geronimo surrendered in September 1886.[35]

By the late 1880s, Horn was a Gila County deputy sheriff in Arizona. He became involved in a fight between cattlemen and sheepmen that would be called the Pleasant Valley War.[36]

In 1890, Pinkerton's National Detective Agency's Denver office hired Horn. The agency considered him an efficient operative, able to track down train robbers and other criminals.[37]

In November 1893, Horn and a small posse including a cowboy named Otto Plaga, arrested a gang of rustlers north of the Iron Mountains. The gang members included four men and Eva Langhoff. Only one gang member was convicted. The rest were set free. Some people believed this made Horn skeptical of the legal system. The rumor spread that Horn would no longer depend on the law to carry out justice but would take matters into his own hands for his employers.[38]

Horn left the Pinkertons in 1894 and went to work for the Swan Land and Cattle Company. However, Horn would continue to work for the Pinkertons off and on until late 1900 or early 1901.[39]

At an 1895 Wyoming Stockgrowers Association meeting in Cheyenne, Horn was said to announce, "Men, I have a system that never fails, when everything else has. Yours has!" Horn's reputation was growing to the point that Wyoming governor William A. Richards met with him to discuss what to do about cattle rustling in Big Horn County, where the governor ran his own cattle.[40]

Badman Billy Lewis was a cattle rustler who had been warned to leave the Iron Mountains. On July 31, 1895, he was loading a skinned beef into a wagon when three bullets slammed into his body, killing him. Rumors circulated that Tom Horn had killed Lewis. There was no proof, but it added to his reputation.[41]

Fred Powell lived on Horse Creek about six miles downstream from Billy Lewis. Powell seemed to enjoy making life miserable for his neighbors. Multiple charges racked up against him over the years—stealing and killing neat cattle, grand larceny, stealing livestock, malicious trespass and destruction of property, incendiarism and malicious trespass, and criminal trespass. He was usually able to get off or pay light fines, except for the incendiarism, for which he had to serve four months in jail. After he was released in 1895, he received three anonymous letters telling him to stop his thieving and to leave the country or he would be killed. He didn't listen.[42]

On September 10, 1895, Powell was outside his house when a shot rang out and a bullet pierced his heart. The killer walked up to Powell's body, leaving a size 8 boot print. The rumor circulated that Tom Horn was the assassin. The story was told that Powell's five-year-old son Billy, referring to Horn, said, "That's the man that killed Daddy." However, Billy was not there at the time of the murder. There was no evidence that Horn had committed either of these killings, but he left Wyoming in November 1895.[43]

Tom Horn returned to Arizona, where the army employed him to help track down renegade Apaches. With the outbreak of the Spanish American War in 1898, Horn served in Cuba as a mule pack master and through his efforts provided the supplies that helped Theodore Roosevelt and his Rough Riders capture San Juan Hill on July 1, 1898.[44]

Horn came down with yellow fever and was discharged in September 1898. Back in the United States, Horn recuperated at John Coble's Iron Mountain ranch.[45]

He was well enough that the Union Pacific hired him to pursue robbers who held up one of their trains between Medicine Bow and Wilcox, Wyoming, on June 2, 1899. He tailed the robbers for months but never caught any of them. On January 15, 1900, he was back at Coble's ranch, where he sent a detailed report to E. C. Harris with the Union Pacific on his activities and who he believed the train robbers were. That same month, Wyoming, Colorado, and Nebraska newspapers created a firestorm of stories swirling around an alleged encounter between Horn and his partner with the last name of Tewksbury and two of the train robbers. The stories varied but the general theme was that Horn and Tewksbury caught the outlaws forty miles west of Jackson Hole, Wyoming, where they shot and killed them, leaving their bodies where they fell. Horn denied it ever happened and nothing came of it except again enhancing his reputation.[46]

Ora Haley, a close friend of John Coble, had a large cattle operation in northwest Colorado in the Brown's Park area. He was losing livestock to rustlers and wanted to put an end to it. At a meeting in Denver, Coble told Haley he would see about sending Tom Horn to do the job. Horn was to be paid five hundred dollars for every cattle thief killed.[47]

Horn, using the alias James Hicks, arrived at Brown's Park in April 1900. Through Horn's investigations he discovered that two of the rustlers were small ranchers Matt Rash and Isom Dart. They were both sent letters to clear out or they would be killed. On July 8, Rash was alone in his cabin preparing lunch when someone stood in the doorway and shot him twice. Rash crawled to his bunk and died. On September 26, Horn dropped his alias, signing a complaint against Isom Dart for horse theft. Dart hunkered down at his ranch along with six friends. It was early morning on October 4 when Dart and his friends emerged from the cabin and walked toward the corral. Two shots were fired, and Dart fell dead with a bullet through his heart.[48]

In the November 18, 1900, edition of Cheyenne's *Wyoming Tribune*, Horn told of the Brown's Park rustler problem and of the time he spent there. He knew both men who had been killed and said about them, "Two more notorious rustlers never infested the Rocky Mountain country."[49]

Personally, Horn was usually quiet, but when he drank, it was to excess, and then he would brag and tell tall tales. His benders could last days. He was a noted cowboy and won riding and roping contests including those contests in the 1901 Cheyenne Frontier Days. He was also well known for his horsehair braiding and leatherwork.[50]

On Saturday, August 3, 1901, tensions flared again in Wyoming's Iron Mountains. Kels Nickell had hired a new sheepherder, an Italian, Vingenzo Biango, who went by the name Jim White. The Millers discovered that Nickell's sheep were on their property and very close to their garden. Of course, there were two sides to the story. White later testified that a coyote had gotten into the herd and scattered the sheep and that was why they were on Miller's land. White was heading after the sheep when Jim Miller, Glendolene Kimmell, and a younger man approached him, the males carrying rifles. They were about two hundred yards away. White said that Miller called out, "Get out from here you son of a bitch, we don't want you around here, this is my place." Then later in his testimony White said, "The old man," referring to Jim Miller, said, "The son of a bitch sent the sheep across to my house. I will fix the son of a bitch before daylight." Miller testified that he did not curse at White but firmly told him three times to get the sheep out of there. White said he sent his dog to bring the sheep back.[51]

It was 5:30 a.m. the next morning, August 4. Kels Nickell was outside milking a cow. Five shots rang out, three bullets hit Nickell—one in each arm and one in the left hip. As he ran to his house, two of Nickell's younger children said they saw two men to the southeast mount their horses and ride away. They couldn't make out who they were, but they said the horses looked like Jim Miller's horses. Later that same day, Jim White said three men shot at him, but he did not get a good look at them. At least thirty sheep were shot and killed while others were crippled. Nickell was put on the train to Cheyenne, where he recovered enough to be jailed there for assault in an unrelated incident on August 15.[52]

The coroner's inquest reconvened on August 6 at the Nickell ranch to investigate the shooting of Kels Nickell and further investigate the murder of Willie. Deputy Sheriff Peter Walaumont arrested and jailed Jim, Gus, and Victor Miller on the suspicion of shooting Kels Nickell, but after being interrogated and having alibis provided for them, they were released. No one was ever charged for the shooting of Kels Nickell.[53]

On August 8, 1901, the coroner's inquest continued in Cheyenne. On Friday, August 9, Tom Horn was called to testify. Laramie County attorney Walter Stoll asked Horn if he had seen any strangers in the area. Horn answered no. Stoll asked if he knew the Nickell and Miller families. He said he knew Kels Nickell, but not the family, and he had met Jim Miller once before but not the family until he had stayed with them for two nights. Much of the questioning was about Horn's whereabouts and movements before and after the murder of Willie Nickell. Horn recounted his movements during that time. On Thursday, July 18, the day Willie was killed, Horn said he was "within seven or ten miles" of Nickell's ranch.[54]

When asked, Horn talked about Jim Miller and Kels Nickell and all the trouble between the two men, saying, "Neither of them are reckoned a very high class of citizens." Horn said Nickell talked about using his sheep to ruin his neighbors. Horn stated that Nickell said, "I left them [the sheep] right in Jim Miller's dooryard. I wonder how the son-of-a-bitch feels about it now." Horn said that Miller and Nickell had started their herds rustling. They had been "pretty pronounced thieves" but for the last five to six years they had been honest.[55]

Horn talked about the cowboy Otto Plaga who had said that Jim Miller had offered a five-hundred-dollar diamond to anyone who would kill Kels Nickell. Horn said that Plaga was "about as unreliable as Miller or Nickell."[56]

The coroner then questioned Horn.

Coroner: I am curious to know if a man that rides around like you do and hears the expressions of people, when a man brings sheep in the country, what the cattlemen think?
Horn: Every cattleman I have heard talk . . . say it was not right, and say so in very strong terms. . . . They say if he had started in the sheep business it would be different. Being in the cattle business and deliberately selling his cattle and putting sheep in than for no other reason than to spite the neighbors about it, and to do them dirt and damage and ruin them if he could, and boast of it then—go and tell them so. He would tell these people how he was going to do them up.
Coroner: It would be easy for you to give the sentiment of the stockmen?
Horn: I know what their sentiment is; their sentiment is that a man that would do as Nickell has, could only do so, being the kind of man Nickell is, troublesome and quarrelsome, turbulent man without character or principal.[57]

The coroner then switched the line of questioning, asking Horn about the two conversations Nickell had said they had in Cheyenne where Nickell stated that if he ever caught Horn off the road on his property, he would kill him.[58]

Coroner: Have you had any words with Nickell that if ever he got you on his place there would be trouble? Did he ever say he would kill you?
Horn: No, sir.
Coroner: Did not he say if he could get a gun first he would kill you?

Horn: No, sir.

Coroner: Didn't he say if you hunted deer or antelope there he would kill you?

Horn: No, sir. He must have told somebody else that.

Coroner: He testified that here.

Horn: He simply lied. I have rode through there a number of years and he has not troubled me yet. I don't know why he should make a statement of that kind.

Coroner: This conversation was entered into in a friendly way?

Horn: He told me in a friendly way to keep out of the country?

Coroner: He said in substance he didn't want you to get off the road, and you could use his place as long as you kept in the road and didn't leave the road, it would be all right to go through his place—was this conversation ever had?

Horn: No sir. I wouldn't allow fifteen of the worst men in the world to tell me that. I am at liberty to go where I please in the country. I wouldn't stand for anybody to tell me anything of the kind. If my business took me through that country I would go. He couldn't tell me that, he wouldn't tell me half before I would got him to stop.

Coroner: He made that statement?

Horn: It was decidedly wrong.[59]

After Stoll questioned Jim Miller about where he was and what he was doing Sunday morning when Kels Nickell was shot, Glendolene Kimmel was brought back for additional questioning. She was asked her opinion of the feud between Miller and Nickell. She said their natures were such that they would never be able to get along. When she was asked who was at fault for the shooting of Kels Nickell, she said it was Nickell's fault because he sent his sheep onto Miller's land and "if it was my land and I ordered him three times to take his sheep off, I would have shot him." She testified that the Millers were home during the time of Kels Nickell's shooting.[60]

The final witness was Joe LeFors. LeFors was born in Texas in 1865 and raised in what would become Oklahoma. He arrived in Wyoming in 1895 on a cattle drive and became a stock inspector. He was involved in a shoot-out with rustlers at Wyoming's notorious Hole-in-the-Wall. In 1899, he led one of the posses after robbers who held up a Union Pacific train between Medicine Bow and Wilcox. They never captured the perpetrators. That same year, US Marshal Frank Hadsell appointed LeFors a deputy. In 1900, he participated in a posse chasing after robbers who held up another Union Pacific train, this time between Tipton and Table Rock, again with no success. Laramie County authorities asked US Marshal Hadsell for LeFors's assistance in investigating Willie Nickell's murder and the shooting of Kels Nickell. When LeFors arrived at the Nickell ranch on August 6, he found a frightened Mrs. Nickell. She did not know who had shot her husband but believed it was because of their sheep. They had received a threatening letter, their sheep had been killed, and their sheepherder run off.[61]

Walter Stoll asked LeFors what he had found at the Nickell ranch. One of the Nickell boys showed him the location from where his father had been shot. LeFors found one set of horse tracks and one footprint. It appeared to be a boot print size 8 or 9. The heel was not sharp but medium. LeFors followed the horse tracks through the rain until they led him to a sandy road. As it was raining and the road was loose sand, he lost the trail.[62]

LeFors was the last witness. Stoll did not have enough evidence for a case against the Millers. The coroner's jury delayed its final report, waiting for more evidence to be uncovered, but nothing was found. On December 26, 1901, the jury reported, "We the jury empaneled to inquire into the death of Willie Nickell, finding that the deceased came to his death on July 18th, from a gunshot wound inflicted by a party or parties unknown."[63]

TOM HORN, GUILTY OF MURDER IN THE FIRST DEGREE
—BILL MARKLEY

Deputy US Marshal Joe LeFors was still on the case, even though the coroner's inquest concluded its active investigation on August 9, 1901. With the consent of the US Marshal's office, LeFors pursued all leads, reporting his findings to Laramie County attorney Walter Stoll. LeFors made several trips to the Iron Mountains but discovered nothing new.[64]

On August 14, Sandy McNeal introduced LeFors to Tom Horn, who was in Frank Meanea's Cheyenne saddle shop having a scabbard made for his Winchester. They had a lively conversation about the attributes of Winchester rifles. LeFors's first impression of Horn was that he was a braggart. As the conversation continued, LeFors referred to the shooting of Kels Nickell and asked Horn why he had let the old man get away. Horn must have felt comfortable with LeFors because he said, "The sun was not shining on the sights of the gun or else it would have been different." Horn also said, "You ought to have seen him run and yell like a Comanche Indian." After his conversation with Tom Horn, Joe LeFors believed Horn was the murderer of Willie Nickell. He also believed cattlemen had hired Horn to take care of Nickell and his sheep. Now he needed proof.[65]

LeFors began investigating Tom Horn and came to believe he was the killer of Billy Lewis and Fred Powell back in 1895. He heard a rumor that, while drunk, Horn had said he "got too handy with a Winchester."[66]

On September 28, Horn traveled to Denver for the annual Carnival. The night of the 29th, he was drinking with three men he had just met. He got into an argument with them, and they beat him, breaking his jaw in two places. He wound up in the hospital for two weeks. Denver newspaper reporters interviewed Horn and built up the story of the dispute between Nickell and him. They wrote that Horn said concerning Nickell, "There is no man who is big bad good or tough enough to bring sheep into a cattle country." After leaving the hospital, Horn went back to John Coble's ranch.[67]

LeFors developed a plan to entrap Horn into admitting he had killed Willie Nickell. LeFors wrote to acquaintances in Montana, including W. D. Smith, Montana's chief livestock inspector, stating he knew of a first-rate cattle detective in need of a job. On December 28, 1901, Smith wrote back, "I want a good man to do some secret work." Rustlers were stealing cattle in the Big Moon River country, and they needed someone to infiltrate the gang.[68]

LeFors happened to be on the train from Rawlins to Cheyenne when he ran into George Prentice, who worked for the Swan Land and Cattle Company. LeFors sat down beside Prentice and began to talk about the murder of Willie Nickell. LeFors told Prentice that he had seen three Pinkerton agents in Cheyenne following Horn for three days as he drank and talked about the Willie Nickell case. LeFors said, "Why don't you send him out of the country? Horn is going to get someone in trouble yet by his talk."[69]

LeFors must have convinced Prentice that he was on his side. Prentice replied that if Horn talked too much, they would have to "bump him off." He told LeFors he had not paid Horn for the last killing, but he had paid him gold and cash on the train between Cheyenne and Denver for previous "jobs committed."[70]

LeFors told Prentice he had a way to make Horn disappear for a while. He told him about the cattle detective job in Montana and showed him the letter from W. D. Smith.[71]

After reading the letter, Prentice agreed that Horn should take the job and leave the country. He said he would discuss it with John Coble and if Horn didn't want the job, they would make him take it.[72]

Prentice must have told Coble right away. Coble was soon in LeFors's Cheyenne office asking to see Smith's letter. LeFors allowed Coble to take the letter with him to show Horn. A rapid exchange of letters followed.[73]

On December 31, 1901, LeFors sent Smith a message, possibly a telegram, informing him of Horn's interest.[74]

On January 1, 1902, Coble gave Horn the letter from Smith. That same day, Horn wrote LeFors stating he wanted the job and enclosed Smith's letter. "I would like to take up that work and I feel sure I can give Mr. Smith satisfaction," Horn wrote. "I don't care how big or bad his men are or how many of them there are, I can handle them. They can scarcely be any worse than the Brown's Hole Gang and I stopped cow stealing there in one summer. . . . I can handle his work and do it with less expense in the shape of lawyer and witness fees than any man in the business."[75]

On January 3, 1902, Smith responded to LeFors's December 31 message with ". . . expect to get my orders to sed [send] for your man Tom Horn."[76]

On January 7, 1902, Horn responded to a letter LeFors had sent him on January 6. "Joe I am much obliged to you for the trouble your [sic] have taken for me in this matter and I will do my best to give satisfaction," Horn wrote. "I will get the men sure, for I have never yet let a cow thief get away from me unless he just got up a [sic] jumped clean out of the country."[77]

That same day, Smith wrote a letter to LeFors stating when Horn reached Montana, they wanted him to stay until the job was done. Smith wanted Horn to arrive as soon as possible, giving instructions on who to meet and where. He also asked LeFors to arrange Horn's railroad transportation and give him any money he needed for expenses, and they would reimburse LeFors.[78]

On January 11, 1902, LeFors sent Horn a telegram telling him to come to Cheyenne. He wanted to hand him a letter of introduction to give the Montana officials. Horn rode to Laramie, started drinking, and took the train to Cheyenne, arriving that night. LeFors met Horn and after leaving him, Horn stayed up drinking through the night.[79]

On January 12, 1902, Sunday morning, LeFors met Horn at the Inter Ocean Hotel for a drink. LeFors told Horn he had to run an errand but wanted to meet again later at the US Marshal's office located on the second floor of the Commercial Block, and Horn agreed.[80]

Unknown to Tom Horn, Joe LeFors was setting him up. LeFors's plan was to get Horn to admit he had killed Willie Nickell in the presence of hidden witnesses. He had met with Laramie County attorney Walter Stoll to go over his plan with him. Stoll told LeFors to make sure the witnesses were reputable. LeFors recruited Charles Ohnhaus, a stenographer, and Les Snow, a deputy sheriff, to act as witnesses. The meeting with Horn was to be held in the US Marshal's private office. Ohnhaus and Snow were in an adjacent room lying on top of a buffalo coat spread out on the floor. Their heads were at a closed, locked door that led into the marshal's office. A mail slot in the door was modified, allowing an inch and a half gap so the two witnesses could see Horn and better hear the conversation. There was also a gap between the bottom of the door and the doorsill. Ohnhaus would later testify, "The sounds from the adjoining room could be heard very distinctly."[81]

Horn met LeFors outside the building and climbed the stairway to the US Marshal's office on the second floor. The meeting between Joe LeFors and Tom Horn started about 11:20 a.m., as Charles Ohnhaus took shorthand notes behind the door.[82]

They first discussed LeFors's letter of introduction to the Montana authorities and what Horn's duties would be when he arrived there.

"I shoot too much," Horn said. "I know; you know me when it comes to shooting. I will protect the people I am working for, but I have never got my employers into any trouble yet over anything I have done. A man can't be too careful because you don't want any God damn officers to know what you are doing."[83]

Then LeFors hoped to trap Horn into admitting he had killed Willie Nickell.

LeFors: Tom, I know you are good man for the place. You are the best man to cover up your trail I ever saw. In the Willie Nickell killing, I could never find your trail, and I pride myself on being a trailer.
Horn: No God damn; I left no trail. The only way to cover up your trail is to go barefooted.
LeFors: Where was your horse?
Horn: He was a God damn long ways off.

LeFors said he would be concerned about being cut off without his horse. Horn replied that was not a concern of his with the people he was dealing with, beside he could always rely on his gun.[84]

LeFors: I never knew why Willie Nickell was killed. Was it because he was one of the victims named, or was it compulsory?
Horn: I think it was this way: Suppose a man was in the big draw to the right of the gate—you know where it is—the draw that comes into the main creek below Nickell's house where Nickell was shot. Well, I suppose a man was in that, and the kid came riding up on him from this way, and suppose the kid started to run for the house, and the fellow headed him off at the gate and killed him to keep him from going to the house and raising a hell of a commotion. That is the way I think it occurred.
LeFors: Tom, you had your boots on when you ran across there to cut the kid off, didn't you?
Horn: No, I was barefooted.

LeFors: You didn't run across there barefooted?
Horn: Yes, I did.

Horn brought up Glendolene Kimmel. He said she had sent him a letter telling him about her testimony at the coroner's inquest. Horn then said, "She told me to look out for you. She said, 'Look out for Joe LeFors; he is not all right; look out for him; he is trying to find out something.'" She told Horn that was what Jim Miller believed about LeFors, but Horn's opinion of the Millers was, "There is nothing to those Millers. They are ignorant old jays. They can't even appreciate a good joke."[85]

Later in the conversation LeFors turned his questions to guns.

LeFors: What kind of gun have you got?
Horn: I used a thirty-thirty Winchester.
LeFors: Tom, do you think that will hold up as well as a thirty-forty?
Horn: No, but I like to get close to my man. The closer the better.
LeFors: How far was Willie Nickell killed?
Horn: About three hundred yards. It was the best shot that I ever made and the dirtiest trick I ever done. I thought at one time he would get away.
LeFors: How about the shells? Did you carry them away?
Horn: You bet your God damn life I did.[86]

They talked more about his trip to Montana. LeFors said he wanted to go home for a little while and then resume their conversation later in the day. LeFors asked one last question before they walked out.[87]

LeFors: Tom, let us go downstairs and get a drink. I could always see your work clear, but I want you to tell me why you killed the kid. Was it a mistake?
Horn: Well, I will tell you all about it when I come back from Montana. It is too new yet.[88]

The morning conversation had lasted two and a half hours. LeFors and Horn went to Harry Hynd's saloon for a drink.[89]

They returned to the US Marshal's office later that afternoon to continue the conversation. Horn went on and on about not being able to hold a conversation in public without being interrupted and then started talking about his life.[90]

Horn: I would like to have had somebody who saw my past and could picture it to the public. It would be the most God damn interesting reading in the country; and if we could describe to the author our feelings at different times it would be better still. The experience of my life, or the first man I killed, was when I was only twenty-six years old. He was a coarse son of a bitch.

LeFors: How much did you get for killing these fellows? In the Powell and Lewis case, you got six hundred dollars apiece. You killed Lewis in the corral with a six-shooter. I would like to have seen the expression on his face when you shot him.

Horn: He was the scaredest son of a bitch you ever saw. How did you come to know that, Joe?

LeFors: I have known everything you have done, Tom for a great many years. I know where you were paid this money.

Horn: Yes. I was paid this money on the train between Cheyenne and Denver.

LeFors: Why did you put the rock under the kid's head after you killed him? That is one of your marks, isn't it?

Horn: Yes, that is the way I hang out my sign to collect money for a job of this kind.

LeFors: Have you got your money yet for the killing of Nickell?

Horn: I got that before I did the job.

LeFors: You got five hundred dollars for that. Why did you cut the price?

Horn: I got twenty-one hundred dollars.

LeFors: How much is that a man?

Horn: That is for three dead men, and one man shot at five times. Killing men is my specialty. I look at it as a business proposition, and I think I have a corner on the market.[91]

They continued swapping tales. Horn's plan was to leave for Montana the next day. The afternoon meeting lasted one and a half hours.[92]

During the two meetings, Ohnhaus took down the conversation in shorthand and occasionally would look at Horn through the door's keyhole. After the two men left, Ohnhaus began transcribing his shorthand notes.[93]

The next day, January 13, 1902, a warrant was issued for Tom Horn's arrest. Sheriff Ed Smalley and Deputy Sheriff Dick Proctor found Horn sitting in the Inter Ocean Hotel. They told him they had a murder warrant for his arrest. He said, "All right," and they escorted him to the county jail.[94]

Horn asked to see Joe LeFors. Smalley telephoned him at Stoll's office. LeFors didn't want to see him, but Smalley insisted and LeFors came to see Horn. At the time, Horn must not have realized LeFors set him up.

"They have got me in here for killing the kid," Horn said.

"The hell they have," LeFors replied. He did not want to hang around there and soon left.[95]

On January 23, a preliminary hearing was held on Tom Horn's murder charge of Willie Nickell. Joe LeFors was called to the witness stand, and it was here for the first time that everyone, including Tom Horn, learned he had confessed to murdering Willie Nickell and that it had been recorded. The presiding judge, Richard H. Scott, ruled there was enough evidence to hold Horn in the Laramie County jail without bail.[96]

The pretrial proceedings began on September 23, 1902, and included jury selection. Horn and many of the initial candidates knew each other. In a strange fluke of fate, Kels Nickell's name was drawn to be a juror. He was quickly dismissed. On October 8, Nickell pulled a knife and threatened a prospective juror accusing him of being bribed to acquit Horn. Nickell was issued an order to show why he should not be held in contempt of court.[97]

The trial was held at the Laramie County Courthouse in Cheyenne beginning at 10:00 a.m. on Friday, October 10, and lasted until Friday, October 24, 1902. Richard H. Scott was the presiding judge. Scott had been the presiding judge in the 1893 trial proceedings concerning the infamous Johnson County War. He had ruled in favor of the big cattle interests leading to no one ever being held accountable for several murders committed by the cattle barons' gunmen. The prosecuting attorney was Laramie County attorney Walter Stoll, who had represented the county during the coroner's inquest. Horn's defense team of five attorneys was headed by Judge John W. Lacey, who had served as Wyoming Territory's first chief justice. Horn's friends paid six thousand dollars to retain his legal team. Over one hundred witnesses were called to testify.[98]

The trial drew national interest. Reporters came from as far away as New York. The courtroom was packed. Outside the courthouse, it was a festive atmosphere. In the saloons, men made bets on the trial's outcome. As the trial proceeded on to October 15, the locally popular Edward "Doc" Moore appeared outside the courthouse and played his fiddle for the enjoyment of witnesses and spectators who danced to his tunes. The music could be heard in the courtroom where many tapped their feet, and some went to the windows to look outside.[99]

Tom Horn's documented confession to the murder of Willie Nickell was the centerpiece of the prosecution's case. To support the case, Stoll had maps prepared to show critical locations and distances for the crime scene and vicinity and presented additional backup evidence and witnesses.[100]

The prosecution and defense spent a majority of the first few days asking physicians about ballistics and the wounds to Willie Nickell's body. The defense argued that Horn could not have committed the murder. He carried a .30-30 Winchester, and the wounds indicated the bullets had been of a larger caliber. This was key. If it could be shown that Horn's weapon had not been used in the murder, the jury could use that to acquit him. The prosecution argued that by the time Willie's body had been examined, three days of decomposition had taken place and the caliber of the bullets could not be determined by the wounds. Dr. L. P. Desmond, one of the prosecution's doctors, stated that there was no way to determine the caliber of a bullet from the wound it produced due to "a hundred and one different causes," including what the bullet struck, the bullet type, if it mushroomed or expanded, and the tissue it went through.[101]

On the fourth day of the trial, Stoll placed fourteen people on the witness stand to bracket Horn's whereabouts on the day Willie Nickell was killed. Thirteen hours before Willie's death, Horn was spotted four to five miles from the murder scene, and four hours after the murder, he was seen riding into Laramie carrying a bundle. Witnesses testified that Horn arrived there about 11:00 a.m., July 18, riding a lathered horse different from the one he had been seen riding in the Iron Mountain area the days previous to the murder. Stoll told the jury that the distance between the murder location and Laramie could be covered by several hours of hard riding.[102]

The prosecution questioned eleven-year-old Freddie Nickell about a .30-30 cartridge he had found at a gate, two miles from the murder scene. The defense wanted it thrown out, but Judge Scott allowed it to remain, saying the jury could "give it such weight as [they] think advisable."[103]

Two witnesses testified that a man resembling Tom Horn had left a blood-stained sweater in their Laramie shoe shop and told them he would return for it. When he didn't return, it was laundered, used, and then sent to Tom Horn in jail. When Sheriff Ed Smalley and Deputy Sheriff Dick Proctor showed the sweater to Horn, he said, "I guess this is my sweater, all right."[104]

Three men testified that Horn bragged about killing Willie Nickell at Denver's annual Carnival. Roy Campbell, a telephone man, said he and two friends were in a saloon. They were talking about detective work when Horn, who was sitting at the bar, introduced himself and said he was a Wyoming stock detective. Campbell said that Horn appeared very intoxicated. One of the men, Frank Mulock, said to Horn, "If you are a Wyoming detective, it seems to me that you would be up there and getting some of that money from the Willie Nickell killing."

"Why, that is all right, I am the main guy in that case. . . . I know all about it."

Later, Horn approached their table and said, "That Nickell shot was the best I ever made in my life."[105]

Mulock, who worked for the Colorado Republican Party, confirmed everything Campbell had said, adding that Horn had said after admitting killing Nickell, "That is the dirtiest trick I ever done."[106]

The third man, Robert G. Cowsley, a civil engineer and in the same national guard unit as Campbell, confirmed what the other two men had said with the addition that Horn had struck their table with his hand when he said, "That Nickell business was the God damned best shot I ever made."[107]

Walter Stoll shifted to Tom Horn's January 12, 1902, confession, setting the stage through witnesses who said they believed Horn had been drinking but did not appear drunk. Stoll then brought Joe LeFors to the witness chair and went through the whole set-up as to how LeFors had obtained Horn's confession. That was followed by Deputy Sheriff Les Snow and stenographer Charles Ohnhaus's testimonies on what they had heard Horn say and what Ohnhaus had transcribed.[108]

It was then the defense team's turn. In his opening statements, T. F. Burke said about Horn's confession, "We will have little trouble, I believe, in showing that Horn was having a little quiet fun with La Fors [sic] when he told him what they claim he did in the United States Marshal's office." The defense team presented five men who testified that Horn was drunk on January 12. The defense brought up the bullet wounds again and had their experts state that the wounds could not have been caused by .30 caliber bullets. Again, the prosecution and defense wrangled back and forth through three physician witnesses, trying to poke holes in each other's positions.[109]

The defense called Otto Plaga to the stand. Plaga testified that he had seen Tom Horn on July 18, 1901, about an hour after Willie Nickell had been killed, about twenty-five miles to the west of the murder scene, riding the horse he usually rode at an easy trot. Plaga said he was about 150 yards away from Horn and could tell his horse was very fresh. When Stoll cross-examined Plaga, he asked why he did not call out to Horn. Plaga responded that he "was cracking this quartz" and "wanted to keep that to myself." The prosecution brought forth witnesses stating that Plaga was unreliable, and the defense brought out witnesses saying that his word was good. Unfortunately for Horn, at the Willie Nickell murder inquest, he had stated that Plaga was unreliable.[110]

On October 17, 1902, at 3:44 p.m., John Lacey called Tom Horn to the witness stand. The crux of Horn's whole testimony boiled down to

Horn having a little fun with LeFors. Horn said, "I never had anything to do with the killing of Willie Nickell; I never had any cause to kill him. . . . There was nothing serious about the talk at all; it was all a josh, all the way through."[111]

Horn said the talk with the three men in Denver never took place. The blue sweater was not his. The people who said he was in Laramie on July 18 were wrong; he claimed he did not arrive there until July 20.[112]

On October 19, Walter Stoll cross-examined Tom Horn. Stoll picked apart differences in Horn's testimony on his whereabouts between the coroner's inquest and his recent testimony at the murder trial. Stoll showed that Horn's testimony on his whereabouts did not correspond to what Otto Plaga had said. Horn had no one to support his testimony on his whereabouts from July 17 to the morning of July 20.[113]

Horn's defense team had been trying to show that LeFors had gotten Horn drunk and had led him into making false statements about killing Willie Nickell—tall tales made in drunken jest. However, Horn undercut his own defense when Stoll, referring to his Denver conversation with Campbell, Mulock, and Cowsley, suggested Horn might have been so drunk he did not remember the conversation.[114]

> *Stoll: You do not wish to say you might have had a conversation of this character, but you were in such a condition you do not recall what it was?*
>
> *Horn: I wish to say that I never saw or spoke or heard of them [Campbell, Mulock, and Cowsley] until they took the witness stand.*
>
> *Stoll: At that time . . . were you in a condition to remember whether you had these conversations with these men or not?*
>
> *Horn: I remember everything that occurred to me in my life.*
>
> *Stoll: You have never been so much under the influence of liquor so as not to remember what you said?*
>
> *Horn: Not if I could talk.[115]*

Stoll led Horn through his discussion with LeFors about doing business for cattlemen and not making reports until the end. Stoll asked Horn about his condition when his conversation with LeFors was recorded.[116]

Stoll: You do not claim that you were so intoxicated that you did not know what you said?
Horn: I know to a certainty I know what I was saying. I had not been to bed the night before; I had been up visiting, drinking, having a good time; I knew perfectly well what I was saying.[117]

Horn admitted that he made the statements about killing Willie Nickell and shooting at Kels Nickell, but he didn't mean anything by it; he was only trying to please LeFors. "I would have said anything else to please him [Lefors], Horn said. "I felt very nice that morning: I felt peaceful I would have told a dozen more lies if he felt inclined to think that way."[118]

When Stoll asked Horn about shooting Willie at a distance of three hundred yards and other details of the killing, Horn responded by saying, "I was just bluffing." Later in the-cross examination, Horn denied he had ever killed anyone, saying, "I never killed a man in my life." Horn admitted that he had made all the recorded statements, including, "Killing men is my specialty. I look at it as a business proposition and I think I have a corner on the market."[119]

When John Lacey conducted his redirect, he had Horn clarify that he lied about murdering people and killing Willie Nickell only to please Joe LeFors. At the end Horn said, "As far as actual killing is concerned I never killed a man in my life or a boy either."[120]

The prosecution and defense went through their final arguments. The *Cheyenne Daily Leader* stated, "Upon Tom Horn's veracity rests his fate," and, "If the jury believes he told the truth when he made his startling confession to Joe LeFors, a verdict of murder in the first degree will be returned against him. If they believe that he is a liar, they will acquit. If there is a division of opinion on the subject, the jury and not the accused will hang."[121]

At 11:30 a.m., Friday, October 24, 1902, the jury left the courtroom to begin its deliberations. The *Denver Times* noted, "All but two are cowmen and familiar with all the conditions of the case," and, "These men have known Horn personally or by reputation for years and may unconsciously let their opinions formed from such acquaintance enter into the rendering of a verdict." The *Times* concluded it was known that Horn had one or two friends on the jury and predicted it would be a hung jury. Many people agreed with the *Times's* observation.[122]

By 4:30 p.m., the jury had made its decision and returned to the courtroom. The *Cheyenne Daily Leader* reported, "Amidst breathless silence, so profound the dropping of a pin could have been heard in the court room, the bailiff took the small piece of paper upon which was written the words that to Tom Horn meant life or death." The court clerk was given the note and read, "We the jury, empaneled in the above entitled case, do find the defendant, Tom Horn, guilty of murder in the first degree, as charged in the information."[123]

On Monday, October 27, Tom Horn's lawyers filed a motion for a new trial. In their forty-seven-page document they listed seventy rulings by Judge Scott that they believed were wrong. The prosecution responded with counter affidavits, and the defense responded to the prosecution's affidavits with its own. Each side presented their arguments before Judge Scott. On Wednesday, November 12, Scott made his decision. He said after reviewing the information presented to him, "I cannot find any error prejudicial to the defendant. The motion for a new trial for the defendant is overruled." Scott then sentenced Horn to be hanged by the neck until dead between 9:00 a.m. and 3:00 p.m. on January 9, 1903.[124]

The next step for the defense was to appeal the verdict to the Wyoming Supreme Court, so Horn was granted a stay of execution until the court could rule. The court would not be hearing the case until August 1903. One fact everyone knew was that up to that time, the Wyoming Supreme Court had never reversed a first-degree murder conviction.[125]

While newspapers groused about the delays in Horn's execution, mobs broke into two Wyoming jails and hanged three murder suspects. There were plots and rumors of plots that Horn's friends would break him out of jail. One plot included blowing up the exercise yard wall with six sticks of dynamite while Horn was in the yard. A saddled horse waited for him to make his escape. There were additional rumors that Horn had his own plans to break out.[126]

One of Horn's attorneys, R. N. Matson, who was also a member of the Wyoming House of Representatives and chairman of the judiciary committee, supported the new House Bill 100 that would abolish capital punishment and would be retroactive, saving Horn from execution. When the public learned that House Bill 100 would spare Horn's life, there was an uproar, and the bill was quickly killed.[127]

Tom Horn's cell was next to a cell belonging to another inmate, Jim McCloud. They were located on a second level atop all the other cells in the Laramie County jail. The doors of the two cells opened onto a corridor with a locked door. A little after 8:00 a.m., on Sunday, August 9, 1903, Deputy Sheriff Dick Proctor opened the corridor door to give McCloud medicine he was taking. Horn and McCloud were sitting on a bench outside their cells. When the door opened, they jumped Proctor, who fought back, but he was overpowered by the two. They tied his hands with window cord and then took him to the sheriff's office where they found a .30-40 Winchester. Proctor was able to reach his Belgian automatic pistol. Horn jumped him and they wrestled to the ground. Proctor got off a couple of shots. One hit McCloud in the leg. Before Horn pried the gun out of his hand, Proctor set the safety. Horn was unfamiliar with how to release it. As this was happening, Deputy Sheriff Les Snow opened the door to the sheriff's office. McCloud pointed the Winchester at him, but he slammed the door and ran, firing his pistol into the air as a warning.[128]

McCloud ran outside to the stable where he found a horse and bridled it. Hearing the commotion around the jail, Sheriff Ed Smalley ran to the stable where he saw McCloud and fired a shot from his gun. McCloud took off running, but after being chased several blocks by various armed men, he was soon captured.[129]

Back in the sheriff's office, Horn had wrestled the gun out of Proctor's hand, leveled it at him, and pulled the trigger, but the safety was on, saving Proctor's life. Horn could not make it work and ran out of the office to the stable. Not finding a horse, he ran out in front of the courthouse in view of roughly fifty people. He started running north. O. M. Aldrich, a Colorado merry-go-round engineer, pulled his pistol, shot at Horn, and chased after him. Horn tried to shoot Aldrich but still could not release the safety. Horn jumped fences and crossed yards with Aldrich in pursuit. As Horn reached Twentieth Street, Aldrich shot again. The bullet creased the top of Horn's head and he dropped to the ground. Horn tried to fire at Aldrich but couldn't get the gun to work. Aldrich jumped on Horn and wrestled with him. Robert Fontaine, a mail clerk, joined Aldrich in the fight. Horn was finally subdued after Aldrich beat him on the head with his gun.[130]

Laramie County peace officers reached Horn and escorted him back to jail as a crowd followed along, some shouting that Horn should be hanged. Kels Nickell joined the mob, trying to stir the men to action.[131]

Horn's failed escape caused quite a stir in Wyoming. He admitted that if he could have taken the safety off the pistol, he would have killed Proctor and others to make his escape.[132]

On August 20, 1903, the Wyoming Supreme Court convened to hear Horn's case. After listening to both sides' arguments, the court reviewed the information submitted and reconvened on September 30. It took Justice Charles Potter two hours to read the court's eighty-seven-page decision. In a nutshell, the Supreme Court upheld the verdict from the lower court, stating, "The objections to the rulings of the court have received our most careful considerations; a very large number of authorities have been consulted, in addition to those cited in this opinion; and it has all resulted in convincing our minds that the record furnishes no justification for a reversal of the case. It seems to have been ably and dispassionately tried. We are, therefore, of the opinion that the judgement should be and same will be affirmed."[133]

The court then pronounced, "And now this court appoints Friday, the 20th day of November, in the year of our Lord 1903, for the execution of the sentence pronounced by the court below."[134]

Tom Horn had one last legal remedy to cheat the hangman—commutation of his sentence to life imprisonment by Acting Governor Fenimore Chatterton. On Saturday, October 31, three of Horn's attorneys appeared before Governor Chatterton presenting papers and affidavits requesting clemency for Tom Horn. Accompanying Horn's attorneys were his friend John Coble and Glendolene Kimmel, who had now changed her story stating Victor Miller had admitted to her that he had killed Willie Nickell. Accompanying the attorneys representing the state of Wyoming was Kels Nickell. After Horn's attorneys made their verbal presentation to the governor, the prosecuting attorneys asked for time to prepare their response. The governor then privately interviewed Glendolene Kimmel about her affidavit for a long period of time. Soon after her revelations, Laramie County attorney Walter Stoll filed perjury charges against Kimmel.[135]

On November 12, the prosecution presented to Governor Chatterton its rebuttal with a stack of affidavits addressing all the defense's points. The defense lawyers countered with their own affidavits. On Saturday, November 14, Governor Chatterton announced his decision. He had reviewed all the affidavits especially Glendolene Kimmel's which if true would mean a pardon for Tom Horn. However, Chatterton did not believe the Kimmel affidavit. He concluded saying, "For these reasons and with more regret than I can express, I do not believe that law and justice would be served by the interposition of Executive clemency." Tom Horn's execution remained set to proceed on Friday, November 20.[136]

Laramie County officials were concerned that Tom Horn's friends might try to break him out of jail. The army loaned the county a gatling gun and an expert gunner. The gatling gun and gunner were placed at the jail in a commanding position covering all points of attack. The day before the execution, Governor Chatterton ordered the adjutant general to station troops around the jail. Horn believed his friends would still spring him even with all the troops present.[137]

That same day, carpenters constructed the gallows just feet from Horn's cell. The hanging mechanism was designed so Horn would basically hang himself. He would be placed on a trap door, where his weight would trigger a valve allowing water into a vessel that when sufficiently filled would jerk a plug and release the trap door.[138]

John Coble visited Horn. Reverend Ira D. Williams also paid Horn a visit and claimed that Horn confessed to him that he had killed Willie Nickell. When later asked about the confession, Horn loudly denied it.[139]

On Friday, November 20, 1903, the day of execution, Horn wrote letters to friends, ate a good breakfast, and had a serious, half-hour conversation with an Episcopal priest, G. C. Rafter. Horn then waited, lying on his bunk, smoking a cigar until it was time to go. As Horn left his cell, his friends the Irwin brothers, Charlie and Frank, stood there and sang his favorite hymn, "Life's Railway to Heaven."[140]

Horn joked with the deputies as they placed straps around his wrists and thighs. He was stoic and continued to banter through the whole process as he was led to the scaffold. Dick Proctor placed the rope around Horn's neck and a hood over his head. Sheriff Ed Smalley and Joe Cahill lifted Horn onto the trap door. All were silent. The only sound was dripping water for thirty-five seconds. The trapdoor sprang open. Horn dropped like a rock and died instantly.[141]

Tom Horn, murderer of Willie Nickell, had paid the ultimate price.

TOM HORN, AN INNOCENT MAN CONDEMNED TO DEATH
—KELLEN CUTSFORTH

Throughout his lifetime, Tom Horn was most known as a stock detective and a bit of a badman. Horn, in many ways, was his own worst enemy. Braggadocious when he had a skin full of liquor, Horn often told tall tales about himself with which he often had little to nothing to do. This character flaw helped lead to Horn's eventual conviction of murder and subsequent death by hanging on November 20, 1903.[142]

When young Willie Nickell was gunned down in 1901, the Cheyenne county commissioner hired US Deputy Marshal Joe LeFors to begin investigating the crime. Coincidentally, in December of that year, LeFors received several letters from prominent ranchers encouraging him to investigate cattle rustling in the area. Suspecting that Horn had something to do with the death of Nickell, LeFors used the ranchers' letters as enticement for Horn to assist in the investigation.

At the time of Nickell's death, Tom Horn had been the favored instrument of justice employed by cattle barons in connection with cattle rustling cases. He was a stock detective and often acted as a hired gun. In 1900, Horn was suspected of killing two known rustlers, Matt Rash and Isom Dart, in Brown's Park, where the Colorado, Utah, and Wyoming borders intersect.[143]

Though Horn was suspected as the assassin of cattle thieves Rash and Dart, there was little to no follow-up on the subject. However, Horn's involvement in several stock theft cases like this and the fact that he was in Wyoming where young Nickell was murdered made him an instant suspect to LeFors.

Tom Horn found the offer of a job helping marshal LeFors track cattle rustlers too enticing and arrived in Cheyenne on Saturday, January 11, 1902. When Horn arrived, LeFors got the stock detective to overimbibe all night and then proceeded to lead him to the US marshal's office early the next morning.[144]

Before Horn arrived at the marshal's office that morning, LeFors secreted a stenographer and a second person to act as witnesses behind a closed door. When a still-inebriated Horn and LeFors entered the office, they began chatting. Over several hours, LeFors led Tom Horn into a conversation about the death of Willie Nickell.[145]

During this conversation, LeFors goaded Horn into speaking about the Nickell case, and Horn reportedly said, "It was the best shot that I ever made and the dirtiest trick I ever done." This circumstance is especially troubling because it amounts to nothing short of entrapment on the part of LeFors.[146]

Tom Horn transformed into a blabbering blowhard when he was drunk. Some of Horn's friends stated, "Tom was lonesome and whisky made him do and say crazy things." John Fullerton, owner of the Inter Ocean Hotel and Horn's friend, corroborated this, mentioning that when Horn was drunk, he "brags and tells big stories."[147]

Supposedly, when Horn was in his cups, he would say anything to make himself sound bigger and more important than he was. He would brag about being a detective and the "best shot in the US." He did this so often that his braggadocio got him involved in several fistfights in western towns, throughout the Great Plains territories.[148] In the case of the Nickell killing, LeFors led Tom into the conversation, made sure he was good and liquored up, and stroked his ego to get him to say something incriminating. In today's terms, this is nothing short of leading and entrapping a suspect. Procedures like this are highly unethical and often inadmissible in a modern court of law.

Another problematic part of Joe LeFors extracting the dubious "confession" was the fact that he and the US Marshals looked at no other suspect in the killing of Nickell other than Tom Horn. Kels Nickell and James Miller had been feuding over Nickell's sheep constantly mixing with Miller's and many other ranchers' cattle for years. There had been accusations of fence cutting, arson-torched haystacks, and fights, especially between members of the Nickell and Miller factions.[149]

As early as 1900, Kels Nickell and James Miller had shot at each other in Wyoming's Iron Mountain region. Though no one was injured in the dust-up, the Millers and Nickells were continuously at each other's throats from then on. In some ways, these two families resembled a western version of the Hatfields and McCoys.

In January 1901, James Miller accosted Kels Nickell in a Cheyenne restaurant. Miller blamed Kels for the accidental death of his son Frank. Because of the shootout with Nickell the previous year, Miller had begun carrying a loaded shotgun all the time. While holding the shotgun, the weapon had accidentally discharged, killing Frank. James became so enraged at this incident that he attacked Nickell. Their fight ended with Miller stabbing Kels. Fortunately for him, he did not die from the wound, and the feud between the Nickells and the Millers intensified to a fevered pace.[150]

Following their confrontation in Cheyenne, James Miller accosted young Willie Nickell. The fourteen-year-old boy, who was eventually felled by an assassin's bullet, was approached by Miller, who aimed his gun at the boy's horse and threatened to pull the trigger. It is also believed that James Miller snapped his breech-load shotgun closed in a threatening manner while the boy was near.[151] With all this menacing and actual violence between the two factions, one would think LeFors and the US Marshal's office would have broadened their search for a suspect in the death of Willie Nickell instead of narrowly focusing on Tom Horn, but they did not. LeFors had it out for Horn, and he would not be deterred.

The whole reason Tom Horn was in the Iron Mountain area of Wyoming was because he had been summoned at the behest of wealthy cattle baron John C. Coble.[152] Coble wanted Horn to investigate to see if Kels Nickell's sheep were straying onto his cattle ranch pastures and if Kels knew it.[153] It is most likely true that Nickell was allowing his sheep to mingle with Miller's cattle and surrounding ranchers' property, allowing them to illegally graze on designated cattle lands. By most accounts from people who knew him, Kels Nickell was an absolute jerk. He purposely allowed his sheep to graze on other ranchers' lands just to spite them.[154]

Furthermore, around a month after the death of Willie Nickell, Kels Nickell was shot three times and severely wounded while milking cows with his youngest daughter. It is estimated that around eighty of his sheep were also slaughtered. Witnesses to this violence noted seeing two men riding away on a pair of horses owned by Jim Miller. Kels Nickell himself said he knew his assailants were James Miller and one of James sons, either Gus or Victor. James Miller was later arrested for the murder attempt and released on bond.[155] Yet, with all this information at his disposal, LeFors never decided to investigate or even interview any of the Millers about the death of Willie Nickell. Instead, he went directly after Horn and only Horn.

The real reason LeFors attacked Tom Horn was the fact that Horn had become a notorious figure in the cattle industry. He was unpopular with many of the smaller cattle ranchers who saw him as an instrument of the large cattle barons, making him a high-profile target. These small-time ranchers felt the cattle barons used Horn to impose their power to disperse troublemakers and dispense a dose of frontier justice if any of them fought back.[156]

It is for certain that Horn killed suspected cattle rustlers in the past through the instruction of the cattle barons. He was also disliked by many people in Wyoming and the surrounding states because of his association with the larger ranching operations. Most historians believe Tom Horn was symbolic of the stranglehold the cattle barons held on the ranching industry and was most likely a killer.[157] However, just because Horn was guilty of one crime did not make him guilty of another. With the conviction and execution of Horn, LeFors made an example of him and inflicted damage to the large cattlemen whose influence was beginning to wane.

When Horn "confessed" to the killing of Willie Nickell, he was stone cold drunk. He was also under the impression that he was going to get a job with LeFors. Horn bragged and told tall tales when inebriated because he thought it improved his stature. He most likely lied about killing Nickell because, in an odd way, he thought he was impressing LeFors. And LeFors goaded Horn to talk about the incident.

After the death of Willie, Kels Nickell believed that either James Miller or one of his sons was responsible. In fact, he accused James's son Gus of being the assassin. There was also consideration amongst the locals that a former sheepherder may have been responsible for the boy's death.[158]

However, during the inquest held after young Willie's death, District Attorney Walter Stoll focused solely on Tom Horn and leading the questioning away from the Miller family members. Stoll, when questioning Kels Nickell about his interaction with Horn, asked specifically if "he [Kels] had heard of his [Horn] making threats." Kels said he had heard "lots of things" but that he and Horn had an agreement with each other.[159]

Tom Horn had earlier mentioned that the rumors circulating that he had made a threat against Kels Nickell's life came from Victor Miller, James's son. During the inquest, Kels mentioned that Horn had said to him that "there was no enmity against you [Kels] for bringing sheep in here" and that "We [cattlemen] were not afraid of sheepmen going to steal our cattle." However, it is noted John Coble was mad at the sheepherders, specifically Nickell, for bringing their sheep into the cattle grazing lands and brought Horn in to investigate.[160]

It is true that Horn was seen near the Nickell property the day before the murder of Willie, but he was not seen on the day of the killing or immediately afterward. Also, there was no direct evidence that he committed the crime. There were no horse tracks, no footprints connected to him, no gun shells, nor any eyewitness accounts putting him in position to assassinate Willie. The only evidence leading to his conviction was his inebriated "confession," which is dubious at best. In fact, had it not been for District Attorney Stoll's insistence on keeping Horn at the center of the investigation, he most likely would not have been mentioned by either the Millers or the Nickell family as the murderer of the Nickell boy.

When it came to the attempt on Kels Nickell's life, Kels himself identified there being two assassins. In fact, he identified one of them as James Miller. His children also identified two killers after the attack. Somehow, US deputy Marshal Joe LeFors, who was conveniently placed in charge of investigating the case, found there to be only one attacker. Guess who he thought that attacker was? When questioned by District

Attorney Stoll about the incident, LeFors said he found hoofprints of a single shod horse, not two, and they did not lead toward the Miller's ranch but toward the home of Billy Clay. Clay was well known for often providing accommodations to Tom Horn while he was working for the cattlemen in that area.[161]

This is crazy! How is it possible that Kels Nickell, who was shot at and hit three times, does not know what he saw. Not only that, but the attack was witnessed by Nickell's children, and they are somehow mistaken about who fired at their father! They are also incorrect about seeing numerous riders racing from the scene! How is it that somehow LeFors found only one set of tracks, and they just so happened to lead to the home of a confidant of Tom Horn? Sorry Kels, you just cannot believe your lying eyes. It was not whom you saw. It was clearly Tom Horn. It was clearly Tom Horn because that is who District Attorney Walter Stoll and US deputy Marshal Joe LeFors decided was responsible.

What is also interesting about the attack on Kels is the fact that if it was Tom Horn who did the shooting, he was apparently unable to kill his mark. In LeFors's description, Horn could apparently pinpoint a shot killing Willie Nickell from two hundred yards away, but he could not finish off Kels with three shots at a much closer distance. LeFors himself even admitted that "his sights must have moved or something [was] wrong with his gun."[162]

The Laramie County commissioners poured thousands of dollars into the murder investigation of Willie Nickell. District Attorney Stoll oversaw all the proceedings. LeFors operated directly under Stoll and did his bidding. As it was with the inquest, Stoll focused his attention directly on Tom Horn.[163] He wanted to catch him in some malfeasance, and LeFors was more than willing to participate.

Punching further holes in the prosecution's investigation of Horn was Glendolene Kimmell. A schoolteacher in the Iron Mountain district and confidant of the Millers, Kimmell implicated them in the murder of Willie Nickell. She said the Millers directed suspicion against Tom Horn, saying Gus and Victor Miller told her, "It's all right to let suspicion fall on Tom Horn, [he] doesn't care."[164]

Both Miller brothers believed that because Horn was under the protection of the cattle barons Tom felt secure that he would never be convicted of any crime. LeFors saw this as misdirection by a Horn sympathizer, and Kimmell would later be accused of perjury during Horn's trial when she testified to this. She was also accused of having a relationship with Horn, which there was absolutely no evidence of and was utter gossip. In fact, Kimmell and Horn barely knew each other. Not surprisingly, her perjury case was dismissed December 16, 1903, conveniently after Horn was hanged.[165]

The mindset of Horn that Glendolene Kimmell described is more in line with his way of thinking than not. It is known that Tom was full of bluster and overly secure that he would never come to grief because of his associations with the big-money cattlemen. He drunkenly bragged to LeFors because he felt there would be no retribution. This is truly egotistical of Horn and certainly baffling, but not out of the ordinary when it came to Tom. Furthermore, Glendolene Kimmell had nothing to gain by supporting Horn. In testifying in favor of him, she told the truth.

Also in defense of Horn was Otto Plaga. Otto was a young cowboy and an acquaintance of Tom's after having helped him arrest a ring of rustlers in 1893. Plaga placed Horn twenty-five miles from the murder scene riding his horse while the killing was to have taken place. Plaga also casually mentioned to his stepfather, Raymond Henecke, that he saw Horn that day.[166]

In response to this obvious alibi for Horn, attorney Stoll nitpicked everything in Plaga's testimony and his earlier deposition. Plaga had said that he was prospecting for gold and he did not point to the specific spot where he saw Horn when presented with a map because he felt he would give away his prospecting spot, which he wanted to keep secret.[167]

When asked why he did not wave to Horn, Plaga said he thought Tom was looking for rustlers and did not want to disturb him. Raymond Henecke corroborated what his stepson testified. Since both Plaga and Henecke were friends of Horn, and waited to report what they saw, their testimonies were questioned. When cross-examined about Plaga seeing him, Horn told the truth and said he had not seen the young man.[168] This truthfulness clearly hurt Horn in the long run and helped lead to his conviction.

When asked about the Miller and Nickell families, Horn said he believed neither one of them would kill anyone. So, detractors of Horn say, "If neither the Nickell nor Miller families are capable of killing each other, then, the killer of Willie Nickell must be Horn." The facts do not bear this out. Both Kels and James had taken shots at each other in 1900. Miller had also stabbed Kels in early 1901. There was no doubt these men were capable of murder, and it did not matter what Tom Horn thought of either family.

The real killer of Willie Nickell was more than likely one or both of James Miller's sons Gus or Victor. Tom Horn certainly killed cattle rustlers, but he did not kill young Willie Nickell. He had no reason to kill him. Tom got liquored up, was goaded into a confession, and was convicted and executed because lawmen in Wyoming wanted to challenge the power of the wealthy cattlemen. What better way to do that than hang the most notorious stock detective of the day.

CHAPTER 10

DID BUTCH CASSIDY DIE IN BOLIVIA?

JUST THE FACTS

Butch Cassidy and the Sundance Kid is one of the great Western movies of all time. The membership of Western Writers of America selected *Butch Cassidy and the Sundance Kid* number four in its top one hundred greatest Westerns.[1]

Most people know about these two outlaws from the 1969 film starring Paul Newman as Butch Cassidy, Robert Redford as the Sundance Kid, and Katharine Ross as Etta Place, Sundance Kid's love interest. (Spoiler alert, if you haven't seen the movie, these two best of friends travel to South America where they continue to commit robberies, are surrounded by the Bolivian army, and die in a hail of bullets.)

Just like many movies, *Butch Cassidy and the Sundance Kid* is based on a true story, but the film is not the real story. What is the truth? Did Butch Cassidy as well as the Sundance Kid die in Bolivia? Let's take a brief look at the lives of Butch Cassidy, whose real name was Robert LeRoy Parker, and the Sundance Kid, whose real name was Harry Longabaugh.

Butch Cassidy was a gentleman outlaw. He did not approve of bloodshed and as far as is known, never killed anyone during his years in the United States. He was courteous to women, generous to those in need, and loyal to friends. Charles Kelly interviewed people who had known him, including law enforcement officers, and all said, in effect, "Butch Cassidy was one of the finest men I ever knew."[2]

Robert LeRoy Parker was born to Maximillian and Ann Parker on April 13, 1866, in Beaver, Utah. Maxi and Ann brought up little Bob and his twelve younger brothers and sisters in a loving, happy Mormon family.[3]

In 1879, Bob was thirteen years old when the Parkers bought a 160-acre ranch in Circle Valley, three miles south of Circleville, Utah. Maxi continued to buy additional land and worked hard to improve it. Fellow Mormons squatted on some of Maxi's land he had developed. He went to the local Mormon bishop to have the squatters removed, but the bishop sided with the squatters, giving them the land. Maxi had little to do with the Mormon Church after that. This could have been one of several reasons Bob would become resentful of those in authority.[4]

That same year, to help the family make ends meet, Bob went to work for Pat Ryan, who owned a ranch outside of Milford, about forty miles north of Circleville. Ryan recognized that Bob was hard working, dependable, and intelligent.[5]

It was payday and Bob needed a new pair of overalls, so he rode into Milford. The store was closed, but Bob found his way into the store, selected the overalls he wanted, and left a note for the owner that the next time he was in town, he would pay for the overalls. The storeowner was not pleased and reported to law enforcement Bob's action as a theft. Bob was arrested, but after reviewing the circumstances, the authorities let him go. The whole experience left a bitter taste in his mouth. He was angry. The incident was an embarrassment to his family, and he felt the law had acted in a heavy-handed manner.[6]

Around 1881 or 1882, Bob along with his mother and two brothers found work closer to home at the Maxwell Ranch and Dairy. During his second year at Maxwell's, Bob met the cowhand Mike Cassidy, who happened to also sideline as cattle rustler and horse thief. Cassidy took a liking to young Bob and gave him a saddle and a pistol. Cassidy taught Bob all he knew of horsemanship, handling cattle, and marksmanship. Bob was a fast learner and soon excelled at marksmanship and horsemanship. However, Cassidy's training of young Bob abruptly ended when the law became suspicious of Cassidy's extracurricular activities and he fled to Mexico.[7]

Parley Christensen, who served as Juab County sheriff for thirty years, said that somewhere during this time Bob was accused of stealing a saddle, arrested, and abused by Garfield County authorities, but there is no official record of his arrest.[8]

It was 1884 and Bob Parker was eighteen years old when he rode away from the family home to seek his fortune in Telluride, Colorado. After Bob left Utah, it was discovered he had signed false bills of sale on cattle belonging to local ranchers. The cattle were discovered in the herds of two friends of Mike Cassidy. The cattle were returned to their rightful owners and no long-term harm was done, but Circle Valley folks now considered Bob to be on the wrong side of the law.[9]

Gold mines were in high production around Telluride. The town was booming with all types of businesses and diversions for gold miners. Nicknamed "the Sodom of the American West," Telluride was a rough town.[10]

Bob, who was now calling himself Roy Parker, found a job outside town, packing ore on mules and then hauling the ore from the mine to the stamp mills. When Roy arrived in town, he had brought an unbroken colt with him and found a rancher who agreed to board it. Every time Roy visited the ranch to work with his colt, the rancher would attempt to buy the horse from him, but Roy said the colt wasn't for sale. Roy became tired of the rancher's pestering and took his colt elsewhere to board.[11]

The rancher wasn't finished with Roy. He went to the law and said that Roy had stolen the colt from him. Roy found out about the rancher's complaint and decided it was time to leave, but he didn't get far before being arrested and placed in jail. Several friends contacted Roy's father, Maxi, and he came to testify at Roy's trial that it was his horse. The court found Roy innocent of stealing his own horse. His father tried to convince him to come home, but Roy was more interested in seeking adventure.[12]

Roy Parker rode to Wyoming and Montana working at a variety of ranch jobs, but, missing the festive life of Telluride, he had returned there by 1888. He found a job with long hours making good money, but he was bored. He became friends with Matt Warner and his brother-in-law Tom McCarty. McCarty, who was over forty, was a hard character and known to be a horse thief, cattle rustler, and gambler. The three of them ran their horses in races against others and usually won. In fact, they were so successful it was hard to find anyone who would race against them.[13]

The three men were soon broke and concocted a plan to rob Telluride's San Miguel Valley Bank. On the morning of June 24, 1889, Roy Parker and Matt Warner walked into the bank while Tom McCarty on horseback held the reins of the two others' mounts. A fourth suspect, who was never clearly identified, was also involved, remaining outside on horseback.[14]

Warner pointed his revolver at a teller's head while Roy filled two sacks with cash. Within five minutes of entering the bank, they were out the door with $20,750. They had relays of fresh horses waiting for them and quickly outdistanced their pursuers.[15]

That summer, Roy Parker changed his name to Roy Cassidy and rode into Brown's Park, a remote valley where eastern Utah and western Colorado come together just south of the Wyoming border. Again changing his name, this time to George Cassidy, he worked for rancher Herb Bassett. The Bassett family liked the hard-working Cassidy, and he became close friends with two of Herb's daughters, Josie and Ann.[16]

Cassidy moved on to Rock Springs, Wyoming, where he worked in a butcher shop; however, he was always welcome in Brown's Park and would often return to visit friends. During this time, he may have received the nickname Butch. There are several theories on how he came by this name—one of the most prevalent is that it's a shortening of "Butcher" Cassidy.[17]

Butch Cassidy was always friendly and charming, easy-going and fun-loving, enjoying a good practical joke. He was likeable and helpful to those in need. However, he had a growing dislike for those in power, the big corporations and cattle barons whom he believed took advantage of people. Butch always tried to avoid violence during any crimes in which he was involved. He eventually became the leader of a loosely organized band of like-minded men who became known as the Wild Bunch. Early on, they were suspected of cattle rustling but there was no hard evidence.[18]

In the fall of 1889, Butch and his friend Al Hainer purchased property on Horse Creek in Fremont County, Wyoming, planning to go into the business of buying and selling horses. In early 1890, Butch supplemented his income by working for Eugenio Amoretti, owner of the EA

Ranch in Wyoming's Wind River country. Amoretti and Butch soon became good friends.[19]

After participating with other ranch hands in the 1890 spring roundup, Cassidy and Hainer sold their horses to local ranchers and left the area. Butch bought land on Blue Creek in Johnson County, Wyoming. His property was just north of the popular outlaw hangout, the Hole-in-the-Wall. During his stay at Blue Creek, it was believed that Butch was involved in horse stealing and cattle rustling. Around Christmas 1890, Butch learned that law enforcement was becoming suspicious of his activities, so he sold his property to a neighbor and left Johnson County. Lawmen and cattlemen now considered Butch Cassidy a member of a loose band of rustlers called the Hole-in-the-Wall Gang.[20]

In August 1891, Butch was living at Mail Camp in Fremont County, Wyoming, when twenty-year-old Billy Nutcher showed up and sold him three horses. Nutcher told Butch he had traded cattle for the horses in Johnson County and that their title was good.[21] However, that was not the case.

Otto Franc, owner of the Pitchfork Ranch and nicknamed the "Little Baron," filed a complaint that one of the three horses belonged to the Grey Bull Cattle Company owned by his absentee neighbor, Englishman Richard Ashworth. Cassidy was arrested ten months later for having the Grey Bull Cattle Company's stolen horse in his possession. His lawyer and two Lander businessmen posted bail for him.[22]

The wheels of justice turned slowly. It was not until June 20, 1893, that Cassidy was tried for stealing the horse said to belong to the Grey Bull Cattle Company. The jury determined that there was not enough evidence to convict him and found Butch not guilty. Anticipating a not guilty outcome, Otto Franc, working with the prosecuting attorney, submitted a new complaint that another of the three horses personally belonged to Richard Ashworth. A year later, in June 1894, Butch was tried for stealing the second horse. This time, the jury found Butch guilty and set the value of the stolen horse at five dollars. The judge sentenced Cassidy to two years in the Wyoming State Penitentiary in Laramie. Butch believed the rich cattle barons had set him up.[23]

Cassidy worked hard and did not cause any problems while in prison. Governor William Alford Richards pardoned him in January 1896, after he had served eighteen months. Butch returned to Brown's Park, where he worked for his old friend Matt Warner at his ranch to earn his keep and renewed his Wild Bunch friendships. Prison had not reformed Butch. He was after adventure, money, and revenge. His targets would become banks, trains, and wealthy corporate interests.[24]

Matt Warner and Bill Wall were hired to provide protection in a dispute over a gold mine claim, which erupted into a gun battle where two men on the opposing side were killed. Warner and Wall were arrested and wound up in jail at Ogden, Utah, with no money to hire attorneys. Warner asked his old pal Butch Cassidy for assistance.[25]

Cassidy did not have the money but knew where he could get it. During the afternoon of August 13, 1896, Butch Cassidy, Elzy Lay, and Bub Meeks robbed the bank at Montpelier, Idaho, escaping with a large amount of money—estimates ranged from seven thousand dollars to higher than thirty thousand dollars.[26]

Attorneys, including Butch's friend Douglas Preston, suddenly appeared to defend Matt Warner and Bill Wall. They said they had received funds from Wall's friends before the Montpelier robbery. They claimed that Butch Cassidy had not been involved in the Montpelier robbery and he did not provide the funds for Warner and Wall's defense. They were able to convince the jury that Warner and Wall had not committed first-degree murder. The jury's verdict was voluntary manslaughter and the judge set their sentence to five years in the Utah State Penitentiary.[27]

Butch and some of his Wild Bunch friends spent the winter of 1896–1897 in the desolate canyonland of southeastern Utah called Robbers' Roost. Their numbers included the Sundance Kid and his wife or girlfriend known as Etta Place.[28]

The Sundance Kid was the moniker for Harry Longabaugh, who was born in 1867 in Mont Clare, a small town across the Schuylkill River from Phoenixville, in southeastern Pennsylvania. In 1882, at the age of fifteen, Harry traveled to Illinois, where he joined his cousin George Longenbaugh and his family on their trek west to Durango, Colorado, where George homesteaded and then two years later moved to Cortez, Colorado.[29]

Harry was good with horses, learning to care for and train them. He worked as a horse wrangler for several ranches, including the LC Ranch outside of Cortez, Colorado. In 1886, Harry was hired by the owners of the N-N Ranch and worked on their cattle drive to Montana. Reaching the N-N Ranch outside of Miles City, the owners kept him on. Toward the end of 1886, the N-N Ranch manager let Harry go when there was little work. He drifted to Deadwood, Dakota Territory, where he worked at odd jobs.[30]

Deciding to return to Miles City, and to help himself get there, Harry stole a horse, saddle, bridal, chaps, spurs, and a pistol from ranch hands working for the VVV Ranch outside of Sundance in Crook County, Wyoming, on February 27, 1887. The Crook County Sheriff tracked down Harry and arrested him in April, but he soon escaped from the sheriff's custody. He was again apprehended in June, convicted, and sentenced to eighteen months' imprisonment. Since Harry was nineteen years old, he served his sentence in the Sundance jail instead of in the Wyoming Territorial Prison. On February 4, 1889, Governor Thomas Moonlight gave Harry a full pardon the day before his release. Harry was nicknamed the Sundance Kid from his stint in the Sundance jail.[31]

The Sundance Kid traveled to Dakota Territory and Colorado, eventually making his way back to Montana and then to Alberta, Canada, working as a wrangler on several ranches. On November 29, 1892, he participated in a train robbery near Malta, Montana. He and two accomplices got away with nineteen dollars, two small paychecks, and a couple of packages. His two partners in crime were arrested and served time in the Montana State Penitentiary. The Sundance Kid was apprehended but managed to escape and hide out at the Hole-in-the-Wall.[32]

Over the years, the Sundance Kid worked in Canada, returned to Montana to wrangle for the N-N Ranch, and later ran with a gang of rustlers near Culbertson in northeastern Montana. During the winter of 1896–1897, he was living at Robbers' Roost in a tent with Etta Place.[33]

Etta Place might have been the most successful outlaw of all. There is no accurate information on her background or what happened to her. There is much speculation, but no one knows her real name.[34]

On April 21, 1897, Butch Cassidy and Elzy Lay robbed the Pleasant Valley Coal Company payroll at Castle Gate, Utah, making off with seven thousand dollars in gold.[35]

The Sundance Kid and other outlaws hid out at the Hole-in-the-Wall after they botched their robbery of the Butte County Bank in Belle Fourche, South Dakota, on June 28, 1897. After several months, they rode to Montana, where a posse tracked them down, captured them, and sent them to South Dakota in late September. Before they could stand trial, they escaped from jail at the end of October.[36]

In July 1898, Sundance along with Harvey Logan and George Currie robbed $450 and jewelry from a Southern Pacific train near Humboldt, Nevada.[37]

Calling himself Jim Lowe, Butch rode into Alma, New Mexico, in the fall of 1898, where an Englishman, Captain William French, hired him as assistant foreman for his WS Ranch. Butch then hired his Wild Bunch friends, including Elzy Lay, Harvey Logan, and the Sundance Kid. Not knowing who was actually working for him, French was pleased the ranch ran smoothly and he never had problems with rustlers.[38]

In March 1899, Sundance, Harvey Logan, and George Currie robbed $550 from the Club Saloon safe in Elko, Nevada.[39]

Butch may have planned the next robbery, which promised to be a big one. On June 2, 1899, Wild Bunch members stopped a Union Pacific train between Wilcox and Medicine Bow, Wyoming. When the mail clerks and express messenger refused to open the railroad car's doors, the gang blew them open with dynamite and then blew the express car safes again with dynamite, which not only opened the doors but blew out and scattered the contents. The bandits gathered over thirty thousand dollars in cash, banknotes, jewelry, and diamonds. They split into two groups and made their escape. None of them were ever captured, even when the Pinkerton Detective Agency was brought in to recover the loot and apprehend the criminals.[40]

In October 1899, a Pinkerton agent visited Captain French at his WS Ranch and informed him that his assistant foreman was none other than Butch Cassidy. French did not fire Butch outright but passed him up when there was a promotion for a better position. Butch soon left on his own accord.[41]

In the spring of 1900, Butch attempted to go straight. He met with Utah governor Heber Wells twice, asking for amnesty, but Wells decided it was too risky and turned him down. Butch's attorney, Douglas Preston, brokered a deal with Union Pacific Railroad officials that if Butch promised not to rob any more Union Pacific trains, they would not prosecute him for past crimes. The deal fell through when the officials failed to show at a prearranged meeting location forty miles north of Rawlins, Wyoming, due to bad weather. Thinking they were setting him up, Butch rode away before the officials arrived. He left a note saying that they had double-crossed him, and the deal was off.[42]

On August 29, 1900, most likely Butch, the Sundance Kid, Harvey Logan, and another robber held up a Union Pacific Railroad train between Tipton and Table Rock, Wyoming. After making sure the passengers and crew were safe, Butch and his men used dynamite to blow up the baggage car and remove fifty-five thousand dollars in cash as well as jewelry. Three posses followed the robbers' trail for two weeks but to no avail.[43]

Butch and the Wild Bunch were not ready to rest on their laurels. They traveled to Winnemucca, Nevada, where the Sundance Kid, Harvey Logan, and Will Carver were the prime suspects in the robbery of the First National Bank of Winnemucca. On September 19, the Sundance Kid, Logan, and Carver entered the bank and within five minutes made their escape with thirty-three thousand dollars. Butch was seen in the area before and after the robbery, but it's not certain what his role was.[44]

Later that fall, five of the Wild Bunch—Butch, Sundance, Harvey Logan, Ben Kilpatrick, and Will Carver—met in Fort Worth, Texas, to celebrate and had their photograph taken together. The Wild Bunch members split up, with Butch and Sundance heading south to San Antonio, where they continued to enjoy themselves. At some point, Etta Place joined them in Texas. Sundance and Etta celebrated the New Year in New Orleans and then visited his family in Pennsylvania, where he introduced Etta as his wife.[45]

The couple visited Buffalo, New York, and then Niagara Falls before joining Butch in New York City. They decided to leave the United States.

It was becoming unsafe with law enforcement and the Pinkertons on their tail. Their destination—Argentina. Argentina was the new hot spot in the world. Its agriculture was rapidly developing, and many considered it a prosperous nation. The British author James Bryce proclaimed Argentina "the United States of the Southern Hemisphere." The Sundance Kid and Etta were calling themselves Harry and Etta Place. Place was Harry's mother's maiden name. After touring New York City for three weeks, Butch, now calling himself James Ryan, and Harry and Etta left on February 20, 1901, for Buenos Aires, Argentina.[46]

The Pinkertons later learned that upon reaching Buenos Aires in late March, Harry and Etta Place stayed at the Hotel Europa and Harry Place opened a bank account, depositing twelve thousand dollars. James Ryan and Harry and Etta Place eventually settled on ranchland in Patagonia in the Cholila Valley along the eastern slopes of the Andes Mountains. They built a four-room American-style cabin with windows imported from the United States. In 1902, Ryan petitioned the Argentine government for twenty-five thousand acres of government land that they were using. In the petition Ryan stated they were running thirteen hundred sheep, five hundred head of cattle, and three dozen horses on the land.[47]

The Places and Ryan were well liked and friendly to their neighbors. In 1902, Harry and Etta returned to the United States, where Etta may have been treated for health issues. They visited Coney Island and Harry's Pennsylvania relatives before returning to Argentina. The couple returned to the United States in 1904 and may have gone to the World's Fair in Saint Louis and visited friends in Fort Worth.[48]

The Pinkertons did not let up, discovering Butch, Sundance, and Etta were living in Argentina. They distributed flyers with the fugitives' photos, offering a ten-thousand-dollar reward for them—dead or alive.[49]

The Pinkertons believed that Butch Cassidy and the Sundance Kid were the two men who robbed a bank in Rio Gallegos in southern Argentina on February 14, 1905, making off with between $70,000 and $130,000. However, documents show that they were at their ranch seven hundred miles to the north in Cholila at the time of the robbery.[50]

Ryan and the Places learned that the Pinkertons knew their whereabouts, and in late 1904, believing they were no longer safe, they began liquidating their assets. On May 9, 1905, the trio left their ranch for good, traveling to Valparaiso, Chile.[51] After this, their movements become even more shadowy.

On December 19, 1905, three men and a woman robbed the bank in Villa Mercedes, Argentina, getting away with $130,000. The Pinkertons believed James Ryan (Butch Cassidy), Harry Longbaugh [sic], Miss E. A. Place, and Harvey Logan committed the robbery, and it was reported as such in the Argentine newspapers.[52]

Historians believe that in 1906, Butch and Sundance were working for the Concordia Tin Mines at Tres Cruces, Bolivia, while Etta disappeared from the record. Butch was using the alias Santiago Maxwell, and Sundance was using Enrique Brown. They were well liked by their employer and fellow workers. They befriended Percy Seibert, a North American mining engineer, working at the mine site. They eventually confided in Seibert who they really were, and the news soon leaked out to the mine managers and employees, but everyone was fine with who Butch and Sundance were. However, the two believed it was time to move on and left in 1908. During this time, they may have committed additional robberies, but nothing can be proven one way or another if it was them or other North American bandits.[53]

After leaving Concordia they may have worked for James "Santiago" Hutcheon's transportation company hauling passengers and freight. According to Percy Seibert, they may have committed a payroll robbery in Peru and a train robbery in Bolivia.[54]

On November 4, 1908, two North Americans held up an official of the Aramayo and Francke Mining Company and stole the payroll he was carrying on a remote trail south of Quechisla, Bolivia. They took fifteen thousand bolivianos, or approximately seven thousand dollars. Two days later, the bandits resisted arrest and were killed in a gun battle at the Indian village of San Vicente and buried in the local cemetery. Percy Seibert said the two men were Butch Cassidy and the Sundance Kid.[55]

End of story—or is it?

DEAD MEN TELL TALL TALES—KELLEN CUTSFORTH

Robert LeRoy Parker, otherwise known as the outlaw Butch Cassidy, was born April 13, 1866, in Beaver, Utah Territory, and died November 17, 1908, in San Vicente, Bolivia. Honestly, this is all that should have to be written about the man as far as his death is concerned, but conspiracy theories persist to this day about Butch having lived into old age.

On November 4, 1908, near Tupiza, Bolivia, the Aramayo and Francke Mining Company payroll was robbed by two heavily armed English-speaking men who are believed to have been Americans. Two days later, on November 6, these same desperadoes were killed in an intense gun-fight with Bolivian police. The bandits were buried with no names.[56]

For years, speculation has swirled around the identity of these crimi-nals. Those who think logically and examine all the facts believe these two robbers to be Robert LeRoy Parker and Harry Longabaugh—or, as they were commonly known, Butch Cassidy and the Sundance Kid. It is a well-known fact that in 1905 Butch and Sundance escaped from New York City to Argentina to avoid authorities who were looking to arrest them for their numerous crimes.[57]

These crimes included bank robbery, train robbery, running protec-tion rackets, and associating with violent criminals. In fact, many of these most violent criminals joined forces with Parker and Longabaugh to form the Wild Bunch gang. These criminals included the likes of Harvey Alex-ander "Kid Curry" Logan, who would eventually be wanted for murder and who would participate in several robberies and shootouts.[58]

The Wild Bunch committed these crimes all over the western United States. After failing to gain amnesty from Utah governor Heber Wells in 1899, Butch decided it was time to go into hiding. After a few more holdups, Butch and Sundance, accompanied by Longabaugh's companion Etta Place, departed from New York City to Buenos Aires, Argentina, on February 20, 1901. The trio settled in a log cabin near Cholila, Argentina, where Butch posed as Etta Place's brother. After finding their footing in the new country, the two bandits would purchase a fifteen-thousand-acre ranch in the area and tried to make an honest living for a period.[59]

Apparently running short on cash, however, it is suspected that Butch and Sundance held up the Banco de Tarapacá y Argentino in Río Gallegos on February 14, 1905, taking over 70,000 pesos. Shortly after this robbery, on May 1 of the same year the two bandits and their confidant Etta Place began selling off all their possessions so they could travel lightly. In truth, the desperadoes were tipped off by their friend local sheriff Eduardo Humphrey after he received a telegram from Argentine authorities instructing him to arrest Cassidy and Longabaugh. Hearing this news and coupled with the fear that the American Pinkerton Detective Agency had caught onto their whereabouts, the trio ran to San Carlos de Bariloche near Buenos Aires.[60]

From Bariloche, Cassidy, Sundance, and Place teamed up with a fourth unknown individual and robbed the Argentine National Bank in Villa Mercedes on December 19, 1905. Unfortunately for Butch and Sundance, they could not keep their noses clean even in a new country and began to "build their savings" accounts the only way they knew how, through theft. By the following year in 1906, Etta Place could no longer stomach life on the lam. So, in June of that year Sundance took her back to the United States and left her in San Francisco.[61]

The fact that both Butch and Sundance had returned to a life of crime to make a living gives a great deal of credence to them being the men who robbed the Aramayo and Francke Mining Company payroll in November 1908. The outlaws were running low on cash and needed the money. It is a fact that they had turned to a life of crime while living in South America and were on the run from both Argentine and American authorities. The mining payroll was an easy target with little to no protection and would have made for a great score.

Following this robbery, the legendary Butch and Sundance would go on to collect their final reward in San Vicente, Bolivia. There are several facts that support this. When Parker and Longabaugh robbed the Aramayo and Francke Mining Company payroll they attempted to hideout in a small boarding house in Bolivia.[62]

When authorities discovered where they were, they dispatched three soldiers, the local police chief, the local mayor, and a few other officials who intended to arrest the duo. Cassidy and the Kid had other plans, however. After realizing they were surrounded, the bandits engaged in a gunfight with the men, killing one of the soldiers as he approached the cabin.[63]

Following the death of the soldier, the shootout started. During what was reported to have lasted a few minutes, the mayor of San Vicente heard "three screams of desperation" followed by gunshots. When the soldiers eventually entered the boarding house the following morning, they found Parker and Longabaugh inside, dead from apparent murder suicide. Riddled with bullets in their arms and legs from the previous day's gun battle, Butch apparently shot Sundance out of mercy then turned the gun on himself.[64]

All the descriptions of the desperado duo matched those of Butch and Sundance. They were said to be Americans, both blonde, one thin (Sundance) the other more heavyset (Butch). The Pinkerton Detective Agency, which had been keeping tabs on the bandits since learning of their presence in South America, continued to keep files on the numerous sightings of the outlaws over the years after their death. But the Pinkertons made no attempt to follow up on these because most accounts had little to no verification.[65]

In August 1908, Butch and Sundance were known to be in Tupiza, Bolivia, which put them in the area to participate in the Aramayo payroll robbery. The mining payroll leader who was there during the holdup, Carlos Peró, gave some interesting descriptions of the bandits to the authorities.[66]

There were multiple descriptions of the desperadoes from people who were confronted by them. Because they had masks covering their faces, the witnesses described their clothes. There was some discrepancy between what the bandits were said to be wearing and what they had on when they were eventually killed. Some witnesses said they wore suits, one light-brown cashmere while the other was a dressed in a yellow cashmere suit.[67]

Peró's description did not match this at all. He stated that they wore red thin-wale corduroy suits. This has led many conspiracy theorists to believe the robbers were not the men shot in San Vicente. But clothes can easily be changed. It is not illogical to think that Butch and Sundance changed their outfits to better hide their identity when it was something obvious they could be identified by since their facial features were covered by masks.

Furthermore, when an inventory of the dead bandit's belongings was taken, authorities discovered 14,400 bolivianos on the men. The total of the Aramayo payroll was 15,000 bolivianos.[68] Butch and Sundance could have lost some of that money along the way to San Vicente, or they could have spent a portion as well. However, the fact that what was found on the bandits was so close to the payroll total gives further credence that the dead desperadoes were the ones who executed the hold-up.

There have been literally dozens of accounts of people who have said they witnessed Butch Cassidy walking around healthy and well after the 1908 gunfight in San Vicente. Some have been completely debunked as mistaken identity, while others have been harder to determine as truth. None of them, however, have proven beyond a shadow of a doubt to be the bandit Butch Cassidy.

What is also intriguing about these myriad tales is that most reference Butch surviving while Sundance does not. Somehow, he survives the shootout but the man right next to him dies. Many of the theories hold that Cassidy disguises himself or hides out while some other bandits are gunned down. In almost all the cases, Butch survives the shootout and lives on in hiding. Nearly all these stories have been completely debunked as quite laughable outright lies.[69]

In fact, the problem with most of the stories and theories regarding Butch and Sundance's survival, whether someone else killed them, they both got away, or just one lives on into old age is that most Americans had not heard about the shootout in Bolivia until the 1930s. The two desperadoes were gunned down in San Vicente in 1908, yet sightings and stories of Butch do not reach a fever pitch until over two decades later.[70]

After the truth came out, suddenly a bevy of "old timers" remembered that Butch had died in Vernal, Utah, in 1927, or in Oregon in 1930, or he was seen walking the same streets as Wyatt Earp had in Tombstone, Arizona. Some even recalled Butch shooting an off-duty marshal in Mount Pleasant, Utah, when he was seventy-seven . . . or eighty-one . . . or maybe he was ninety-four.[71] And so, the stories go, on and on into infinity.

One of the most interesting and more credible cases of a Butch Cassidy survival story is that of William T. Phillips. Phillips was a resident of Spokane, Washington, and spread a rumor to his closest friends that he was the bandit Butch Cassidy. Phillips's tale unfolds that during his lifetime, he made the trek to Wyoming numerous times to look for Butch's lost caches and to visit his old friends from his outlaw days. He supposedly "knew" facts that only the real Butch Cassidy could have known.[72]

Many people who knew Phillips claimed that he looked like Butch in his early photos. He was even able to convince several of Cassidy's real friends in Wyoming that he was Butch with the stories he regaled them with. Although Phillips convinced many that he was Butch, there were several old timers who did not believe his tall tales. One of these included Lula Parker Betenson, Butch's real sister.[73]

Lula, throughout her life, maintained that Phillips was not her brother and that he was perpetrating a fraud. Phillips bought into his lie of being Butch Cassidy so fully that he even drafted a novel titled *The Bandit Invincible* covering the life and crimes of Butch Cassidy. His story, however, eventually came to an end when historian Larry Pointer scrutinized his windy tales.[74]

Pointer, through meticulous research, discovered that Phillips's identity was that of William T. Wilcox, a former convicted felon. Pointer also discovered that Wilcox was a prisoner during the 1890s when the real Butch Cassidy was in jail and Wilcox most likely picked up some of his stories. It is also believed that Wilcox took the name William T. Phillips from his cousin to hide his identity as a criminal. Pointer's unearthing of Wilcox's mugshot from his prison days proved unequivocally that he was posing as not only Phillips but as Butch Cassidy too.[75]

Lula Parker Betenson, although unconvinced that Wilcox was her brother, also gave in to the idea that Butch had survived. In her book *Butch Cassidy, My Brother,* Lula divulged that Butch arrived at the Parker Ranch, where she was living, in 1925. He stayed with the family and regaled them with stories of being a bandit and his time in South America. He noted that he had not returned until then because he said he was ashamed of his past as a wanted criminal.[76]

This man posing as Butch apparently died in 1937 and was buried on the property, but Lula would never reveal where the body was buried.

She said this was because she did not want to see his body exhumed or treated as a tourist attraction.[77] In 2019 a local researcher by the name of Marylin Grace told other researchers that she believed the body was buried at "Tom's Cabin," which was a former sheepherder's cabin on the Parker property.[78]

When a dig took place on the grounds after this information was aired, a human toe bone and a spinal bone were discovered on the underside of the cabin. But when a DNA analysis was performed on the remains, it could not be determined who the bones belonged to.[79] In all likelihood, these bones belonged to another imposter posing as the long dead Robert LeRoy Parker. As is often the case with myth and folklore, people want the fantastical to be true, but in the case of Butch Cassidy the facts remain that he most likely died in Bolivia on that fateful day in 1908.

WHERE IN THE WORLD ARE BUTCH AND SUNDANCE?
—BILL MARKLEY

The world learned of the demise of Butch Cassidy and the Sundance Kid in Arthur Chapman's article "'Butch' Cassidy" published in *Elks Magazine's* April 1930 issue. Chapman contacted Percy A. Seibert, a Santiago, Chile, attorney, who said he had known Butch and Sundance when he had employed them while working as the manager for the Concordia tin mine in Bolivia. Seibert gave Chapman the details of the outlaws' last fight.[80]

Chapman's article related that in early 1909 [actually November 4, 1908], bandits held up Aramayo mine employees transporting the mine's payroll near Quechisla, in southern Bolivia. Along with taking the payroll, the bandits also took a mule. A few weeks later [actually it was two days later, on November 6], "two heavily armed Americanos, on jaded mules" arrived in the Indian village of San Vicente and rented a room at the only inn in town that was also the police station. The two men, who were Butch Cassidy and the Sundance Kid, piled their equipment including rifles in a room and then entered another room across the plaza where they ordered food and drink.[81]

The San Vicente constable recognized one of Butch and Sundance's mules as being the one taken during the robbery. The constable informed a company of cavalry that was located near town. The cavalry captain had his men quietly surround the police station. With pistol drawn, the captain entered the room where Butch and Sundance were eating. He demanded they surrender, but Butch shot from the hip, killing the captain. A sergeant, leading hand-picked men, was the next to die as they rushed Butch and Sundance's position.[82]

Cassidy and Longabaugh were firing rapidly, and with deadly effect. Those of the detachment who remained on their feet were firing in return. . . . Other soldiers began firing, from behind the shelter of the courtyard wall.

"Keep me covered, Butch," called Longabaugh. "I'll get our rifles."

Shooting as he went, Longabaugh lurched into the courtyard. . . .

The sergeant and most of his file of soldiers were stretched out, dead. A few wounded were trying to crawl to safety. . . .

Soldiers were firing through the open gate and from all other vantage points outside the wall. Longabaugh got halfway across the courtyard and fell, desperately wounded, but not before he had effectively emptied his six-shooter.

When Cassidy saw his partner fall, he rushed into the courtyard. Bullets rained about him as he ran to Longabaugh's side. Some of the shots found their mark, but Cassidy, though wounded, managed to pick up Longabaugh and stagger back to the house with his heavy burden.

Cassidy saw that Longabaugh was mortally wounded. Furthermore, it was going to be impossible to carry on the battle much longer unless the rifles and ammunition could be reached. Cassidy made several attempts to cross the courtyard. At each attempt he was wounded and driven back.

. . . Night came on, and men fired at the red flashes from weapons. There were spaces of increasing length between Cassidy's shots. He had only a few cartridges left. Longabaugh's cartridge belt was empty. . . .

The soldiers, about 9 or 10 o'clock in the evening, heard two shots fired in the bullet-riddled station. Then no more shots came. . . . The soldiers kept on firing all through the night and during the next morning.

About noon an officer and a detachment of soldiers rushed . . . into the station. They found Longabaugh and Cassidy dead. Cassidy had fired a bullet into Longabaugh's head and had used his last cartridge to kill himself.[83]

Were these two outlaws Butch Cassidy and the Sundance Kid? Let's look into the facts of the Aramayo mine payroll robbery, the San Vicente shootout, the last known whereabouts of Butch and Sundance, and their possible sightings after the shootout.

The Aramayo Mine Payroll Robbery

On November 4, 1908, Carlos Peró, an official of the Aramayo and Francke Mining Company, was south of Quechisla, Bolivia, bringing a payroll shipment of fifteen thousand bolivianos to the company mine. He was accompanied by his teenage son Mariano, and his servant Gil González. At 9:15 a.m., Peró was on foot following his son and servant, who were riding mules along the trail, when two well-armed "Yankees," whose faces were covered by bandannas, held them up.[84]

Leveling their rifles at the three men and "in a very threatening manner," the bandits ordered in English for González and Mariano to dismount from their mules. The bandits knew Peró spoke English and that he was carrying the Aramayo payroll and even which package the money was in. Expecting the haul to be eighty thousand bolivianos, the bandits were disappointed to learn the package contained only fifteen thousand. The bandits must have had an informant within Aramayo, but their contact had his information wrong. There was an eighty-thousand-boliviano payroll shipment, but that was scheduled to be sent the week after the robbery.[85]

In his report to Aramayo officials at their Tupiza headquarters, Peró recounted what happened after the bandits found the payroll package: "Then they demanded that I give them our servant's mule—the dark brown named 'Aramayo,' with the Quechisla brand—which is known by all our stable hands in Tupiza. We had to unsaddle the mule and hand it over along with a brand-new hemp rope. Keeping their eyes on us and their rifles ready, they departed with the mule."[86]

Peró then described the bandits: "The two Yankees wore new, dark red, thin-wale corduroy suits with narrow, soft-brimmed hats, the brims turned down in such a way that, with the bandannas tied behind their ears, only their eyes could be seen. One of the bandits, the one who came closest to and talked with me, is thin and of normal stature, and the other, who always maintained a certain distance, is heavyset and taller. Both of them carried new carbines, which appeared to be of the Mauser-type. . . . But they were completely new, which is to say, never used. The bandits also carried Colt revolvers, and I believe they also had very small Browning revolvers outside their cartridge belts, which were filled with rifle ammunition."[87]

Peró stated in the same report there may have been more bandits since "our servant noted various animals hidden in the ravine." Years later, Mariano told his son that there were six in the party who robbed them. He could see two of them were *gringos* but could not make out the others.[88]

Later that day, Aramayo's Tupiza headquarters sent a telegram to the company agent in Uyuni stating, "This morning Mr. Peró was robbed between Salo and Guadalupe by two tall individuals, one slender and the other heavyset, a gringo and a Chilean; armed with rifles. . . . The heavyset man's name is said to be Madariaga." However, headquarters sent the company agent a follow-up letter on November 5, calling the two men "Yankees." The same day, headquarters sent a letter to the Aramayo general administrator at Quechisla. When mentioning the bandits, it read, "From what information we have, one must be English and the other Chilean, perhaps the same two who asked Mr. Peró for work here in Tupiza."[89]

In his first report Peró writes, "Don Manuel [Aramayo] should not send any more cash shipments without an armed guard, because it is clear that the Yankees in Tupiza are there with the expectation of assaulting whatever shipment the company makes." In his second report Peró again stressed that there were lots of Yankees: "It is also possible, given the relative increase in unemployed North Americans in Tupiza and Uyuni, that there are enough of them to assault and seize our company's cash shipments from all sides." It is quite clear there were many Yankees in this area of Bolivia at this time.[90]

Peró wrote, "Upon arrival in Cotani, I encountered two North Americans who were carrying only some saddlebags and a woman's saddle, but they were armed with rifles and pistols. They had slept in Cotani last night and were going to sleep in Guadalupe today. They said that they had lost a revolver in Cotani, and because only a boy had been in their room, they were taking the boy, whose name was Faustino Duran, to Tupiza to report him to the police."[91]

On November 6, Peró wrote another letter to the Aramayo managers in Tupiza stating that the two North Americans he had encountered in Cotani had been captured in Salo. The Oruro newspaper *La Prensa* described the two men: "They were armed to the teeth: Each one had a fine rifle, two revolvers and a dagger. They also had a pack mule, leather cords for binding hands, chemicals sufficient to drug someone, and a total of five hundred bolivianos in cash." Four articles in Buenos Aires *La Prensa* stated that the two gringos claimed to be Ray A. Walters, a North American, and Frank Harry Murray, an Englishman. One unusual item they had in their possession was a woman's saddle.[92]

Did Peró and other Bolivians use the term "Yankee" to describe anyone who appeared to be a northern European Caucasian? When describing Walters and Murray, Peró wrote, "The other two Yankees—who look like Austrians, individuals much taller than the two bandits and much heavier." Walters and Murray had earlier asked Peró for work, but he had told them the company was not hiring at the time.[93]

There are no official reports stating that Butch Cassidy under any of his aliases or the Sundance Kid under any of his aliases were responsible for the Aramayo robbery. The only name associated with the crime was Madariaga. Madariaga is a Basque surname.

SAN VICENTE SHOOTOUT

On the evening of November 6, 1908, two men on mules rode into San Vicente, looking for a room for the night. San Vicente was a small village about thirty miles southwest of the Aramayo robbery site. Remigio Sanchez, who was a miner living there, later testified he saw the two "gringos" ride into the village from the east.[94]

The men found Cleto Bellot, the corregidor,[95] and asked where they might find lodging. He directed them to Bonifacio Casasola's house where Casasola agreed to rent them a room for the night. After unsaddling and feeding their mules, they piled their saddles and gear along with their rifles in the patio outside the entrance to their room. Bellot stayed and talked with them about where they were coming from and going. They gave Casasola money to go buy them beer and sardines.[96]

Bellot must have been suspicious of the two men. He went to where "the commission" was lodging. The members of the commission were an inspector and two soldiers in pursuit of the bandits. He told the inspector about the two "foreigners." The inspector and two soldiers loaded their rifles and then had Bellot accompany them to the foreigners' room.[97]

As the men entered the patio, the lead soldier, Victor Torres, was closest to the door of the room, when one of the foreigners shot him with a revolver. Torres shot back once. The other soldier shot twice, and the inspector shot once, as they all quickly retreated.[98]

Captain Concha arrived and asked Bellot to gather men to surround the house. As Bellot was finding men, he later testified, "I heard three screams of desperation. After the guards were posted, no more shots were heard, except that the inspector fired one shot at about midnight.

"At about six in the morning, we were able to enter the room and found the two foreigners dead, one in the doorway and the other behind the door on a bench."[99]

Remigio Sanchez added additional information in his testimony that the smaller gringo had appeared in the doorway and shot twice at Torres. The gun battle lasted a little more than half an hour, but before it was over, Victor Torres was dead from his gunshot wound.[100]

Sanchez testified, "We remained all night until at dawn, the captain ordered the owner of the house to go inside. The captain entered with a soldier, and then all of us entered and found the smaller gringo stretched out on the floor, dead, one bullet wound in the temple and another in the arm. The taller one was hugging a ceramic jug. He was dead, also, with a bullet wound in the forehead and several in the arm." Cantonal Agent Aristides Daza arrived on scene on November 7 at 6:00 a.m. and described the bodies and their wounds the same as Sanchez.[101]

In Sanchez's testimony, he described the clothing and appearance of the two dead men: "The tall gringo was dressed in a light-brown cashmere suit, a grey hat, red gaiters, a belt with about twenty-eight bullets, a gold watch, a dagger (so I was told), and a silk handkerchief. The smaller one wore a yellow suit, apparently cashmere, red gaiters, a grey hat. He had a silver watch, a blue silk handkerchief, a cartridge belt with about thirty bullets. The pair also had bullets in all their pockets. Both were unshaven blonds, with somewhat turned-up noses, the small one a bit ugly and the large one good looking."[102]

Anne Meadows wrote in her book *Digging Up Butch and Sundance*, "The words *blond* and *turned-up noses* cover a lot of territory in South America. They apply to anyone whose hair isn't black and whose nose doesn't turn down."[103]

The officials took an inventory of what was found on each man and what they had piled in the patio. The items found on the shorter man included a six-shot Colt revolver, holster and belt with thirty cartridges, sixteen pounds sterling and two half-pounds sterling, seven cards inscribed with the name Enrique B. Hutcheon, and seven inscribed cards with the name Edward Graydon. The items the taller man had on him included currency totaling 93.05 bolivianos, an English dictionary, a new modified Winchester carbine along with 121 Winchester cartridges. Among the baggage pile was a map of Bolivia, eighty-eight pounds sterling, 14,400 boliviano bills in various denominations, a pair of binoculars, one Argentine-model Mauser carbine and sheath, and 149 Winchester, Mauser, and modified Mauser cartridges, one English saddle, two saddle blankets, one pair of spurs, one bridle, one saddle skin, one cinch, one set of reins, one whip, and two mules which were said to belong to the Aramayo mining company.[104]

The Bolivians had recovered most of the stolen payroll. Sanchez testified, "In the afternoon, after Delfín Rivera identified them [the two dead men], we interred them."[105]

On November 20, 1908, an inquest was held to determine the facts concerning the three deaths in San Vicente on November 6. The cadavers of the two bandits were exhumed and Carlos Peró, Mariano Peró, and Gil González examined the bodies. They gave sworn testimony that the bodies were those of the two men who had robbed them. The official summary signed document stated, "They said that they recognized the cadavers on sight . . . that from their size and constitution they were certain to be the same persons who carried out the assault."[106]

Carlos Peró testified, "Today, having had to identify the exhumed cadavers here, despite having seen no more than the robbers' eyes and the corresponding parts of their faces at the time of the robbery, I recognize both of them, without any sort of doubt, as well as the hats they wore, with the exception of their clothing, which is different from what they wore at Huaca Huañusca [the robbery site]. The mule recovered by the Uyuni commission that captured the robbers is the same one that was taken from me at the scene of the robbery."[107]

A week after the inquest, Juan Félix Erazo from the town of Estarca was interviewed. Erazo stated, "About a month ago, Mr. Graydon introduced me to a tall, blond, mustachioed, plump foreigner, whose name I don't remember. At that time, we drank a few glasses of beer in Estarca in the home of Fortunato Valencia. They told me that they came from Esmoraca and brought another foreigner, shorter than the other, and three of them passed through Tomahuaico. . . . On the sixth of November, I was in Cucho when, at seven in the morning, two gringos arrived. One was the same one Graydon introduced to me in Estarca; the other I don't remember having met. When I saw them in Tiburcio Bolívar's house, I went there, and they were at the door with their two saddled mules, one solid black and the other dark brown. Both carried revolvers and rifles on their saddles, but instead of revolvers, there apparently were pistols conveniently placed in their belts and many bullets, which were also displayed in their belts. I asked them where they were going, and they responded that they were going to inspect or study the wagon trail to San Vicente. I advised them to take a guide, then excused myself and left them. They went at seven-thirty in the morning.

"[Bolívar] assured me that they had slept the previous night at the home of Narcisa, the widow of Burgos. Sunday night, the eighth of November, I learned that two gringos had been killed in San Vicente because they had stolen a cash shipment from Señor Peró. With the reports I have had from San Vicente, by the animals, weapons, and date upon which they left Cucho, I am convinced that they are the same."[108]

Through the years, the people of San Vicente have believed one of the two men was a North American and the other a Chilean. Dan Buck found in his research of Bolivian vital statistics the 1908 death of "*n. n.* Madariaga." The letters "*n. n.*" stand for *ningun nombre,* which mean "no name."[109] Was Madariaga the alleged Chilean who some reports and the people of San Vicente mentioned? Is that who Delfín Rivera identified?

What do we have up to this point? There is no mention of Butch Cassidy or Harry Longabaugh in any official report. The fight was not a big battle and did not go on for very long, ending when the shorter bandit shot and killed his companion and then committed suicide.

Who was Edward Graydon? Who was Enrique B. Hutcheon? Why did the shorter outlaw have seven of each of their cards?

Edward Graydon is most likely the "Mr. Graydon" who was the friend of the tall, blond, plump gringo that Erazo drank a few glasses of beer with in Estarca. All we currently know about Graydon is that he was not one of the two bandits Erazo met in Cucho on November 6.

There is a little more information on Enrique B. Hutcheon. His half-brother was James "Santiago" Hutcheon, who owned a successful Bolivian transportation company in the early 1900s. Percy Seibert would later claim that Butch Cassidy and the Harry Longabough worked for Santiago Hutcheon.[110]

So, the cards do not identify the two dead outlaws; no one else could or would identify them. Some thought for whatever reason one of their names was Madariaga. Officially they remain *ningun nombre,* or "no name."

The two bandits certainly did not run out of ammunition, and they were able to retrieve one of the rifles. They both received bullet wounds in their arms, but nowhere else, so why did the short one shoot the tall one and then commit suicide? No one knows.

Three days after the two bandits were killed in San Vicente, the Tupiza authorities released Ray A. Walters and Frank Harry Murray, who had been captured in Salo.[111] Who were Walters and Murray? Were they also involved in the Aramayo robbery? Walters and Murray had 500 bolivianos in cash on them when arrested. The San Vicente bandits had 14,493.05 bolivianos in their possession. The Aramayo payroll was 15,000.

At 9:00 p.m., on November 15, 1908, nine days after the San Vicente gunfight, American explorer Hiram Bingham, who would later rediscover the Inca city of Machu Picchu, and a friend arrived at a hotel in La Quiaca, Argentina, sixty miles south of Tupiza, Bolivia. Bingham wrote, "We received a call from two rough-looking Anglo-Saxons who told us hair-raising stories of the dangers of the Bolivian roads where highway robbers driven out of the United States by the force of law and order and hounded to death all over the world by Pinkerton detectives, had found a pleasant resting-place in which to pursue their chosen occupation without let or hindrance. We found out afterwards that one of our informants was one of this same gang of robbers. Either he decided that we were disposed to regard his 'pals' in a sufficiently lenient manner to make our presence in Bolivia immaterial to them, or else he came to the conclusion that we had nothing worth stealing, for we were allowed to proceed peaceably and without any annoyance wherever we journeyed in Bolivia. He put the case quite emphatically to us that it was necessary for them to make a living, that they were not allowed to do so peaceably in the States, that they desired only to be let alone and had no intention of troubling travelers except those that sought to get information against them. They relied entirely for their support on being able to overcome armed escorts accompanying loads of cash going to the mines to liquidate the monthly payroll. This they claimed was legitimate plunder taken in fair fight. The only individuals who had to suffer at their hands were those who took up the case against them. Having laid this down for our edification, he proceeded to tell us what a reckless lot they were and how famous had been their crimes, at the same time assuring us that they were all very decent fellows and quite pleasant companions."[112] Who were these outlaws? Unfortunately, Bingham did not record the names of the two men.

The next morning, Bingham and his friend traveled to Tupiza, Bolivia. They rode in a coach pulled by an eight-mule team and driven by the owner James "Santiago" Hutcheon. Hutcheon allegedly hired Butch and Sundance after they left Concordia, according to Percy Seibert.[113]

This was the same James Hutcheon who was the half-brother of Enrique Hutcheon whose cards were found on the body of the shorter outlaw in San Vicente.

Bingham wrote, "Don Santiago [Hutcheon], who in his capacity as coach-master and stage-driver, has had to carry hundreds of thousands of dollars in cash over the unprotected Bolivian highways, assured us that he had never been molested by any of these highwaymen because he never troubled them in any way either by carrying arms or spreading information of their doings. If the Bolivian bandits are half as bad as they were painted to us that night, Don Santiago must lead a charmed life for he and his stages certainly offer an easy mark for any enterprising outlaw."[114]

At Tupiza, Bingham heard the Aramayo payroll robbery and shootout in San Vicente stories, which were already becoming distorted: "After a fight, in which three or four of the soldiers were killed and as many more wounded, the thatch roof of the hut was set on fire and the bandits forced out into the open where they finally fell, each with half a dozen bullets in his body."[115]

Writing about the two dead outlaws, Bingham recorded, "a couple of bandits, one of whom had been hunted out of Arizona by Pinkerton detectives." Neither Butch nor Sundance had been hunted out of Arizona. Bingham continued, "The robbers and their friends, of whom there seemed to be a score or more, let it be carefully understood that they would take a definite revenge for any lives that might be lost in pursuit of the highwaymen."[116] It would be interesting to know the names of the robbers' friends, and it's also interesting that Hutcheon could transport hundreds of thousands of dollars of cash and not be robbed. Could he have been connected to local gringo robbers?

As a minor point, Bingham wrote about the bandits' mules: "Their mules were captured and sold to Don Santiago [Hutcheon] who let me have one of them for my journey. He turned out to be a wonderfully fine saddle mule."[117]

On July 31, 1909, Frank Aller, the US vice consul in Antofagasta, Chile, sent a letter to the US legation in La Paz, Bolivia, seeking help to determine if an American citizen, Frank Boyd, was alive or dead, and if dead, to send his death certificate so Boyd's estate could be settled. "Mr.

Wm. Gray of Oruro, Mr. Thomas Mason of Uyuni and many others" had informed Aller that Boyd, who was known as H. A. Brown in Bolivia, was killed along with a companion named Maxwell at San Vicente and both buried as unknowns. The Pinkertons believed that Longabaugh had used the alias "Frank Boyd" during his visit to Chile, in 1905. Many historians believe "Maxwell" was an alias for Butch Cassidy. Alexander Benson with the American legation in La Pas wrote in one of his letters to the Bolivian Minister of Foreign Affairs, "Legal proof of his [Brown's] death is wanted by a Judge of the Court of Chile, in order to settle his estate. Brown and Maxwell were the men who held up several of the Bolivian Railway Company's pay trains and also the stage coaches of several mines."[118]

After much back-and-forth correspondence between the two embassy staffs and letters to and from Bolivian government officials, the Bolivian government provided a death certificate stating that the names of the bandits killed at San Vicente were unknown.[119]

There was never any proof that Longabaugh and Cassidy were responsible for the robberies mentioned by Benson. The attempt to settle Frank Boyd's estate may have been a ploy to flush out Boyd if he tried to protect his assets. In any event, the Chilean efforts failed.

A. G. Francis's Story

British engineer A. G. Francis wrote a story called "The End of an Outlaw" published in the May 1913 issue of *Wide World Magazine*. Francis was in charge of transporting a river dredge for a gold mining operation upriver to the headwaters of the Rio San Juan de Oro in Bolivia. Hauling the large machinery through the rough terrain was a slow, arduous venture. Francis wrote, "One evening during the month of August, 1908, I was enjoying a solitary meal, when a loud outcry on the part of my dogs announced the arrival of visitors. Going to the door of my house I was in time to greet two riders, who, from their saddles and general appearance, I judged to be Americans. This opinion was confirmed when one of the new-comers, a burly, pleasant-looking man with a moustache, said cheerily—'How do? We have seen Teddy'—my friend—'in town, and he told us you wouldn't object to having us stop here a while to rest our animals.'"[120]

Francis invited them in, and they wound up staying with him for a few weeks. The two men introduced themselves as Frank Smith and George Low. Smith was the larger man and Low was "a rather slightly-built man of middle height, with a fair beard and moustache and eyes like gimlets." Francis said they were "pleasant and amusing companions."[121]

Francis doesn't state how, but he wrote that he later learned that Smith was Kid Curry, the alias of Harvey Logan, and Low was Butch Cassidy.[122]

Francis relates a violent confrontation Curry had with Francis's laborers and a later run-in that Curry had with Argentine officials who he believed tried to capture him. Later, Francis had his headquarters set up at Tomahuiaco. Cassidy borrowed Francis's big grey horse, and he and Curry rode to Tupiza where they stayed at the Hotel International and scouted targets to rob, finally selecting the Aramayo mine payroll shipment.[123]

At 1:00 a.m., on November 5, Curry and Cassidy returned to Tomahuiaco after robbing the Aramayo mine shipment. Cassidy, appearing ill, went to bed, while Curry stayed awake to tell Francis about the robbery. Later that morning, "At about ten a.m., the two bandits and the writer being seated on the veranda, we received our first tidings from Tupiza by the arrival of an acquaintance on a spent horse, who exclaimed as he dismounted—'You had better get out of this, boys; they are saddling up a hundred men to come after you.'"[124]

After eating breakfast, Curry and Cassidy prepared to leave, insisting that Francis come with them. They saddled their animals and rode out leading the Aramayo mule. The three of them spent the night in a room in the town of Estarca. Francis fell asleep and did not awake until sunup on November 6. At 8:00 a.m. they were on the road traveling north toward Uyuni, when Curry and Cassidy let Francis go.[125]

The next day, Francis learned of two gringos being killed in San Vicente. He rode there and learned from details told to him that it must have been Curry and Cassidy. He did not say that he saw the bodies. One interesting tidbit, Francis wrote, was that "both men were buried in San Vicente, in unconsecrated ground," so if Francis was correct, their bodies would not have been buried in the San Vicente cemetery.[126]

There are a few inconsistencies with Francis's story. He said that when he first saw Curry and Cassidy ride into his camp, he could tell they were Americans by their saddles and clothing. However, the Bolivian inventory of the items from the two dead bandits list one of the saddles as English, and the other was a saddle skin and a saddle blanket used by South Americans. Several times Francis refers to Curry's mount as being a horse. He never mentions what Cassidy's mount was. Francis said they led the stolen mule, making three animals, but the dead bandits only had two. Both deceased bandits' mounts were riding mules. Francis's timing of events and places differ from Juan Félix Erazo's recollection, which was recorded closer to the date of the gun battle. On November 6, 1908, Erazo said he was in Cucho when he saw the two robbers at 7:00 a.m. and learned that they had stayed the night in the home of Narcisa, the widow of Burgos, but he made no mention of Francis staying there.

According to Francis, the two bandits and he stayed in Estarca ten miles to the south of Cucho and began their journey toward Uyuni. At 8:00 a.m., they left Francis behind and continued north toward Cucho. So Erazo said the robbers were in Cucho at 7:00 a.m. when Francis indicated they would have to still be in Estarca, ten miles to the south. One or the other is wrong.

Francis wrote that the smaller man who he said was Cassidy was "a rather slightly built man of middle height." When Cassidy entered the Wyoming Territorial Prison, his height was recorded at five feet nine inches and from his photographs he does not appear of slight build.[127]

The larger man told Francis that he was Kid Curry. However, a posse killed a train robber named Tap Duncan on June 8, 1904, at Glenwood Springs, Colorado. Detectives later had Duncan's body exhumed and they claimed it belonged to Kid Curry. Others believed that was not the case, and there were reports that Curry had escaped to South America and teamed up with Butch Cassidy and the Sundance Kid. In the September 1910 issue of *Wide World Magazine*, John H. McIntosh wrote an article entitled "The Evolution of a Bandit" stating that the US State Department had sent a team of detectives to Argentina to help rid the country of Kid Curry and his gang of outlaws.[128]

Were Frank Smith and George Low imposters pretending to be famous outlaws? Did Francis make up his story based on information about the robbery he had heard?

After reading Francis's account in *Wide World Magazine*, William Pinkerton wrote to a colleague stating, "I believe the whole story to be fake."[129]

Arthur Chapman's Butch Cassidy and the Sundance Kid Story with Percy Seibert's Contribution

In Arthur Chapman's article "'Butch' Cassidy" in *Elks Magazine's* April 1930 issue, it can be hard to determine when Percy Seibert is relating what he believes, what Chapman already knows from previous writings, and what Seibert has said that Chapman has embellished. Even stories that Seibert may have believed could have been concocted by the two men he said claimed to be Cassidy and Longabaugh. For instance, Seibert told Chapman that Butch had robbed his first train when he was fifteen years old. There is no record of that.[130]

In the article, the statement is made, "In Bolivia, Cassidy was known as James Maxwell, Santiago Maxwell, and Lowe."[131] This statement was most likely made by Seibert to Chapman. It was later discovered that Seibert had a letter in a scrapbook written by J. P. Maxwell dated November 12, 1907, from Santa Cruz, Bolivia, addressed "To the Boys at Concordia." In Chapman's article, he does not give the alias of Harry Longabaugh. Anne Meadows in her book *Digging up Butch and Sundance* writes that Seibert told authors James D. Horan, Charles Kelly, and Arthur Chapman that Sundance's alias was Enrique Brown and Butch's was Santiago Maxwell.[132]

Seibert said that Sundance got drunk one night in Uyuni, Bolivia, and "dropped some boastful remarks to another American about the holdups that he and Cassidy had staged in Argentina." Butch and Sundance decided it was time to move on, so Butch squared their accounts at Concordia's company store, and they left.[133]

Chapman wrote, "A few weeks [it should be a few days] after this holdup [the Aramayo payroll holdup] two heavily armed Americanos, on jaded mules, rode into the patio of the police station at the Indian village of

San Vicente, Bolivia, and demanded something to eat. . . . One of the men was 'Butch' Cassidy, and the other was Harry Longabaugh. After the Aramayo mines remittance holdup, the bandits had proceeded to Tupiza, where they took employment with a transportation outfit. [This would have been a very short job.] Learning that they had been identified as the perpetrators of the Aramayo holdup, they hurriedly departed for Uyuni, Bolivia."[134]

Seibert does not explain how he knew that these two men were Butch and Sundance. When comparing what Chapman wrote of the account and the accounts of on-scene witnesses, Chapman and Seibert embellished the whole story. Seibert was not at San Vicente. He did not see the bandits' bodies. Whatever he told Chapman was hearsay or his own theories.

These same two bandits claimed to A. G. Francis that they were Kid Curry and Butch Cassidy. They did not look like or act like Butch Cassidy or the Sundance Kid.

What about Butch and Sundance

Twentieth-century residents of San Vicente believed they knew where the two gringo bandits were buried in the local cemetery. In 1991, Anne Meadows and Dan Buck participated with forensic scientists in a US Public Broadcasting Service NOVA project to exhume the remains of the bandits and hopefully identify them. The remains of a Caucasian male were found. DNA testing revealed that the bones were not those of Butch or Sundance; maybe they belonged to a German named Gustav Zimmer[135]—or maybe someone else, like one of the actual bandits.

Personally, one item kept bothering me as I reviewed the information on Butch and Sundance's time in Bolivia. It was the letter that J. P. "Santiago" Maxwell wrote in Santa Cruz, Bolivia, on November 12, 1907, and sent to "the Boys at Concordia."[136]

All that I have read about Butch Cassidy shows he was respectful to women, but Maxwell's letter commented on the large number of women in town and how he believed he was appealing to them. He wrote, "One never gets too old if he has blue eyes and a red face and looks capable of making a blue eyed Baby Boy." He bragged about having an affair with a married woman, and if he had to give up the affair "there is plenty more."

Butch Cassidy loved and understood animals and as a boy had a variety of pets. I have not read of him mistreating an animal. Describing the terrain, Maxwell wrote in his letter, "not a level spot on it to whip a dog" and then later he wrote about a mule he and his companion Ingersoll had trouble with: "Ingersoll hobbled her and tied her to a tree and wore a nice green pole out on her, but I didn't think he had done a good job so I worked a little while with rocks. Between us, we broke her jaw and we have been feeding her on mush ever since."

I do not believe J. P. Maxwell, the writer of the letter to "the Boys at Concordia," was Butch Cassidy.

The two men killed at San Vicente were not following Butch Cassidy and the Sundance Kid's usual procedures to plan for and be secretive before committing a robbery. According to Francis, after Cassidy and Logan saw Peró leave Tupiza with the mine payroll, they "returned to the hotel, saddled their animals, and entering the bar for a last drink exchanged remarks with several men whom they knew. 'Where are you off to, boys?' said one. 'We're going to get a nice little packet,' replied Parker [Cassidy], smiling. 'Such a nice little packet.'"[137]

Butch and Sundance always had relays of mounts ready for them to speed away from the crime scene as quickly as possible. These two men did not do that; in fact, it appeared they dawdled in the area until it was too late.[138]

Their actions when confronted in San Vicente seem out of character for Butch and Sundance. Why did they start shooting before they knew what the police and soldiers wanted? Butch was not known to have killed anyone and tried to prevent violence if he could. In addition, why would the shorter man kill the larger man and then commit suicide since they still had plenty of ammunition?

After reviewing the available information, there are three options:

- The two men were Butch and Kid Curry.
- The two men were Butch and Sundance.
- The two men were not Butch and Sundance.

William Pinkerton, the head of the top detective agency in the world, said about Francis's article on the death of Cassidy and Curry, "I believe the whole story to be fake."[139]

When I began this project, I did not know much about the deaths of Butch and Sundance in Bolivia. My knowledge of the event was pretty much based on the movie *Butch Cassidy and the Sundance Kid*, which I thoroughly enjoyed when I first saw it in 1969. After reviewing the evidence, I believe Butch Cassidy and the Sundance Kid were not killed at San Vicente and continued to live on after the incident.

Butch Cassidy died many times. He "died" on Friday, May 13, 1898, when a posse out of Price, Utah, caught up with the rustler Joe Walker and three other men near Robbers' Roost. Two of the men gave up but the other two shot back and the posse killed both men. The posse found that they had killed Walker and, examining the second man, declared he was Butch Cassidy even though the two survivors said the man killed was a cowboy named Johnny Herring. When the bodies were brought back to town, a large crowd gathered to view the outlaws. They were buried that Sunday, but on Monday, the body of "Butch" was exhumed to be examined by law enforcement officers who knew Butch. They declared that the body did not belong to Butch. It really was the cowboy Johnny Herring. The Saturday before the burial, the bodies had been on display. The story is told that Butch hid in a wagon and had a friend drive him through town past the hall where his body was being viewed so he could joke that he attended his own funeral. Butch's sister Lula Parker Betenson wrote, "Looking through peepholes . . . Butch watched the 'mourners' and was surprised to see a number of women wiping their eyes. He was touched by such a display of emotion at his passing." He later told his family, "No, it sure wasn't me. He was better looking."[140]

During the course of their research on Butch and Sundance, Anne Meadows and Dan Buck found numerous references to their demise. A posse shot and killed Butch near Vernal, Utah, in the late 1890s. He was killed in a "tropical saloon brawl" in the early 1900s. In 1904, Butch and Sundance were surrounded and killed by soldiers on the border between Argentina and Chile. They were attacked and killed in a cabin on the eastern slopes of the Andes Mountains, killed by bounty hunters in Brazil, and Sundance was killed in Venezuela, all during 1906. Butch was shot and killed at Green River, Wyoming, the winter of 1905–1906, and finally in the fall of 1908, he was knifed in the back in a Paris slum.[141]

William Allan Pinkerton managed the western division of Pinkerton's National Detective Agency. In November 1907, he gave an address at the annual convention of the International Association Chiefs of Police in Jamestown, Virginia. In his address Pinkerton talked about the Wild Bunch members.[142]

He talked about Harvey Logan, alias Kid Curry, stating, "On November 29, 1902, while awaiting transfer to that institution [the United States Penitentiary in Columbus, Ohio], he made his escape by 'holding-up' the guards in the Knoxville jail; fleeing to the mountains on horseback. He has not been recaptured."[143] Based on this comment, Pinkerton did not believe that Tap Duncan, who had died on June 8, 1904, at Glenwood Springs, Colorado, was Harvey Logan.

Later in Pinkerton's speech, he discussed what his agency believed about the whereabouts of Butch, Sundance, and Etta: "'Butch' Cassidy and Harry Longbaugh [sic] and Etta Place, a clever horsewoman and rifle shot, fled to Argentine Republic, South America, where they, it is said, have been joined by Logan. Being expert ranchmen, they engaged in cattle raising on a ranch they had acquired, located on a piece of high table land from which they commanded a view of 25 miles in various directions, making their capture practically impossible. During the past two years, they committed several 'hold-up' bank robberies in Argentina in which Etta Place, the alleged wife of Harry Longbaugh [sic], it is said, operated with the band in male attire. We advised the Argentine authorities of their presence and location, but they became suspicious of preparations for their arrest, fled from Argentine Republic and were last heard from on the Southwest Coast of Chile, living in the wild open country."[144]

If Pinkerton's Detective Agency's information was correct, placing Butch Cassidy and Harry Longabaugh in Southwest Chile in 1907, then the men who Percy Seibert claimed were Butch and Harry working for the Concordia tin mine in Bolivia were frauds since they were working at the mine at that time. And if they were frauds, then Butch Cassidy and the Sundance Kid did not die at San Vicente.

Back on June 28, 1905, Harry Longabaugh was in Valparaíso, Chile, when he sent a letter to his Argentine neighbor Dan Gibbons, writing, "We are writing to you to let you know that our business went well, and we received our money. We arrived here today, and the day after tomorrow my wife and I leave for San Francisco." Continuing, he wrote, "I don't want to see Cholila ever again, but I will think of you and of all of our friends often, and we want to assure you of our good wishes."[145]

It's believed that Harry and Etta returned from San Francisco to South America to participate with Butch Cassidy and maybe Harvey Logan in the December 19, 1905, Villa Mercedes bank robbery in Argentina.[146]

A January 1906 Pinkerton memorandum stated that the Chilean government had some problems with Longabaugh, and with the aid of Frank Aller, the US vice consul in Antofagasta, Chile, and the payment of 1,500 pesos, the matter was taken care of. There were also reports that Longabaugh returned to Cholila in 1906 to sell some remaining livestock.[147]

The Pinkertons expanded their search worldwide for Cassidy and Longabaugh, believing that Butch, Sundance, and Etta went to Buenos Aires and sailed to Europe where they were spotted in Paris buying clothing and jewelry, visiting the opera and museums, and dining in fine restaurants. They traveled to Monte Carlo and resided in a villa on the Riviera. Learning that Pinkerton detectives had discovered their whereabouts, they disappeared before the Pinkertons raided their villa.[148]

The *San Antonio Light* reported that three people matching the descriptions of Butch, Sundance, and Etta were spotted at Cape Horn in early 1907. Local law enforcement did not follow through, and the threesome disappeared.[149]

In the September 1910 issue of *Wide World Magazine*, John H. McIntosh wrote about Kid Curry's Argentinian gang: "The American members of his band are George Leroy Parker, alias 'Butch' Cassidy, and Harry Longbaugh [sic], alias 'The Sun-Dance Kid.'" Notice that McIntosh, who was a detective, uses the present tense "are" when referring to Butch Cassidy and the Sundance Kid, acknowledging that they are alive, almost two years after their supposed death.[150]

Where did they go? Their trail grows cold at this point.

There were plenty of Butch Cassidy sightings in the United States, years after the San Vicente shootout. Butch Cassidy relative Bill Betenson, in his book *Butch Cassidy: My Uncle,* has a long list of people and the circumstances under which they said they met Butch. The Butch Cassidy imposter William T. Wilcox, also known as William T. Phillips, may have been the cause of some of these sightings.[151]

Lula Parker Betenson, Butch's sister, wrote in her book *Butch Cassidy, My Brother* that Butch returned to the Parker family home in the fall of 1925. Butch stayed at his father Maxi's place for about a week, and Lula sat along with other siblings and listened to his tales and heard his regrets for taking the outlaw trail. Lula Parker Betenson said she knew her brother and she was adamant that William T. Phillips was not Butch Cassidy.[152]

As to the sightings of Butch Cassidy, plenty of people claimed they saw him after San Vicente, but there are no legal documents or newspaper reports to support them. It boils down to whether you believe these people or not. As for the two bandits buried at San Vicente, they are still *ningun nombre.* So, what happened to Butch, Sundance, and Etta? I do not know, but it's nice to speculate that they lived in comfort to a ripe old age anywhere in the world they wanted.

ACKNOWLEDGMENTS

BILL AND KELLEN'S ACKNOWLEDGMENTS

We want to thank everyone who has lent us a hand in the completion of this book. Special thanks to Erin Turner, Sarah Parke, Kristen Mellitt, Sally Jaskold, and all the other folks at TwoDot and Rowman & Littlefield for believing in us and giving us the opportunity to write this sequel. Thanks to Nancy Shoup for your great review of the manuscript. Barry Williams, thanks for your wordsmithing expertise. Thanks to both of you for going over the entire book searching for inconsistencies, weird sentence constructions, misspellings, and odd things that just don't make sense.

Specifically, we want to thank Bill Groneman for his assistance and review of the many deaths of Davy Crockett. Will Bagley and Terry Del Bene, thank you for your help with the Donner Party. Thank you, Dennis Hagen, for your commentary on Crook and Custer. Thanks to George Gilland, aka *Tatanka Owichakuya*, Brings Back Buffalo, for your review and support on Sitting Bull's two graves.

We would like to thank the various institutions, collections, and individuals that provided research materials that made this publication possible. Thank you to the Western History Department of the Denver Public Library for use of their images. We want to especially thank Chad Coppess for the use of his photographs and to the South Dakota Historical Society Press for permission to use the Wild Bill Hickok assassination image.

Thanks to the Western Writers of America and its members providing constant support and encouragement throughout our writing careers. We want to acknowledge and thank all those who have written books, magazine and newspaper articles, letters, journals, and memoirs, and all those who have preserved and maintained those documents to keep the memory of the Old West alive.

BILL'S ACKNOWLEDGMENTS

Thank you to my son Chris for the review of the Donner Party and Lost Dutchman chapters. Thanks to Doctor Tom Huber for his medical evaluation of the Donner Party bodies. Jim Swanson, thank you for providing your insight into the stories of the Lost Dutchman. Thanks Brennan Jordan for your evaluation of the possible Lost Dutchman ore sample. Stuart Rosebrook, thanks for putting me on the trail of good Butch Cassidy books. Chris Enss, thank you for your help on Butch Cassidy, the Sundance Kid, and Etta Place. Mike Pellerzi, as always thanks for your cowboy point of view and moral support. A big thank you to my wife, Liz, for putting up with my long hours in the basement plunking away on the computer keyboard, helping with the occasional spelling of a word, and traveling with me to obscure places on my research trips. Thanks to my entire family for their continued support. Most of all, thanks to the Lord for giving me this opportunity and for the ability to think and write.

KELLEN'S ACKNOWLEDGMENTS

I would like to first thank my beautiful and wonderful wife, Meghan. I thank my amazing daughters, Cora and Vivian, who inspire me everyday and are the reason I write. Thank you to my parents, Allen and Patricia Cutsforth, for the continuous love and support you have shown me through the years. I want to thank Dennis Hagen, a brilliant historian and great friend, for reviewing this book and making much needed corrections. And thanks to all of those who have supported me through my career.

ENDNOTES

CHAPTER 1: THE MANY DEATHS OF DAVY CROCKETT

1. Stephen L. Hardin, "Battle of the Alamo," Texas State Historical Association, Handbook of Texas, online, accessed August 10, 2020, https://tshaonline.org/handbook/online/articles/qea02.

2. J. R. Edmondson, *The Alamo Story: From Early History to Current Conflicts* (Plano, TX: Republic of Texas Press, 2000), 237.

3. Timothy J. Todish and Terry Todish, *Alamo Sourcebook 1836: A Comprehensive Guide to the Alamo and the Texas Revolution* (Austin, TX: Eakin Press, 1998), 31.

4. Ibid.

5. Ibid., 32.

6. Walter Lord, *A Time to Stand* (Lincoln, NE: University of Nebraska Press, 1961), 67.

7. Ibid.

8. Albert A. Nofi, *The Alamo and the Texas War of Independence, September 30, 1835 to April 21, 1836: Heroes, Myths, and History* (Conshohocken, PA: Combined Books, 1992), 76.

9. Edmondson, *The Alamo Story*, 301.

10. Dan Kilgore, *How Did Davy Die? And Why Do We Care So Much?* (comm. ed., Elma Dill Russell Spencer Series in the West and Southwest) (College Station, TX: Texas A&M University Press, 2010).

11. Todish and Todish, *Alamo Sourcebook*, 43–44.

12. Robert Scott, *After the Alamo* (Plano, TX: Republic of Texas Press, 2000), 100–101.

13. Thomas Ricks Lindley, *Alamo Traces: New Evidence and New Conclusions* (Lanham, MD: Republic of Texas Press, 2000), 142.

14. Todish and Todish, *Alamo Sourcebook*, 50.

15. Edmonson, *The Alamo Story*, 362.

16. Todish and Todish, *Alamo Sourcebook*, 52.

17. Edmonson, *The Alamo Story*, 367.

18. Bill Groneman, *Death of a Legend: The Myth and Mystery Surrounding the Death of Davy Crockett* (Dallas, TX: Republic of Texas Press, 1999), 29.

19. "The War in Texas," *Vermont Chronicle*, May 12, 1836. Newspapers.com, accessed September 27, 2020, https://www.newspapers.com/image/489182233/?terms=Davy%2BCrockett%2C&match=2.

20. Ron J. Jackson Jr., "POW Crockett?" *Wild West Magazine*, February 2020, 48; Groneman, *Death of a Legend*, 31–33.

21. Alan C. Huffines, *Blood of Noble Men: The Alamo Siege and Battle* (Fort Worth, TX: Eakin Press, 1999), 4, 158–159. 181. James Donovan, *The Blood of Heroes: The 13-Day Struggle for the Alamo—And the Sacrifice that Forged a Nation* (New York, NY: Little, Brown and Company, 2012), 291, 292, 294.

22. Donovan, *The Blood of Heroes*, 294; Huffines, *Blood of Noble Men*, 185; Groneman, *Death of a Legend*, 88.

23. Huffines, *Blood of Noble Men*, 4, 173, 175, 182.

24. Groneman, *Death of a Legend*, 78; Huffines, *Blood of Noble Men*, 4.

25. Lon Tinkle, *13 Days to Glory: The Siege of the Alamo* (College Station, TX: Texas A&M University Press, 1958), 225; Huffines, *Blood of Noble Men*, 4; Groneman, *Death of a Legend*, 12.

26. Groneman, *Death of a Legend*, 79, 80.

27. Ibid., 78–79, 82–84.

28. Ibid., 79, 84–85.

29. Ibid., 86, 265.

30. Ibid., 41.

31. Bill Groneman, "Follow the Money," *The Alamo Journal*, 172, August 2014, 3–9; Groneman, *Death of a Legend*, 29, 41.

32. Groneman, *Death of a Legend*, 46.

33. Groneman, "Follow the Money," 3–9.

34. Seymour V. Connor, "New Washington, TX," *Texas State Historical Association Handbook of Texas*, accessed October 3, 2020, https://www.tshaonline.org/handbook/entries/new-washington-tx; Groneman, "Follow the Money," 3–9.

35. Ray Allen Billington, *Westward Expansion: A History of the American Frontier* (New York, NY: The MacMillan Company, 1949), 498; David Nevin, *The Texans* (Alexandria, VA: Time-Life Books, 1975), 141.

36. Groneman, "Follow the Money," 3–9

37. Groneman, "Follow the Money," 3–9; Groneman, *Death of a Legend*, 52, 54.

38. Groneman, *Death of a Legend*, 53.

39. Ibid., 55–56.

40. Donovan, *The Blood of Heroes*, 333, 447; Groneman, "Follow the Money," 3–9; Groneman, *Death of a Legend*, 54.

41. Groneman, *Death of a Legend*, 42, 61.

42. Ibid., 62.

43. Ibid., 62–63.

44. Ibid., 63–65.

45. Ibid., 65.

46. Ibid., 65–66, 67.

47. Ibid., 67, 68.

48. Ibid., 42, 67, 68, 69, 241n32.

49. Ibid., 42, 70, 71.

50. Ibid., 70.

51. Ibid., 70, 71.

52. Ibid., 71.

53. Ibid., 73.

54. Ibid., 73–74.

55. Ibid., 75.

56. Groneman, *Death of a Legend*, 124, 128, 136.

57. Ibid., 129–130, 136, 138.

58. Donovan, *The Blood of Heroes*, n448, n449.

59. Ibid., n449.

60. Groneman, *Death of a Legend*, 157.

61. Jackson Burk, "The Secret of the Alamo," *Man's Conquest Magazine*, April 1960, 18, 20, 92–93, 96; Bill Groneman, *Eyewitness to the Alamo* (Lanham, MD: Republic of Texas Press, 2001), 216–217.

62. Donovan, *The Blood of Heroes*, n447–n448.

63. David Crockett, *A Narrative of the Life of David Crockett of the State of Tennessee* (Coppell, TX: CreateSpace, 2016), title page.

64. Michael Wallis, *David Crockett: The Lion of the West* (New York: W.W. Norton & Company, 2011), 123–130.

65. Ibid., 159–160.

66. Ibid., 275.

67. Bob Palmquist, "A Home or Perish," *Wild West*, Vol. 29, No. 5, February 2017, 41–43.

68. Ibid., 43.

69. Donovan, *The Blood of Heroes*, 277–289.

70. Ibid., 282–283.

71. Ibid., 291.

72. Ibid., 292.

73. William Groneman III, "Davy's Death at the Alamo Is Now a Case Closed—Or Not," *Wild West*, February 2015, accessed August 28, 2020, https://www.historynet.com/davys-death-at-the-alamo-is-now-a-case-closed-or-not.htm.

74. Hardin, *Battle of the Alamo*, 146.

75. Groneman, *Davy's Death at the Alamo Is Now a Case Closed—Or Not*.

76. Paul Andrew Hutton, "Out on a Limb," *Wild West*, Volume 30, No. 5, February 2018, page 43.

77. Ibid., 43–44.

78. Ibid.

79. Ibid.

80. Ibid., 43.

81. Hardin, "Battle of the Alamo," 146.

CHAPTER 2: WHERE AND WHEN DID SACAGAWEA DIE?

1. James P. Rhonda, *Lewis and Clark among the Indians* (Lincoln, NE: University of Nebraska Press, 2002), 256–257; W. Dale Nelson, *Interpreters with Lewis and Clark: The Story of Sacagawea and Toussaint Charbonneau* (Denton, TX: University of North Texas Press, 2003), 11.

2. Bill Markley, *Up the Missouri River with Lewis and Clark: From Camp Dubois to the Bad River* (New York, NY: iUniverse, 2005), xxii.

3. Jon Kukla, *A Wilderness So Immense: The Louisiana Purchase and the Destiny of America* (New York, NY: Alfred A. Knopf, 2003), 218–225.

4. James Crutchfield, Candy Moulton, and Terry Del Bene, eds., *The Settlement of America: Encyclopedia of Western Expansion from Jamestown to the Closing of the Frontier*, Vol. 1 (Armonk, NY: M. E. Sharp, 2011), 308–309.

5. Markley, *Up the Missouri*, 1–2.

6. Ibid.

7. Gary E. Moulton, ed., *The Definitive Journals of Lewis and Clark: Up the Missouri River to Fort Mandan*, Vol. 3 (Lincoln, NE: University of Nebraska Press, 1987), 2; Dayton Duncan, *Out West: An American Journey* (New York, NY: Viking Penguin, 1987), 179; Crutchfield, Moulton, and Del Bene, *The Settlement of America*, Vol. 2, 314–315; Nelson, *Interpreters*, 13, 16.

8. Moulton, *The Definitive Journals*, Vol. 3, 228; Nelson, *Interpreters*, 5–7.

9. Moulton, *The Definitive Journals*, Vol. 3, 228n1; Nelson, *Interpreters*, 8.

10. Crutchfield, Moulton, and Del Bene, *The Settlement of America*, Vol. 2, 433.

11. Nicholas Biddle, *The Journals of the Expedition Under the Command of Captains Lewis and Clark*, Vol. 2 (Norwalk, CT: The Heritage Press Edition, 1993), 233; Stephen E. Ambrose, *Undaunted Courage: Meriwether Lewis, Thomas Jefferson, and the Opening of the American West* (New York, NY: Simon & Schuster, 1996), 187. Dayton Duncan, *Out West*, 164.

12. Rhonda, *Lewis and Clark*, 257; Nelson, *Interpreters*, 30.

13. Moulton, *The Definitive Journals*, Vol. 3, 239; Nelson, *Interpreters*, 9, 15.

14. Ambrose, *Undaunted Courage*, 187; Rhonda, *Lewis and Clark*, 116–117.

15. Moulton, *The Definitive* Journals, Vol. 3, 291; Nelson, *Interpreters*, 22.

16. Moulton, *The Definitive Journals*, 327; Nelson, *Interpreters*, 24.

17. George Drouillard's father was a French Canadian and his mother was a Shawnee. He was fluent in French, English, and several Indian languages as well as proficient in sign language. Ambrose, *Undaunted Courage*, 118–119.

18. Ambrose, *Undaunted Courage*, 211.

19. Bernard DeVoto, *The Journals of Lewis and Clark* (Boston, MA: Houghton Mifflin Company, 1953), 93; Nelson, *Interpreters*, 27.

20. Ibid., 94–95.

21. Nelson, *Interpreters*, 27.

22. DeVoto, *The Journals of Lewis and Clark*, 109–111; Nelson, *Interpreters*, 29.

23. Nelson, *Interpreters*, 29–34; Ambrose, *Undaunted Courage*, 241–243.

24. Ambrose, *Undaunted Courage*, 259–260; Nelson, *Interpreters*, 35.

25. Nelson, *Interpreters*, 30, 37, 38; DeVoto, *The Journals of Lewis and Clark*, 189–191; Ambrose, *Undaunted Courage*, 274.

26. Ibid., 277

27. Biddle, *The Journals of the Expedition*, 233.

28. Ibid.

29. Ibid.

30. Ibid.

31. Ibid, 233–234.

32. Nelson, *Interpreters*, 39–40.

33. DeVoto, *The Journals of Lewis and Clark*, 207.

34. Nelson, *Interpreters*, 41–43; Ambrose, *Undaunted Courage*, 283.

35. Ambrose, *Undaunted Courage*, 289.

36. Nelson, *Interpreters*, 44; Ambrose, *Undaunted Courage*, 289, 290.

37. Gary E. Moulton, ed., *The Definitive Journals of Lewis and Clark: Patrick Gass*, Vol. 10 (Lincoln, NE: University of Nebraska Press, 1996), 146; Nelson, *Interpreters*, 44–45.

38. Ambrose, *Undaunted Courage*, 303; Nelson, *Interpreters*, 45–46.

39. Ambrose, *Undaunted Courage*, 304; Nelson, *Interpreters*, 45.

40. Biddle, *The Journals of the Expedition*, 328; Ambrose, *Undaunted Courage*, 310, 313; Nelson, *Interpreters*, 47.

41. Ambrose, *Undaunted Courage*, 316; Nelson, *Interpreters*, 49.

42. DeVoto, *The Journals of Lewis and Clark*, 294; Ambrose, *Undaunted Courage*, 317, 319.

43. DeVoto, *The Journals of Lewis and Clark*, 294; Nelson, *Interpreters*, 51.

44. DeVoto, *The Journals of Lewis and Clark*, 300–301; Ambrose, *Undaunted Courage*, 319.

45. Biddle, *The Journals of the Expedition*, 351–351, 355; Nelson, *Interpreters*, 51–52.

46. Nelson, *Interpreters*, 54.

47. Gary E. Moulton, ed., *The Definitive Journals of Lewis and Clark: John Ordway and Charles Floyd*, Vol. 9 (Lincoln, NE: University of Nebraska Press, 1995), 299; Ambrose, *Undaunted Courage*, 358–359; Nelson, *Interpreters*, 57.

48. Ambrose, *Undaunted Courage*, 360; Nelson, *Interpreters*, 57.

49. Nelson, *Interpreters*, 58–59.

50. Ibid., 59–60.

51. Ambrose, *Undaunted Courage*, 375–376; Nelson, *Interpreters*, 55, 60.

52. Nelson, *Interpreters*, 60.

53. Ibid., 60–62.

54. Clark's inscription can still be seen today. Nelson, *Interpreters*, 62.

55. Landon Y. Jones, *William Clark and the Shaping of the West* (New York, NY: Farrar, Straus and Giroux, 2004), 145; Nelson, *Interpreters*, 62–64.

56. Ambrose, *Undaunted Courage*, 398.

57. Ambrose, *Undaunted Courage*, 399; Nelson, *Interpreters*, 65.

58. Jones, *William Clark and the Shaping of the West*, 145.

59. Nelson, *Interpreters*, 69.

60. Irving W. Anderson, "Probing the Riddle of the Bird Woman," *Montana the Magazine of Western History*, Vol. 23, No. 4, (Helena, MT: Montana Historical Society, Autumn 1973), 6; Jones, *William Clark and the Shaping of the West*, 194; Nelson, *Interpreters*, 70, 71.

61. Hiram Martin Chittenden, *The American Fur Trade of the Far West*, Vol. 1 (Stanford, CA: Academic Reprints, 1954), 188; R. G. Robertson, *Competitive Struggle: America's Western Fur Trading Posts, 1764–1865* (Boise, ID: Tamarack Books, 1999), 157.

62. Ray A. Mattison, "Report on Historical Aspects of the Oahe Reservoir Area, Missouri River, South and North Dakota," *South Dakota Historical Collections and Report*, Vol. XXVII (Pierre, SD: South Dakota State Historical Society, 1954), 112; Hiram Martin Chittenden, *The American Fur Trade of the Far West*, Vol. 2, 957.

63. John C. Luttig, *The Journal of a Fur-Trading Expedition on the Upper Missouri 1812–1813*, Mountain Men and the Fur Trade, Sources of the History of the Fur Trade in the Rocky Mountain West website, accessed August 31, 2020, http://mtmen.org/mtman/html/Luttig/luttig.html.

64. Anderson, "Probing the Riddle of the Bird Woman," 16.

65. Luttig, *The Journal of a Fur-Trading Expedition*.

66. Ibid.

67. Anderson, "Probing the Riddle of the Bird Woman," 12, 15, 16.

68. Nelson, *Interpreters*, 124–125.

69. Ibid., 123.

70. Ibid., 125.

71. Grace Raymond Hebard, *Sacajawea: A Guide and Interpreter of the Lewis and Clark Expedition, with an Account of the Travels of Toussaint Charbonneau, and of Jean Baptiste, The Expedition Papoose* (Mineola, NY: Dover Publications, 1932), 89, 113.

72. Ibid., 89–90.

73. Ibid., 91, 93.

74. Ibid., 113.

75. Ibid., 112–113.

76. Ibid., 153.

77. Ibid., 153–154.

78. Raymond J. DeMallie, volume editor, *Plains*, Handbook of North American Indians, Vol. 13, Part 2 (Washington DC: Smithsonian Institution, 2001), 886; S. C. Gwynne, *Empire of the Summer Moon: Quanah Parker and the Rise and Fall of the Comanches, the Most Powerful Indian Tribe in American History* (New York, NY: Simon & Schuster, 2010), 27; Hebard, *Sacajawea*, 154.

79. Hebard, *Sacajawea*, 155.

80. Ibid.

81. Ibid., 158.

82. Ibid., 159, 160, 161, 165.

83. Ibid., 165, 166, 167, 169.

84. Ibid., 175, 176.

85. Ibid., 187.

86. Ibid., 227.

87. Ibid., 272–273.

88. Ray A. Mattison, "Report on Historical Aspects of the Oahe Reservoir Area, Missouri River, South and North Dakota," *South Dakota Historical Collections and Report*, 116; Hebard, *Sacajawea*, 207, 211.

89. Irving W. Anderson, "Sacagawea: Inside the Corps," pbs.org, accessed August 29, 2020, http://www.pbs.org/lewisandclark/inside/saca.html.

90. Ibid.

91. Donald Jackson, ed., *The Letters of the Lewis and Clark Expedition with Related Documents, 1783–1854* (Urbana: University of Illinois Press, 1978), 527.

92. Nelson, *Interpreters*, 123.

93. Ibid., 123–124.

94. Ibid., 124–126.

95. Ibid.

96. Bonnie Butterfield, "Sacagawea: What Happened to Sacagawea after the Expedition Returned?" accessed September 11, 2020, http://www.bonniebutterfield.com/sacagawea-death.html.

97. Nelson, *Interpreters*, 126–127.

98. Ibid., 126.

99. Ibid., 125.

100. Ibid., 127.

101. Ibid.

102. Ibid.

103. Ibid.

104. Ibid., 125.

CHAPTER 3: DONNER PARTY CANNIBALISM

1. Ethan Rarick, *Desperate Passage: The Donner Party's Perilous Journey West* (England: Oxford University Press, 2008), 33.

2. Ibid., 8.

3. Ibid., 18.

4. Thomas F. Andrews, "Lansford W. Hastings and the Promotion of the Great Salt Lake Cutoff: A Reappraisal," *The Western Historical Quarterly* 4 (2), April 1973, pp. 133–150.

5. Charles McGlashan, *History of the Donner Party: A Tragedy of the Sierra Nevada* (San Francisco: A. Carlisle & Company, 11th edition, 1918), 16.

6. Ibid.

7. Rarick, *Desperate Passage*, 95.

8. George R. Stewart, *Ordeal by Hunger: The Story of the Donner Party* (suppl. ed.) (New York: Houghton Mifflin, 1988), 105–107.

9. Ibid., 211–212, 217.

10. Mark McLaughlin, "Donner Party Weather," Mic Mac Publishing, accessed May 14, 2020, https://www.thestormking.com/Donner_Party/Donner_Party_Weather/donner_party_weather.html.

11. Ibid., 190–196.

12. Ibid., 247–252.

13. Ibid., 258–265.

14. Kristin Johnson, "Donner Party Cannibalism: Did They or Didn't They? (Spoiler Alert: They Did)," *Wild West* 26 (2013): 35.

15. Ibid., 35–36

16. Ibid.

17. Ibid., 31.

18. Ibid.

19. Ibid., 32.

20. Ibid.

21. Ibid., 33.

22. Ibid.

23. Ibid.

24. Ibid., 33–34.

25. Ibid., 36.

26. Ibid.

27. Ibid., 36–37.

28. Ibid.

29. Ibid., 37.

30. Terry Del Bene, *Donner Party Cookbook: A Guide to Survival on the Hastings Cutoff* (Norman, OK: Horse Creek Publications, 2003), 25; Huston Horn, *The Pioneers*

(Alexandria, VA: Time-Life Books), 114; Frank Mullen Jr., *The Donner Party Chronicles: A Day-by-Day Account of a Doomed Wagon Train, 1846–1847* (Reno, NV: Nevada Humanities Committee, 1997), 108–109.

31. Stewart, *Ordeal by Hunger*, 41; Bene, *Donner Party Cookbook*, 29, 33, 35; Mullen, *The Donner Party Chronicles*, 132–133.

32. J. Roderic Korns and Dale L. Morgan, eds. (revised and updated by Will Bagley and Harold Schindler), *West from Fort Bridger: The Pioneering of the Immigrant Trails across Utah, 1846–1850* (Logan, UT: Utah State University Press, 1995), 309–310; Bene, *Donner Party Cookbook*, 39.

33. Kristin Johnson, *"Unfortunate Emigrants": Narratives of the Donner Party* (Logan, UT: Utah State University Press, 1996), 263, 275.

34. Bene, *Donner Party Cookbook*, 41.

35. Ibid.

36. Mullen, *The Donner Party Chronicles*, 146; Bene, *Donner Party Cookbook*, 41.

37. Stewart, *Ordeal by Hunger*, 58; Mullen, *The Donner Party Chronicles*, 160; Bene, *Donner Party Cookbook*, 41.

38. Bene, *Donner Party Cookbook*, 43.

39. Bene, *Donner Party Cookbook*, 43; Mullen, *The Donner Party Chronicles*, 168–169.

40. Rarick, *Desperate Passage*, 84; Stewart, *Ordeal by Hunger*, 21, 64–65, 69, 95; Bene, *Donner Party Cookbook*, 45, 47.

41. Bene, *Donner Party Cookbook*, 47–48.

42. Bene, *Donner Party Cookbook*, 48; Mullen, *The Donner Party Chronicles*, 170.

43. Bene, *Donner Party Cookbook*, 48; Mullen, *The Donner Party Chronicles*, 174.

44. Stewart, *Ordeal by Hunger*, 76–77; Mullen, *The Donner Party Chronicles*, 174, 176.

45. Some historians give the date of October 25, 1846, for Stanton's return to the Donner Party.

46. Charles F. McGlashan, *History of the Donner Party: A Tragedy of the Sierras* (Mineola, NY: Dover Publications, 2013), 40; Bene, *Donner Party Cookbook*, 51.

47. Stewart, *Ordeal by Hunger*, 81, 82; Mullen, *The Donner Party Chronicles*, 184.

48. Bene, *Donner Party Cookbook*, 53; Mullen, *The Donner Party Chronicles*, 188; Stewart, *Ordeal by Hunger*, 82, 83.

49. Bene, *Donner Party Cookbook*, 53; Stewart, *Ordeal by Hunger*, 84.

50. Bene, *Donner Party Cookbook*, 53–54, 107n2; Rarick, *Desperate Passage*, 116–117.

51. Kelly J. Dixon, Julie M. Schablitsky, and Shannon A. Novak, eds., *An Archaeology of Desperation: Exploring the Donner Party's Alder Creek Camp* (Norman: University of Oklahoma Press, 2011), 5; Bene, *Donner Party Cookbook*, 54; Rarick, *Desperate Passage*, 117–118.

52. Rarick, *Desperate Passage*, 118.

53. Stewart, *Ordeal by Hunger*, 108; Bene, *Donner Party Cookbook*, 54.

54. Stewart, *Ordeal by Hunger*, 101–103; Bene, *Donner Party Cookbook*, 57, 59.

55. Stewart, *Ordeal by Hunger*, 110–111; Bene, *Donner Party Cookbook*, 54, 59.

56. Stewart, *Ordeal by Hunger*, 112–113; Bene, *Donner Party Cookbook*, 59, 61.

57. Stewart, Ordeal by Hunger, 115, 116; Bene, *Donner Party Cookbook*, 61.

58. Mullen, *The Donner Party Chronicles*, 226, 228; Bene, *Donner Party Cookbook*, 61, 71.

59. McGlashan, *History of the Donner Party*, 51.

60. Stewart, *Ordeal by Hunger*, 125; Bene, *Donner Party Cookbook*, 61, 63.

61. Will Bagley, *So Rugged and Mountainous: Blazing the Trails to Oregon and California, 1812-1848* (Norman: University of Oklahoma Press, 2010), 321; Stewart, *Ordeal by Hunger*, 146–149; Bene, *Donner Party Cookbook*, 65, 67.

62. Bene, *Donner Party Cookbook*, 71.

63. Mullen, *The Donner Party Chronicles*, 248, 264, 270; Bene, *Donner Party Cookbook*, 71.

64. Mullen, *The Donner Party Chronicles*, 276, 278, 286; Bene, *Donner Party Cookbook*, 71, 73; Stewart, *Ordeal by Hunger*, 177–178, 186.

65. Rarick, *Desperate Passage*, 171; Mullen, *The Donner Party Chronicles*, 288; Bene, *Donner Party Cookbook*, 75.

66. Stewart, *Ordeal by Hunger*, 197–198; Mullen, *The Donner Party Chronicles*, 290; Bene, *Donner Party Cookbook*, 75.

67. Rarick, *Desperate Passage*, 187; Bene, *Donner Party Cookbook*, 77.

68. Bagley, *So Rugged and Mountainous*, 323; Bene, *Donner Party Cookbook*, 79.

69. Mullen, *The Donner Party Chronicles*, 294, 295; Bene, *Donner Party Cookbook*, 81, 83.

70. Bene, *Donner Party Cookbook*, 81; Stewart, *Ordeal by Hunger*, 213.

71. Stewart, *Ordeal by Hunger*, 213, 214, 334.

72. Ibid., 211.

73. Ibid., 211–212.

74. Ibid., 212.

75. Jessy Quinn Thornton, *Oregon and California in 1848*, Vol. 2 (New York, NY: Harper & Brothers Publishers, 1849), 199. Google Books, accessed June 1, 2020, https://books.google.com/books?id=T1pHswEACAAJ&printsec=frontcover&source=gbs_ge_summary_r&cad=0#v=onepage&q&f=false.

76. Thornton, *Oregon and California in 1848*, 199–200; Stewart, *Ordeal by Hunger*, 215, 216.

77. Stewart, *Ordeal by Hunger*, 215, 216.

78. Ibid., 215–219.

79. Ibid., 220–221, 363, 364.

80. Ibid., *Ordeal by Hunger*, 222.

81. Bene, *Donner Party Cookbook*, 85. Stewart, *Ordeal by Hunger*, 227.

82. Stewart, *Ordeal by Hunger*, 228–229.

83. Eliza P. Donner Houghton, *The Expedition of the Donner Party and Its Tragic Fate* (Chicago, IL: A. C. McClurg & Co., 1911), 107, accessed June 6, 2020, https://tile.loc.gov/storage-services//service/gdc/calbk/187.pdf; Stewart, *Ordeal by Hunger*, 231, 232–233.

84. Houghton, *The Expedition of the Donner Party*, 107–108; Stewart, *Ordeal by Hunger*, 233.

85. Stewart, *Ordeal by Hunger*, 235.

86. Ibid., 238.

87. Ibid., 239, 240–241.

88. Ibid., 243, 245.

89. Ibid., 248–249.

90. Ibid., 249–250.

91. Dixon, Schablitsky, and Novak, *An Archaeology of Desperation*, 52; Stewart, *Ordeal by Hunger*, 249.

92. Stewart, *Ordeal by Hunger*, 249.

93. Ibid., 251.

94. Mullen, *The Donner Party Chronicles*, 314–318; Stewart, *Ordeal by Hunger*, 254.

95. Stewart, *Ordeal by Hunger*, 257.

96. Mullen, *The Donner Party Chronicles*, 336; Stewart, *Ordeal by Hunger*, 259–260.

97. Houghton, *The Expedition of the Donner Party*, 141; Stewart, *Ordeal by Hunger*, 261, 264, 265.

98. Dixon, Schablitsky, and Novak, *An Archaeology of Desperation*, 54.

99. Stewart, *Ordeal by Hunger*, 334.

100. Mullen, *The Donner Party Chronicles*, 278.

101. Dale Morgan, ed., *Overland in 1846: Diaries and Letters of the California-Oregon Trail*, Vol. 1 (Lincoln, NE: University of Nebraska Press, 1963), 352–353.

102. Thornton, *Oregon and California in 1848*, 198, 199.

103. Stewart, *Ordeal by Hunger*, 214.

104. Joseph A. King, *Winter of Entrapment: A New Look at the Donner Party* (Lafayette, CA: K&K Publications, 1994), 181–182, 183; Morgan, *Overland in 1846*, 352–353; Kristin Johnson, *"Unfortunate Emigrants,"* 8, 49n66. Morgan gave as an example of Eddy's unreliability that he told three different versions of the Forlorn Hope's journey.

105. King, *Winter of Entrapment*, 108.

106. Ibid., 180–181.

107. Ibid., 56.

108. James Frazier Reed, "The Snow-Bound, Starved Emigrants of 1846," *Pacific Rural Press*, Vol. 1, No. 13, April 1, 1871, California Digital Newspaper Collection, accessed June 3, 2020, https://cdnc.ucr .edu/?a=d&d=PRP18710401.2.5&e=-------en--20--1--txt-txIN--------1.

109. Morgan, *Overland in 1846*, 321.

110. It is interesting to note that George R. Stewart in his book *Ordeal by Hunger* made the same mistake, at first calling Clark as Stone, making the correction two paragraphs later on page 215.

111. Thornton, *Oregon and California in 1848*, 199.

112. Ibid., 200.

113. Mullen, *The Donner Party Chronicles*, 293; Rarick, *Desperate Passage*, 192–193, 266n192.

114. Rarick, *Desperate Passage*, 193.

115. Johnson, *"Unfortunate Emigrants,"* 4–5.

116. Dixon, Schablitsky, and Novak, *An Archaeology of Desperation*, 188.

117. Reed, "The Snow-Bound, Starved Emigrants of 1846."

118. Houghton, *The Expedition of the Donner Party*, 350.

119. King, *Winter of Entrapment*, 171.

120. Dixon, Schablitsky, and Novak, *An Archaeology of Desperation*, 332n10.

121. Morgan, *Overland in 1846*, 352–353; Johnson, *"Unfortunate Emigrants,"* 8, 49n66. As an example of Eddy's unreliability, he gave three different versions of the Forlorn Hope's journey.

122. King, *Winter of Entrapment*, 97.

123. McGlashan, *History of the Donner Party*, 155, 161.

124. Dixon, Schablitsky, and Novak, *An Archaeology of Desperation*, 164, 175, 178, 326.

125. Ibid., 178.

126. Ibid., 95, 190–191.

127. Ibid., 103.

128. Johnson, *"Unfortunate Emigrants,"* 137, 164.

129. McGlashan, *History of the Donner Party*, 155, 159.

130. Stewart, *Ordeal by Hunger*, 260, 277.

131. Stewart, *Ordeal by Hunger*, 276; Dixon, Schablitsky, and Novak, *An Archaeology of Desperation*, 65.

132. Dixon, Schablitsky, and Novak, *An Archaeology of Desperation*, 189.

133. Ibid., 190.

134. Ibid., 8–9, 19–21, 54; Rarick, *Desperate Passage*, 241.

CHAPTER 4: WHY DID JACK MCCALL KILL WILD BILL HICKOK?

1. Joseph G. Rosa, *Wild Bill Hickok: The Man and His Myth* (Lawrence, KS: University Press of Kansas, 1996), 1, 3, 216–240; J. W. Buel, *Heroes of the Plains* (Philadelphia, PA: Historical Publishing Co., 1881), 21–221; Joseph G. Rosa, *Wild Bill Hickok, Gunfighter: An Account of Hickok's Gunfights* (Norman: University of Oklahoma Press, 2003), 68, 69.

2. Joseph G. Rosa, *They Called Him Wild Bill: The Life and Adventures of James Butler Hickok* (Norman: University of Oklahoma Press, 1974), 4; Rosa, *Wild Bill Hickok: The Man and His Myth*, 217; Bill Markley and Kellen Cutsforth, *Old West Showdown: Two Authors Wrangle Over the Truth About the Mythic Old West* (Guilford, CT: Rowman & Littlefield, 2018), 36.

3. Troy Grove was originally named Homer, but there already was a Homer, Illinois, so the name was changed later.

4. Rosa, *They Called Him Wild Bill*, 10, 14–16.

5. Ibid., 17–18, 22.

6. W. F. Cody, *Buffalo Bill's Life Story: An Autobiography* (New York: Cosmopolitan Book Corporation, 1920), 52.

7. Rosa, *Wild Bill Hickok, Gunfighter*, 71; James D. McLaird, *Wild Bill Hickok and Calamity Jane: Deadwood Legends* (Pierre, SD: South Dakota State Historical Society Press, 2008), 8, 12–13; Markley and Cutsforth, *Old West Showdown*, 35–37.

8. Rosa, *They Called Him Wild Bill*, 350–351.

9. McLaird, *Wild Bill Hickok and Calamity Jane*, 28–39.

10. Rosa, *Wild Bill Hickok: The Man and His Myth*, 20; McLaird, *Wild Bill Hickok and Calamity Jane*, 41, 42, 44.

11. Rosa, *They Called Him Wild Bill*, 352–353; McLaird, *Wild Bill Hickok and Calamity Jane*, 45.

12. Crutchfield, Moulton, and Del Bene, *The Settlement of America*, Vol. 1, 158–159; Bill Markley, "Custer's Gold," *True West Magazine*, April 2018, 70.

13. Herbert Krause and Gary D. Olson, *Prelude to Glory: A Newspaper Accounting of Custer's 1874 Expedition to the Black Hills* (Sioux Falls, SD: Brevet Press, 1974), 26; Crutchfield, Moulton, and Bene, *The Settlement of America*, Vol. 1, 158–159; Paul Horsted and Ernest Grafe, *Exploring with Custer: The 1874 Black Hills Expedition* (Custer,

SD: Golden Valley Press, 2002), 87–89; Paul Andrew Hutton, *Phil Sheridan and His Army* (Norman: University of Oklahoma Press, 1985), 298–299.

14. Watson Parker, *Deadwood: The Golden Years* (Lincoln, NE: University of Nebraska Press, 1981), 15–18, 58–59.

15. Watson Parker, *Gold in the Black Hills* (Pierre, SD: South Dakota Historical Press, 2003), 106–108, 130–133.

16. William B. Secrest, ed., *I Buried Hickok: The Memoirs of White Eye Anderson* (College Station, TX: Creative Publishing Co., 1980), 92–93; Rosa, *They Called Him Wild Bill*, 286.

17. Richard B. Hughes and Agnes Wright Spring, eds., *Pioneer Years in the Black Hills* (Rapid City, SD: Dakota Alpha Press, 2002), 122–123; Secrest, *I Buried Hickok*, 97.

18. Harry "Sam" Young, *Hard Knocks: A Life Story of the Vanishing West* (Pierre, SD: South Dakota Historical Society Press, 2005), 213.

19. Secrest, *I Buried Hickok*, 99, 104, 116; Rosa, *They Called Him Wild Bill*, 289.

20. Young, *Hard Knocks*, 215.

21. Young, *Hard Knocks*, 220; Thad Turner, *Wild Bill Hickok: Deadwood City—End of Trail* (Deadwood, SD: Old West Alive! Publishing, 2001), 125.

22. Young, *Hard Knocks*, 220; Rosa, *They Called Him Wild Bill*, 297.

23. Young, *Hard Knocks*, 220.

24. Ibid.

25. Ibid.

26. Rosa, *They Called Him Wild Bill*, 297, 299.

27. Ibid., 298.

28. Rosa, *They Called Him Wild Bill*, 298; Young, *Hard Knocks*, 221; Secrest, *I Buried Hickok*, 120.

29. Secrest, *I Buried Hickok*, 120; McLaird, *Wild Bill Hickok and Calamity Jane*, 53.

30. Secrest, *I Buried Hickok*, 120; McLaird, *Wild Bill Hickok and Calamity Jane*, 58; Turner, *Wild Bill Hickok*, 146, 148.

31. Turner, *Wild Bill Hickok*, 149–150.

32. Turner, *Wild Bill Hickok*, 152–153; McLaird, *Wild Bill Hickok and Calamity Jane*, 54.

33. McLaird, *Wild Bill Hickok and Calamity Jane*, 54.

34. Aaron Woodard, *The Revenger: The Life and Times of Wild Bill Hickok* (Guilford, CT: Rowman & Littlefield Publishing Group, 2018), 117; Joe E. Milner and Earle R. Forrest, *California Joe: Noted Scout and Indian Fighter* (Lincoln, NE: University of Nebraska Press, 1935), 258.

35. Frank J. Wilstach, *Wild Bill Hickok: The Prince of Pistoleers* (Garden City, NY: Doubleday, Page & Company, 1926), 295; Secrest, *I Buried Hickok*, 116; McLaird, *Wild Bill Hickok and Calamity Jane*, 55–56.

36. Rosa, *They Called Him Wild Bill*, 289; Milner and Forrest, *California Joe*, 246, 250.

37. Wilstach, *Wild Bill Hickok*, 299–300, 302.

38. Wilstach, *Wild Bill Hickok*, 301; Secrest, *I Buried Hickok*, 121.

39. Rosa, *They Called Him Wild Bill*, 317.

40. Wilstach, *Wild Bill Hickok*, 295; Milner and Forrest, *California Joe*, 258; Secrest, *I Buried Hickok*, 121.

41. Rosa, *Wild Bill Hickok, Gunfighter*, 164.

42. Rosa, *They Called Him Wild Bill*, 317.

43. Milner, *California Joe*, 251–252, 257.

44. Milner, *California Joe*, 258; Rosa, *They Called Him Wild Bill*, 317–318.

45. Secrest, *I Buried Hickok*, 121.

46. Milner, *California Joe*, 260.

47. Joseph G. Rosa, *Alias Jack McCall: A Pardon or Death?* (Kansas City, MO: The Kansas City Posse, The Westerners, 1967), 5; Aaron Woodward, "The Coward Who Shot Wild Bill," *Wild West Magazine*, August 2019, 40–41; Woodard, *The Revenger*, 117–118.

48. Woodward, "The Coward Who Shot Wild Bill," 41; Woodard, *The Revenger*, 118.

49. Rosa, *Wild Bill Hickok: The Man and His Myth*, 201; Woodard, *The Revenger*, 118–119; Rosa, *Alias Jack McCall*, 8–9.

50. "Wild Bill: A Sequel to the Tragedy," *Black Hills Weekly Pioneer*, November 11, 1876, Newspapers.com, accessed July 19, 2020, https://www.newspapers.com/image/262594576/?terms=%2C%2BWild%2BBill.

51. Rosa, *Wild Bill Hickok, Gunfighter*, 173.

52. Kathy Weiser, "Jack McCall—Cowardly Killer of Wild Bill Hickok," legendsof america.com, accessed July 18, 2020, https://www.legendsofamerica.com/we-jackmccall/.

53. Woodward, "The Coward Who Shot Wild Bill," 38–40.

54. Weiser, "Jack MCall—Cowardly Killer of Wild Bill Hickok."

55. Ibid.

56. Ibid.

57. Woodward, "The Coward Who Shot Wild Bill," 41.

58. Wilstach, *Wild Bill Hickok*, 295.

59. Lucius Beebe and Charles Clegg, *The American West: The Pictorial Epic of a Continent* (New York: E. P. Dutton and Company, 1955), 383.

60. Woodward, "The Coward Who Shot Wild Bill," 41.

61. Ibid.

62. Ibid.

63. Ibid., 42.

CHAPTER 5: DID GENERAL GEORGE CROOK DOOM CUSTER AND THE SEVENTH CAVALRY?

1. Richard I. Wiles Jr., *The Battle of the Rosebud: Crook's Campaign on 1876* (Fort Leavenworth, KS: US Army Command and General Staff College, 1993), 49.

2. "Indians hammer U.S. soldiers at the Battle of the Rosebud," History .com, accessed May 25, 2020, https://www.history.com/this-day-in-history/indians-hammer-u-s-soldiers-at-the-battle-of-the-rosebud.

3. Ibid.

4. Paul L. Hedren, *Rosebud, June 17, 1876: Prelude to the Little Big Horn* (Norman, OK: University of Oklahoma Press, 2019), 139–141.

5. Joseph C. Porter, *Paper Medicine Man: John Gregory Bourke and his American West* (Norman, OK: University of Oklahoma Press, 1986) 38–39.

6. Thomas Powers, *The Killing of Crazy Horse* (New York, NY: Alfred A. Knopf, 2010), 140; Robert M. Utley, *The Lance and the Shield: The Life and Times of Sitting Bull* (New York, NY: Ballantine Books, 1993), 176; Hedren, *Rosebud*, 176.

7. Charles D. Collins Jr., *Atlas of the Sioux Wars*, 2d ed.(Fort Leavenworth, KS: Combat Studies Institute Press, 2006), Map 19.

8. Ibid., Map 22.

9. Stanley Vestal, *Sitting Bull: Champion of the Sioux* (Norman, OK: University of Oklahoma Press, 1932), 152.

10. Collins, *Atlas*, Map 19.

11. Ibid., Map 22.

12. Ibid., Map 20–21.

13. J. W. Vaughn, *Indian Fights; New Facts on Seven Encounters* (Norman: University of Oklahoma Press, 1966), 139.

14. Collins, *Atlas*, Map 20–21.

15. Vaughn, *Indian Fights*, 136-143.

16. Collins, *Atlas*, Map 23.

17. Markley and Cutsforth, *Old West Showdown*, 65.

18. Ibid.

19. Ibid., 76.

20. Thomas Powers, *The Killing of Crazy Horse* (New York, NY: Alfred A. Knopf, 2010), 185, 189; Utley, *The Lance and the Shield*, 141; Hutton, *Phil Sheridan and His Army*, 313; John G. Bourke, *On the Border with Crook* (New York, NY: Skyhorse Publishing, 2014), 302–303.

21. Hedren, *Rosebud*, 155, 301; James Donovan, *A Terrible Glory: Custer and the Little Big Horn: The Last Great Battle of the American West* (New York, NY: Little, Brown and Company, 2008), 153.

22. Hedren, *Rosebud*, 304.

23. Hedren, *Rosebud*, 340–341; Utley, *The Lance and the Shield*, 140, 141–142.

24. Hedren, *Rosebud*, 169, 342; Utley, *The Lance and the Shield*, 141–142.

25. Alfred H. Terry, *The Field Diary of General Alfred H. Terry: The Yellowstone Expedition—1876*, 2nd ed. (Bellevue, NE: Old Army Press, 1970), 15, 21; Donovan, *A Terrible Glory*, 144–145, 160; Hutton, *Phil Sheridan and His Army*, 311.

26. Donovan, *A Terrible Glory*, 161, 162, 164–165.

27. Bourke, *On the Border with Crook*, 318; Hedren, *Rosebud*, 308–309, 341.

28. Hedren, *Rosebud*, 311.

29. Hedren, *Rosebud*, 309; Donovan, *A Terrible Glory*, 131–132; Bourke, *On the Border with Crook*, 278–280.

30. Bourke, *On the Border with Crook*, 318; Hedren, *Rosebud*, 311–312.

31. Hedren, *Rosebud*, 345; Utley, *The Lance and the Shield*, 141–142.

32. Utley, *The Lance and the Shield*, 142.

33. Donovan, *A Terrible Glory*, 165; Terry, *The Field Diary of General Alfred H. Terry*, 22.

34. Bourke, *On the Border with Crook*, 318; Hedren, *Rosebud*, 312, 313; the south fork of Goose Creek is known today as Little Goose Creek.

35. Hedren, *Rosebud*, 313, 314.

36. Donovan, *A Terrible Glory*, 165, 167; Terry, *The Field Diary of General Alfred H. Terry*, 22–23.

37. Hedren, *Rosebud*, 314–317.

38. Donovan, *A Terrible Glory*, 168, 170.

39. Bourke, *On the Border with Crook*, 319; Hedren, *Rosebud,* 317, 318; James D. McLaird, *Calamity Jane: The Woman and the Legend* (Norman, OK: University of Oklahoma Press, 2005), 53.

40. Bourke, *On the Border with Crook*, 319; Hedren, *Rosebud,* 317.

41. Donovan, *A Terrible Glory*, 172, 173, 178.

42. Hedren, *Rosebud,* 318, 335; Utley, *The Lance and the Shield*, 141, 142–143; Hutton, *Phil Sheridan and His Army*, 313; Powers, *The Killing of Crazy Horse*, 192; Bourke, *On the Border with Crook*, 325, 327, 329; Donovan, *A Terrible Glory*, 153.

43. Bourke, *On the Border with Crook*, 321–322.

44. Terry, *The Field Diary of General Alfred H. Terry*, 23; Markley and Cutsforth, *Old West Showdown*, 65, 67; Donovan, *A Terrible Glory*, 190, 192, 300.

45. Hedren, *Rosebud,* 347; Utley, *The Lance and the Shield*, 142; Vestal, *Sitting Bull,* 154.

46. Donovan, *A Terrible Glory*, 195-196.

47. Terry, *The Field Diary of General Alfred H. Terry*, 23.

48. Hedren, *Rosebud,* 347; Utley, *The Lance and the Shield*, 142–143; Vestal, *Sitting Bull,* 154.

49. Donovan, *A Terrible Glory*, 196–198; Markley and Cutsforth, *Old West* Showdown, 67.

50. Donovan, *A Terrible Glory*, 300–301.

51. Joe De Barthe, *The Life and Adventures of Frank Grouard* (St. Joseph, MO: Combe Printing Company, 1894), 255; Mac H. Abrams, *Sioux War Dispatches: Reports from the Field, 1876–1877* (Yardley, PA: Westholme Publishing, 2012), 168–169.

52. Hedren, *Rosebud,* 339.

53. Powers, *The Killing of Crazy Horse*, 192.

54. Barthe, *The Life and Adventures of Frank Grouard*, 243–244, 255.

55. Gregory F. Michno, *Lakota Noon: The Indian Narrative of Custer's Defeat* (Missoula, MT: Mountain Press Publishing Company, 1997), 20, 23, 24, 31, 32; Hedren, *Rosebud,* 340.

56. Markley and Cutsforth, *Old West Showdown*, 67.

57. Ibid., 67–68.

58. Ibid., 68.

59. Markley and Cutsforth, *Old West Showdown*, 68; Donovan, *A Terrible Glory*, 190.

60. Donovan, *A Terrible Glory*, 297, 306; Terry, *The Field Diary of General Alfred H. Terry*, 24.

61. Bourke, *On the Border with Crook*, 334; Powers, *The Killing of Crazy Horse*, 197; Hedren, *Rosebud,* 349; Abrams, *Sioux War Dispatches*, 208.

62. Hedren, *Rosebud,* 353.

63. Ibid., 353–354.

64. Ibid., 354.

CHAPTER 6: DID ROBERT FORD KILL JESSE JAMES?

1. Bill O'Neal, *Encyclopedia of Western Gunfighters* (Norman, OK: University of Oklahoma Press, 1979), 164–165, 166–167; Markley and Cutsforth, *Old West Showdown*, 22–23.

2. *History of Clay and Platte Counties, Missouri* (St. Louis, MO: National Historical Company, 1885), 259–261; William A. Settle Jr., *Jesse James Was His Name or, Fact and*

Fiction Concerning the Careers of the Notorious James Brothers of Missouri (Lincoln, NE: University of Nebraska Press, 1966), 33, 34; Ted P. Yeatman, *Frank and Jesse James: The Story Behind the Legend* (Naperville, IL: Sourcebooks 2000), 85; T. J. Stiles, *Jesse James: Last Rebel of the Civil War* (New York, NY: Random House, 2002), 172.

3. O'Neal, *Encyclopedia of Western Gunfighters*, 165, 346–347.

4. William Allan Pinkerton, *Train Robberies, Train Robbers and the "Holdup" Men* (Reprint Andesite Press, 1907), 20.

5. Jesse James Jr., *Jesse James, My Father: The First and Only True Story of His Adventures* (Cleveland, OH: Buckeye Publishing Co., 1899), 39; Stiles, *Jesse James*, 298, 340.

6. Yeatman, *Frank and Jesse James*, 212, 213; Settle, *Jesse James Was His Name*, 102; Stiles, *Jesse James*, 353, 354.

7. Bill Markley, *Billy the Kid and Jesse James: Outlaws of the Legendary West* (Guilford, CT: Rowman & Littlefield Publishing, 2019), 240; Yeatman, *Frank and Jesse James*, 253, 254; Settle, *Jesse James Was His Name*, 111; Stiles, *Jesse James*, 368; Carl W. Breihan, *Saga of Jesse James* (Caldwell, ID: The Caxton Printers, 1991), 111.

8. Yeatman, *Frank and Jesse James*, 260, 263–264; Breihan, *Saga of Jesse James*, 119; Stiles, *Jesse James*, 373.

9. Breihan, *Saga of Jesse James*, 113–114; Yeatman, *Frank and Jesse James*, 262; Settle, *Jesse James Was His Name*, 116.

10. Yeatman, *Frank and Jesse James*, 262; Settle, *Jesse James Was His Name*, 116; Breihan, *Saga of Jesse James*, 114.

11. Stiles, *Jesse James*, 373; Yeatman, *Frank and Jesse James*, 265.

12. Stiles, *Jesse James*, 372.

13. Stiles, *Jesse James*, 372; Yeatman, *Frank and Jesse James*, 266.

14. Settle, *Jesse James Was His Name*, 116; Yeatman, *Frank and Jesse James*, 266.

15. Yeatman, *Frank and Jesse James*, 267; Stiles, *Jesse James*, 374.

16. Frank Triplett, *Jesse James: The Life, Times, and Treacherous Death of the Most Infamous Outlaw of All Time* (New York, NY: Skyhorse, 2013), 286; Stiles, *Jesse James*, 374; Breihan, *Saga of Jesse James*, 124.

17. Breihan, *Saga of Jesse James*, 123; Settle, *Jesse James Was His Name*, 116.

18. Stiles, *Jesse James*, 375; Yeatman, *Frank and Jesse James*, 268.

19. Breihan, *Saga of Jesse James*, 123–124; Triplett, *Jesse James*, 288.

20. Breihan, *Saga of Jesse James*, 124.

21. Ibid.

22. Yeatman, *Frank and Jesse James*, 269; Triplett, *Jesse James*, 289–290; Robertus Love, *The Rise and Fall of Jesse James* (Lincoln, NB: University of Nebraska Press, 1990), 343; Breihan, *Saga of Jesse James*, 124.

23. Breihan, *Saga of Jesse James*, 124–127; Yeatman, *Frank and Jesse James*, 268–269.

24. Breihan, *Saga of Jesse James*, 126.

25. Breihan, *Saga of Jesse James*, 126; Yeatman, *Frank and Jesse James*, 269.

26. Breihan, *Saga of Jesse James*, 128, 131.

27. Settle, *Jesse James Was His Name* 107, 116, 118, 119; Breihan, *Saga of Jesse James*, 129–130.

28. Breihan, *Saga of Jesse James*, 131.

29. Ibid.

30. Ibid.
31. Settle, *Jesse James Was His Name*, 119.
32. Breihan, *Saga of Jesse James*, 131.
33. Settle, *Jesse James Was His Name*, 118; Breihan, *Saga of Jesse James*, 131–132.
34. Settle, *Jesse James Was His Name*, 118.
35. Yeatman, *Frank and Jesse James*, 269; Breihan, *Saga of Jesse James*, 133; Settle, *Jesse James Was His Name*, 118, 119.
36. Breihan, *Saga of Jesse James*, 134, 135; Stiles, *Jesse James*, 377.
37. Settle, *Jesse James Was His Name*, 119.
38. Breihan, *Saga of Jesse James*, 135; Yeatman, *Frank and Jesse James*, 296.
39. Yeatman, *Frank and Jesse James*, 323–324; Settle, *Jesse James Was His Name*, 170.
40. Yeatman, *Frank and Jesse James*, 323–324.
41. Ibid., 324.
42. Settle, *Jesse James Was His Name*, 170; Yeatman, *Frank and Jesse James*, 324.
43. Settle, *Jesse James Was His Name*, 170–171; Yeatman, *Frank and Jesse James*, 328.
44. Breihan, *Saga of Jesse James*, 154–155; Yeatman, *Frank and Jesse James*, 328.
45. Yeatman, *Frank and Jesse James*, 329.
46. Breihan, *Saga of Jesse James*, 156.
47. Ibid.
48. Yeatman, *Frank and Jesse James*, 339.
49. Ibid., 329, 331, 332.
50. Breihan, *Saga of Jesse James*, 159–160.
51. Ibid.
52. Yeatman, *Frank and Jesse James*, 335, 336, 337, 375.
53. Ibid., 371, 374.
54. Stiles, *Jesse James*, 363–375.
55. Ibid., 381
56. Ibid., 395.
57. Cy Warman, *Frontier Stories*, *"A Quiet Day in Creed"* (New York, NY: Charles Scribner's Sons, 1898), 93–101.
58. Philip Steele, *The Best of NOLA: Outlaws and Lawmen*, *"James Brothers' Death Hoax"* (Laramie, WY: The National Association for Outlaw and Lawman History, 2001), 256.
59. Ibid., 260.
60. Ibid., 260–261.
61. Ibid.
62. Ibid.
63. Ibid., 261.
64. Ibid.
65. Ibid., 260, 262.
66. "Jesse James is Alive! In Lawton," *The Lawton Constitution* (May 19, 1948): 1.
67. Anne C. Stone, James E. Starrs, and Mark Stoneking, "LAST WORD SOCIETY Mitochondrial DNA Analysis of the Presumptive Remains of Jesse James," accessed June 25, 2020, https://web.archive.org/web/20100719085854/http://class.csueastbay.edu/faculty/gmiller/3710/DNA_PDFS/mtDNA/mtDNA_JesseJames.pdf.
68. Ibid.

69. Ibid.
70. Betty Dorsett Duke, "Fraudulent Jesse James DNA Results?" jessejamesintexas.com, accessed June 25, 2020, http://www.jessejamesintexas.com/2Fraudulent_DNAMedia.pdf.
71. Steele, *The Best of NOLA*, 262.

CHAPTER 7: SITTING BULL'S TWO GRAVES

1. Deanne Stillman, *Blood Brothers: The Story of the Strange Friendship between Sitting Bull and Buffalo Bill* (New York: Simon & Schuster, 2017), 217–218; Rex Alan Smith, *Moon of the Popping Trees: The Tragedy at Wounded Knee and the End of the Indian Wars* (Lincoln, NE: University of Nebraska Press, 1975), 156.
2. Norman E. Matteoni, *Prairie Man: The Struggle between Sitting Bull and Indian Agent James McLaughlin* (Guilford, CT: TwoDot, 2015), 235.
3. Smith, *Moon of the Popping Trees*, 70, 71; Eileen Pollack, *Woman Walking Ahead: In Search of Catherine Weldon and Sitting Bull* (Albuquerque, NM: University of New Mexico Press, 2002), 123.
4. Utley, *The Lance and the Shield*, 284; Vestal, *Sitting Bull*, 269.
5. Ibid.
6. Smith, *Moon of the Popping Trees*, 88–89.
7. James McLaughlin, *My Friend the Indian* (Lincoln, NE: University of Nebraska Press, 1989), 184, 185; Smith, *Moon of the Popping Trees*, 103.
8. Vestal, *Sitting Bull*, 272–273; Roger L. Di Silvestro, *In the Shadow of Wounded Knee: The Untold Final Story of the Indian Wars* (New York, NY: Walker & Company, 2007), 70; McLaughlin, *My Friend the Indian*, 190.
9. Dennis C. Pope, *Sitting Bull, Prisoner of War* (Pierre, SD: South Dakota State Historical Society Press, 2010), 130–134.
10. McLaughlin, *My Friend the Indian*, 208, 209.
11. Smith, *Moon of the Popping Trees*, 149.
12. Smith, *Moon of the Popping Trees*, 149; Vestal, *Sitting Bull*, 282.
13. McLaughlin, *My Friend the Indian*, 216.
14. Matteoni, *Prairie Man*, 271.
15. Ibid.
16. Matteoni, *Prairie Man*, 271–272; Smith, *Moon of the Popping Trees*, 151.
17. Smith, *Moon of the Popping Trees*, 149–150; Utley, *The Lance and the Shield*, 296; Vestal, *Sitting Bull*, 285.
18. Roger L. Nichols, *American Indians in U.S. History* (Norman, OK: University of Oklahoma Press, 2003) 160.
19. Utley, *The Lance and the Shield*, 296; Vestal, *Sitting Bull*, 288.
20. Stillman, *Blood Brothers*, 218–219; Utley, *The Lance and the Shield*, 300; Vestal, *Sitting Bull*, 295, 296.
21. Stillman, *Blood Brothers*, 218–219.
22. Ibid., 219.
23. Ibid., 219–220.

24. Stillman, *Blood Brothers*, 220; Stanley Vestal, *New Sources of Indian History, 1850–1891, the Ghost Dance, the Prairie Sioux, a Miscellany* (Norman, OK: University of Oklahoma Press, 1934), 28–29, 30; Utley, *The Lance and the Shield*, 302; Vestal, *Sitting Bull*, 302–303.

25. Utley, *The Lance and the Shield*, 303; Vestal, *Sitting Bull*, 305.

26. Stillman, *Blood Brothers*, 220.

27. "Sitting Bull Killed by Indian Police," History.com, accessed March 25, 2020, https://www.history.com/this-day-in-history/sitting-bull-killed-by-indian-police.

28. Bill Markley, "Sitting Bull Rests, but Is He at Peace?" historynet.com, accessed April 5, 2020, https://www.historynet.com/sitting-bull-rests-peace.htm.

29. Paul T. Hellmann, *Historical Gazetteer of the United States* (New York, NY: Routledge, 2013), p. 993.

30. Megan Chelsea and John Brandon, "A Brief History of Mobridge, South Dakota," slideshare.net, accessed April 4, 2020, https://www.slideshare.net/argyleist/mobridge-history.

31. Rod Thomas, "Sitting Bull's Burials: A History," friendslittlebighorn.com. Accessed April 4, 2020, http://www.friendslittlebighorn.com/sittingbullsburials.htm.

32. Bill Markley, "Sitting Bull Rests, But Is He at Peace?" *Wild West Magazine*, June 2008.

33. Thomas, "Sitting Bull's Burials."

34. Ibid.

35. "Sitting Bull, Where Do You Lie?" roadsideamerica.com, accessed March 25, 2020, https://www.roadsideamerica.com/story/28961.

36. Ibid.

37. Ibid.

38. Vestal, *Sitting Bull*, 312.

39. Ibid.

40. "Sitting Bull, Where Do You Lie?"

41. Rob De Wall, *The Saga of Sitting Bull's Bones* (Crazy Horse, SD: Korczak's Heritage, 1984), 63; Markley, "Sitting Bull Rests, But Is He at Peace?"; Utley, *The Lance and the Shield*, 305.

42. McLaughlin, *My Friend the Indian*, 222; Wall, *Sitting Bull's Bones*, 124.

43. Josephine Waggoner, *Witness: A Hunkpapha Historian's Strong-Heart Song of the Lakotas*, (Lincoln, NE: University of Nebraska Press, 2013), 680.

44. John C. Bailar, Jr., editor, *General Chemistry*, (Boston, MA: Raytheon Education Company, 1968), 200–201, 318–319, 578–579.

45. Wall, *Sitting Bull's Bones*, 128.

46. "Where's Bull's Body?", *Bismarck Daily Tribune*, December 20, 1890. (Bismarck, ND). Newspapers.com. Accessed April 19, 2020. https://www.newspapers.com/image/7414407/?terms=

47. "Sitting Bull's Remains," *Chicago Tribune*, December 20, 1890. (Chicago, IL) Newspapers.com. Accessed April 14, 2020. https://www.newspapers.com/image/349506643/?terms=Sitting%2BBull%2Bdeath%2C

48. Pollack, *Woman Walking Ahead*, 156, 342npp.152-156. McLaughlin, *My Friend the Indian*, 414–415.

49. McLaughlin, *My Friend the Indian*, 416.

50. Ibid.

51. Ibid, 416–417.

52. Wall, *The Saga of Sitting Bull's Bones*, 41.

53. Ibid., 127–129.

54. Ibid., 129.

55. "Sitting Bull's Grave, Fort Yates, N.D.," Digital Horizons, Life on the Northern Plains, State Historical Society of North Dakota, accessed April 22, 2020, http://www.digitalhorizonsonline.org/digital/collection/uw-ndshs/id/5941/.

56. "N.D.'s Sitting Bull Action Draws Tribal Council Ire," *Rapid City Journal*, March 23, 1953 (Rapid City, SD), Newspapers.com, accessed April 21, 2020, https://www.newspapers.com/image/351451843/?article=4ddf931f-cd89-40f3-b399-95d225d65dcc.

57. Bob Lee, "The Story Behind the Story," *Rapid City Journal*, March 29, 1953 (Rapid City, SD), Newspapers.com, accessed April 22, 2020, https://www.newspapers.com/image/351456933.

58. Ibid.

59. Ibid.

60. McLaughlin, *Sitting Bull's Bones*, 36, 38–39, 42, 43, 65.

61. "N.D.'s Sitting Bull Action Draws Tribal Council Ire," *Rapid City Journal*, March 23, 1953 (Rapid City, SD), Newspapers.com, accessed April 21, 2020, https://www.newspapers.com/image/351451843/?article=4ddf931f-cd89-40f3-b399-95d225d65dcc.

62. McLaughlin, *Sitting Bull's Bones*, 72 and 79.

63. Ibid., 83–104, 113, 129.

64. Ibid., 104–111; Markley, "Sitting Bull Rests, But Is He at Peace?"

65. "S.D. Ghouls Steal Sitting Bull's Bones," *Bismarck Tribune*, April 8, 1953 (Bismarck, ND), Newspapers.com, accessed April 22, 2020, https://www.newspapers.com/image/413317996/?terms=.

66. "Sitting Bull's Body taken to S.D.," *Rapid City Journal*, April 8, 1953 (Rapid City, SD), Newspapers.com, accessed April 22, 2020, https://www.newspapers.com/image/351205623/?terms=.

67. Wall, *Sitting Bull's Bones*, 138, 262; Markley, "Sitting Bull Rests, But Is He at Peace?"

CHAPTER 8: THE LOST DUTCHMAN MINE

1. Robert Sikorsky, *Fool's Gold: The Facts, Myths and Legends of the Lost Dutchman Mine and the Superstition Mountains* (Phoenix, AZ: Golden West Publishers, 1983) 15.

2. Ibid.

3. "Goldfield, Arizona—Given a Third Rebirth," Legends of America, accessed March 15, 2020, https://www.legendsofamerica.com/az-goldfield/.

4. Robert Blair, *Tales of the Superstitions: The Origins of the Lost Dutchman's Legend* (Tempe, AZ: Arizona Historical Foundation, 1975) 29.

5. Ibid., 59.

6. Ibid.

7. Ibid., 73–74.

8. Ibid., 59.

9. Tom Kollenborn, "Robert K. Corbin's Legacy," blogspot, accessed March 16, 2020, https://superstitionmountaintomkollenborn.blogspot.com/2009/08/robert-k-corbins-legacy.html.

10. Blair, *Tales of the Superstitions*, 12.

11. Ibid., 11.

12. Sikorsky, *Fool's Gold*, 110.

13. Ibid., 111.

14. Ibid.

15. Blair, *Tales of the Superstitions*, 11.

16. Ibid., 98.

17. Ibid, 11.

18. Ibid., 59.

19. Estee Conatser, *Sterling Legend: The Facts Behind the Lost Dutchman Mine Gem* (Baldwin Park, CA: Gem Guides Book Co., 1987).

20. Gene Botts, "Peralta Stones and Lost Dutchman Gold Mine: The Peralta Stones are Fakes!" DesertUSA, accessed March 23, 2020, https://www.desertusa.com/lost-dutchman/peralta-stones-fake.html.

21. Ibid., 21–22.

22. Khatri Vikas, *World Famous Treasures Lost and Found* (India: Pustak Mahal, 2013), 64.

23. Blair, *Tales of the Superstitions*, 96.

24. Byrd Howell Granger, *A Motif Index For Lost Mines and Treasures Applied to Redaction of Arizona Legends, and to Lost Mine and Treasure Legends Exterior to Arizona* (Tucson, AZ: University of Arizona Press, 1977) 99.

25. Halka Chronic, *Roadside Geology of Arizona* (Missoula, MT: Mountain Press Publishing Company, 1983), 95.

26. James Swanson and Tom Kollenborn, *Superstition Mountain: A Ride Through Time* (Phoenix, AZ: Arrowhead Press, 1981), 155, 158.

27. "Superstition Wilderness Area," U.S. Department of Agriculture, Forest Service, Tonto National Forest website, accessed June 9, 2020, https://www.fs.usda.gov/detail/tonto/specialplaces/?cid=fsbdev3_018739.

28. Estee Conatser, *The Sterling Legend: The Facts Behind the Lost Dutchman Mine* (Upland, CA: Gem Guide Books, 1972), 7, 8; Swanson and Kollenborn, *Superstition Mountain*, 3, 6; Tom Kollenborn, "Don't Blame the Thunder God," *Tom Kollenborn Chronicles*, December 16, 2013, accessed June 9, 2020, http://superstitionmountaintom kollenborn.blogspot.com/search?q=Apache+Thunder+Gods.

29. Swanson, *Superstition Mountain*, 16.

30. Swanson, *Superstition Mountain*, 16–17; Conatser, *The Sterling Legend*, 11.

31. Conatser, *The Sterling Legend*, 12.

32. Ibid., 12–13.

33. Ibid., 13.

34. Ibid.

35. Ibid., 14.

36. Ibid.

37. Conatser, *The Sterling Legend*, 15–16.

38. Swanson, *Superstition Mountain*, 31.

39. Ibid., 32.

40. Ibid., 34–35.

41. Ibid., 27, 34.

42. Ibid., 27, 33.

43. P. C. Bicknell, "One of Arizona's Lost El Dorados," *San Francisco Chronicle*, January 13, 1895, Newspapers.com, accessed June 14, 2020, https://www.newspapers.com/image/27596373/; Conatser, *The Sterling Legend*, 34; Swanson, *Superstition Mountain*, 33–34.

44. Swanson, *Superstition Mountain*, 35.

45. Ibid., 35, 40, 43.

46. Ibid., 35–36.

47. Blair, *Tales of the Superstitions*, 73; Swanson, *Superstition Mountain*, 36.

48. Swanson, *Superstition Mountain*, 39, 44.

49. Tom Kollenborn, "An Affliction," *Tom Kollenborn Chronicles*, May 4, 2015, accessed June 12, 2020, http://superstitionmountaintomkollenborn.blogspot.com/search?q=gold.

50. Swanson, *Superstition Mountain*, 39–40, 44.

51. Ibid., 43.

52. James Swanson personal conversation with Bill Markley at Superstition Mountain Lost Dutchman Museum, March 10, 2020.

53. "The Lost Dutchman Gold Mine, Jacob Waltz's Mining Tools exhibit," Superstition Mountain Lost Dutchman Museum, viewed by Bill Markley, March 10, 2020.

54. Ibid.

55. Swanson, *Superstition Mountain*, 34, 44.

56. Ibid., 47–48.

57. Ibid., 50.

58. Ibid.

59. Ibid., 57.

60. Ibid.

61. Ibid., 57, 60.

62. Ibid., 61–62.

63. Tom Kollenborn, "What Dreams Are Made Of," *Tom Kollenborn Chronicles*, September 23, 2013, accessed June 14, 2020.

64. Tom Kollenborn and the Superstition Mountain Historical Society, "Jacob Waltz 'Lost Dutchman' Exhibit," The Superstition Mountain Lost Dutchman Museum, accessed June 12, 2020, http://superstitionmountainmuseum.org/exhibits/jacob-waltz-lost-dutchman-exhibit/.

65. "Prospecting, Mining, And Searching for Treasure In Wilderness Areas," USDA Forest Service, Tonto National Forest, accessed June 13, 2020, https://www.fs.usda.gov/detail/tonto/specialplaces/?cid=fsbdev3_018726.

66. "Walter Brennan: Dutchman's Gold Lyrics," LyricWiki. accessed June 13, 2020, https://lyrics.fandom.com/wiki/Walter_Brennan:Dutchman%27s_Gold.

CHAPTER 9: WAS TOM HORN GUILTY OR INNOCENT?

1. Chip Carlson, *Tom Horn: Blood on the Moon: Dark History of the Murderous Cattle Detective* (Glendo, WY: High Plains Press, 2001), 135, 142, 155.

2. Ibid., 142, 143.

3. Ibid., 141–142.

4. Ibid., 134–136.

5. John W. Davis, *The Trial of Tom Horn* (Norman, OK: University of Oklahoma Press, 2016), 15–16.

6. Carlson, *Tom Horn*, 137–138; Davis, *The Trial of Tom Horn*, 14–15.

7. Carlson, *Tom Horn*, 139–140; Davis, *The Trial of Tom Horn*, 15.

8. Davis, *The Trial of Tom Horn*, 15.

9. Carlson, *Tom Horn*, 143.

10. Davis, *The Trial of Tom Horn*, 4.

11. Ibid.

12. Ibid.

13. Ibid., 4, 5, 13.

14. Carlson, *Tom Horn*, 149.

15. Davis, *The Trial of Tom Horn*, 14.

16. Coroner's Inquest for William Nickell, Testimony, Part 1 (CR4-58 State vs Tom Horn, Laramie County District Court, Wyoming State Archives), 27, accessed September 5, 2020, https://drive.google.com/file/d/1a2c1FpuXCv0j1xgZQkJzxfGoUnOF OGl7/view.

17. Ibid., 39.

18. Ibid., 39–40.

19. Ibid., 40.

20. Ibid., 41.

21. Ibid., 42.

22. Ibid., 45–53.

23. Ibid., 53–55.

24. Ibid. 58–59.

25. Ibid., 66–67.

26. Ibid., 67.

27. Coroner's Inquest, Part 2, 80; Carlson, *Tom Horn*, 166.

28. Coroner's Inquest, Part 1, 62, 64; Davis, *The Trial of Tom Horn*, 21, 22.

29. Coroner's Inquest, Part 1, 63; Davis, *The Trial of Tom Horn*, 22, 27.

30. Coroner's Inquest, Part 2, 91, 94.

31. Davis, *The Trial of Tom Horn*, 30.

32. Tom Horn, *Life of Tom Horn, Government Scout and Interpreter* (Scotts Valley, CA: CreateSpace, 2016), 9, 12; Carlson, *Tom Horn*, 22–27.

33. Horn, *Life of Tom Horn*, 12.

34. Ibid., 13.

35. Monty McCord, *Calling the Brands: Stock Detectives in the Wild West* (Guilford, CT: Rowman & Littlefield Publishing Group, 2018), 71; Horn, *Life of Tom Horn*, 13, 127.

36. McCord, *Calling the Brands*, 71; Davis, *The Trial of Tom Horn*, 41.

37. McCord, *Calling the Brands*, 71–72; Horn, *Life of Tom Horn*, 132–134.

38. Davis, *The Trial of Tom Horn*, 41.

39. Horn, *Life of Tom Horn*, 134; Carlson, *Tom Horn*, 133.

40. Davis, *The Trial of Tom Horn*, 41; Carlson, *Tom Horn*, 67, 69.

41. Carlson, *Tom Horn*, 70–72.

42. Ibid., 74–75.
43. Davis, *The Trial of Tom Horn*, 42; Carlson, *Tom Horn*, 77.
44. Carlson, *Tom Horn*, 83–84; Davis, *The Trial of Tom Horn*, 42.
45. Davis, *The Trial of Tom Horn*, 42.
46. Davis, *The Trial of Tom Horn*, 42–43; Carlson, *Tom Horn*, 93;95, 97, 98.
47. Carlson, *Tom Horn*, 109.
48. Ibid., 114, 120, 121.
49. Davis, *The Trial of Tom Horn*, 44, 304n29.
50. Ibid., 44.
51. Coroner's Inquest, Part 3, 150, 152; Davis, *The Trial of Tom Horn*, 37; Carlson, *Tom Horn*, 152, 155.
52. Carlson, *Tom Horn*, 152, 153; Davis, *The Trial of Tom Horn*, 38.
53. Carlson, *Tom Horn*, 152–153.
54. Coroner's Inquest, Part 4, 283–288; Carlson, *Tom Horn*, 176, 177.
55. Ibid., 289–290, 293–294.
56. Ibid., 291–292.
57. Ibid., 295–296.
58. Carlson, *Tom Horn*, 189.
59. Coroner's Inquest, Part 4, 296–297.
60. Coroner's Inquest, Part 6, 355–376; Davis, *The Trial of Tom Horn*, 47–48.
61. Joe LeFors, *Wyoming Peace Officer: An Autobiography* (Laramie, WY: Laramie Printers, 1953), 131–134; Carlson, *Tom Horn*, 195–196; Davis, *The Trial of Tom Horn*, 48–49.
62. Coroner's Inquest, Part 7, 402–405.
63. Davis, *The Trial of Tom Horn*, 49, 51.
64. LeFors, *Wyoming Peace Officer*, 135–136; Davis, *The Trial of Tom Horn*, 58–59.
65. LeFors, *Wyoming Peace Officer*, 136; Davis, *The Trial of Tom Horn*, 58–59, 61.
66. LeFors, *Wyoming Peace Officer*, 137; Davis, *The Trial of Tom Horn*, 59.
67. Davis, *The Trial of Tom Horn*, 59, 60; Carlson, *Tom Horn*, 196.
68. Davis, *The Trial of Tom Horn*, 60; Carlson, *Tom Horn*, 197.
69. LeFors, *Wyoming Peace Officer*, 137; Davis, *The Trial*, 60–61.
70. LeFors, *Wyoming Peace Officer*, 137; Davis, *The Trial of Tom Horn*, 61.
71. LeFors, *Wyoming Peace Officer*, 138; Davis, *The Trial of Tom Horn*, 61.
72. LeFors, *Wyoming Peace Officer*, 138; Davis, *The Trial of Tom Horn*, 61–62.
73. LeFors, *Wyoming Peace Officer*, 138; Davis, *The Trial of Tom Horn*, 62.
74. Carlson, *Tom Horn*, 199.
75. Ibid., 197–199.
76. Ibid., 199.
77. Ibid., 199–200.
78. Ibid., 200–201.
79. Davis, *The Trial of Tom Horn*, 62; Carlson, *Tom Horn*, 201.
80. Ibid.
81. Davis, *The Trial of Tom Horn*, 62, 112; Carlson, *Tom Horn*, 202.
82. Davis, *The Trial of Tom Horn*, 63, 109; Carlson, *Tom Horn*, 201.
83. Carlson, *Tom Horn*, 205.
84. Ibid., 206.

85. Ibid., 207.

86. Ibid., 208–209.

87. Ibid., 209.

88. Ibid.

89. Davis, *The Trial of Tom Horn*, 111; Carlson, *Tom Horn*, 209.

90. Carlson, *Tom Horn*, 209.

91. Ibid., 210.

92. Carlson, *Tom Horn*, 210; Davis, *The Trial of Tom Horn*, 111.

93. Davis, *The Trial of Tom Horn*, 63, 116; Carlson, *Tom Horn*, 210.

94. Davis, *The Trial of Tom Horn*, 52, 63.

95. Carlson, *Tom Horn*, 211.

96. Carlson, *Tom Horn*, 213; Davis, *The Trial of Tom Horn*, 53, 54–55.

97. Davis, *The Trial of Tom Horn*, 69.

98. Carlson, *Tom Horn*, 216, 217; Davis, *The Trial of Tom Horn*, 53, 54–55, 69–71.

99. Carlson, *Tom Horn*, 216; Davis, *The Trial of Tom Horn*, 69, 105.

100. Davis, *The Trial of Tom Horn*, 75.

101. Carlson, *Tom Horn*, 220; Davis, *The Trial of Tom Horn*, 87, 88, 89.

102. Davis, *The Trial of Tom Horn*, 75, 94.

103. Ibid., 94, 95.

104. Ibid., 100–102.

105. Ibid., 75, 103.

106. Ibid., 106–107.

107. Ibid., 108.

108. Ibid., 108–116.

109. Ibid., 120–129, 133–136.

110. Carlson, *Tom Horn*, 224–225, 226; Davis, *The Trial of Tom Horn*, 137.

111. Davis, *The Trial of Tom Horn*, 139, 162.

112. Carlson, *Tom Horn*, 236–237; Davis, *The Trial of Tom Horn*, 162.

113. Davis, *The Trial of Tom Horn*, 165, 169, 170.

114. Ibid., 171.

115. Ibid.

116. Ibid., 173.

117. Ibid., 174.

118. Ibid., 176.

119. Ibid., 178, 179.

120. Ibid,. 180, 181.

121. Ibid., 192.

122. Ibid., 219–220.

123. Ibid., 222.

124. Ibid., 228, 231, 234, 236, 237.

125. Carlson, *Tom Horn*, 289; Davis, *The Trial of Tome Horn*, 244, 254–255.

126. Carlson, *Tom Horn*, 288–289; Davis, *The Trial of Tome Horn*, 243–245, 246–247.

127. Davis, *The Trial of Tom Horn*, 247.

128. Carlson, *Tom Horn*, 290–291; Davis, *The Trial of Tom Horn*, 248–249.

129. Carlson, *Tom Horn*, 291–292; Davis, *The Trial of Tom Horn*, 250–251.

130. Carlson, *Tom Horn*, 292–293; Davis, *The Trial of Tom Horn*, 250, 251.

131. Davis, *The Trial of Tom Horn*, 251.

132. Ibid., 252.

133. Ibid., 255, 257, 258, 259, 265.

134. Ibid., 265.

135. Ibid., 267, 269, 270, 271.

136. Ibid, 271, 272, 277.

137. Carlson, *Tom Horn*, 298–299; Davis, *The Trial*, 279, 281.

138. Davis, *The Trial of Tom Horn*, 280–281.

139. Ibid., 280, 282.

140. Carlson, *Tom Horn*, 335; Davis, *The Trial of Tom Horn*, 282.

141. Carlson, *Tom Horn*, 301; Davis, *The Trial of Tom Horn*, 283.

142. Larry D. Ball, *Tom Horn: In Life and Legend* (Norman, OK: University of Oklahoma Press, 2014), 435.

143. Chip Carlson, "Tom Horn: Wyoming Enigma," wyohistory.org, November 8, 2014, accessed September 25, 2020, https://www.wyohistory.org/encyclopedia/tom-horn-wyoming-enigma#:~:text=Horn%20remains%20controversial%20for%20two,questionable%20nature%20of%20his%20trial.

144. Ibid.

145. Ibid.

146. Ibid.

147. Ball, *In Life and Legend*, 252–253.

148. Ibid, 254.

149. Ibid., 262–263.

150. Ibid., 264.

151. Ibid., 264, 267.

152. Kevin Killough, "Was Tom Horn Innocent?" county17.com, July 20, 2018, accessed September 26, 2020, https://county17.com/2018/07/20/was-tom-horn-innocent-thisweekinwyhistory/.

153. Ball, *In Life and Legend*, 262–263.

154. Ibid.

155. Killough, "Was Tom Horn Innocent?"

156. Ibid.

157. Ibid.

158. Ball, *In Life and Legend*, 265–266.

159. Ibid., 267.

160. Ibid., 266.

161. Ibid., 270–271.

162. Ibid., 277.

163. Ibid.

164. Ibid., 281.

165. Ibid., 427.

166. Ibid., 342

167. Ibid.

168. Ibid., 342–343.

CHAPTER 10: DID BUTCH CASSIDY DIE IN BOLIVIA?

1. Kaspar M., "Western Writers of America's 100 Greatest Westerns," Internet Movie Database website, accessed July 21, 2020, https://www.imdb.com/list/ls006229256/. The Western Writers of America selected *Shane* as number one, *High Noon* as number two, and *The Searchers* as number three.

2. Charles Kelly, *The Outlaw Trail: A History of Butch Cassidy and His Wild Bunch* (Lincoln, NE: University of Nebraska Press, 1938, 1959), 4.

3. Bill Betenson, *Butch Cassidy: My Uncle* (Glendo, WY: High Plains Press, 2017), 29–30; Mac Blewer, *Wyoming's Outlaw Trail* (Charleston, SC: Arcadia Publishing, 2013), 60; W. C. Jameson, *Butch Cassidy: Beyond the Grave* (Lanham, MD: Rowman & Littlefield Publishing, 2014), 5.

4. Richard Patterson, *Butch Cassidy: A Biography* (Lincoln, NE: University of Nebraska Press, 1998), 2,4; Jameson, *Beyond the Grave*, 13–14.

5. Jameson, *Beyond the Grave,* 16; Patterson, *Butch Cassidy*, 2.

6. Jameson, *Beyond the Grave,* 16; Patterson, *Butch Cassidy*, 5.

7. Jameson, *Beyond the Grave,* 16 17–18; Patterson, *Butch Cassidy*, 4–5, 7–8.

8. Kelly, *The Outlaw Trail*, 11; Patterson, *Butch Cassidy*, 5.

9. Jameson, *Beyond the Grave*, 19, 21; Patterson, *Butch Cassidy*, 11.

10. Jameson, *Beyond the Grave*, 22.

11. Jameson, *Beyond the Grave*, 22; Patterson, *Butch Cassidy*, 14.

12. Jameson, *Beyond the Grave*, 22, 23; Patterson, *Butch Cassidy*, 14 , 15.

13. Jameson, *Beyond the Grave*, 23, 24; Patterson, *Butch Cassidy*, 15, 17.

14. Jameson, *Beyond the Grave*, 24, 25; Patterson, *Butch Cassidy*, 24.

15. Jameson, *Beyond the Grave*, 25; Patterson, *Butch Cassidy*, 25.

16. Jameson, *Beyond the Grave*, 26, 27, 31; Patterson, *Butch Cassidy*, 44, 45.

17. Jameson, *Beyond the Grave*, 32, 34; Patterson, *Butch Cassidy*, 56.

18. Jay Robert Nash, *Encyclopedia of Western Lawmen & Outlaws* (New York, NY: Da Capo Press, 1994), 67; Jameson, *Beyond the Grave*, 32, 34–35; Patterson, *Butch Cassidy*, 46, 58, 121.

19. Jameson, *Beyond the Grave*, 37; Patterson, *Butch Cassidy*, 46.

20. Larry Pointer, *In Search of Butch Cassidy* (Norman, OK: University of Oklahoma Press, 1977), 69; Jameson, *Beyond the Grave*, 50; Patterson, *Butch Cassidy*, 49, 50–53.

21. Jameson, *Beyond the Grave*, 40; Patterson, *Butch Cassidy*, 59.

22. Blewer, *Wyoming's Outlaw Trail,* 48; Jameson, *Beyond the Grave*, 40; Patterson, *Butch Cassidy*, 62, 64, 65.

23. Patterson, *Butch Cassidy*, 62, 64, 65, 67; Jameson, *Beyond the Grave*, 41.

24. Anne Meadows, *Digging Up Butch and Sundance* (Lincoln, NE: University of Nebraska Press, 2003), 24; Patterson, *Butch Cassidy*, 78, 79; Jameson, *Beyond the Grave*, 42, 43.

25. Patterson, *Butch Cassidy*, 86.

26. Patterson, *Butch Cassidy*, 88–92; Jameson, *Beyond the Grave*, 47–48.

27. Patterson, *Butch Cassidy*, 93, 97; Jameson, *Beyond the Grave*, 49.

28. Meadows, *Digging Up Butch and Sundance*, 25; Patterson, *Butch Cassidy*, 101; Jameson, *Beyond the Grave*, 51.

29. Pointer, *In Search of Butch Cassidy*, 99; Meadows, *Digging Up Butch and Sundance*, 26; Patterson, *Butch Cassidy*, 111–112.

30. Patterson, *Butch Cassidy*, 112–113.

31. Meadows, *Digging Up Butch and Sundance*, 27, 28, 30; Patterson, *Butch Cassidy*, 114–115, 116–117.

32. Meadows, *Digging Up Butch and Sundance*, 31, 32; Patterson, *Butch Cassidy*, 117, 121, 122.

33. Meadows, *Digging Up Butch and Sundance*, 31–32.

34. Meadows, *Digging Up Butch and Sundance*, 120–121; Jameson, *Beyond the Grave*, 51.

35. Patterson, *Butch Cassidy*, 105.

36. Meadows, *Digging Up Butch and Sundance*, 32; Patterson, *Butch Cassidy*, 125.

37. Meadows, *Digging Up Butch and Sundance*, 33.

38. Pointer, *In Search of Butch Cassidy*, 148; Meadows, *Digging Up Butch and Sundance*, 33; Patterson, *Butch Cassidy*, 141–143.

39. Meadows, *Digging Up Butch and Sundance*, 33.

40. Meadows, *Digging Up Butch and Sundance*, 34; Patterson, *Butch Cassidy*, 143, 144, 146.

41. Meadows, *Digging Up Butch and Sundance*, 34; Patterson, *Butch Cassidy*, 156.

42. Meadows, *Digging Up Butch and Sundance*, 35; Patterson, *Butch Cassidy*, 160, 161.

43. Meadows, *Digging Up Butch and Sundance*, 35; Patterson, *Butch Cassidy*, 161–165.

44. Meadows, *Digging Up Butch and Sundance*, 34; Patterson, *Butch Cassidy*, 166–169.

45. Meadows, *Digging Up Butch and Sundance*, 35, 36, 37; Patterson, *Butch Cassidy*, 175, 177, 181, 183–184.

46. Patterson, *Butch Cassidy*, 184–185, 186, 192; Meadows, *Digging Up Butch and Sundance*, 37; Jameson, *Beyond the Grave*, 57.

47. Jameson, *Beyond the Grave*, 92, 93, 95.

48. Ibid., 93, 94, 96.

49. Ibid., 95.

50. Jameson, *Beyond the Grave*, 98; Meadows, *Digging Up Butch and Sundance*, 363.

51. Jameson, *Beyond the Grave*, 97; Patterson, *Butch Cassidy*, 204, 206.

52. Patterson, *Butch Cassidy*, 207–208.

53. Jameson, *Beyond the Grave*, 99–100, 102–103; Patterson, *Butch Cassidy*, 209, 210.

54. Patterson, *Butch Cassidy*, 214.

55. Arthur Chapman, "'Butch' Cassidy," *Elks Magazine*, April 1930, 62–63, accessed August 11, 2020, https://www.elks.org/magazinescans/1930-04A.pdf; Patterson, *Butch Cassidy*, 215, 216; Jameson, *Beyond the Grave*, 105, 107.

56. Betenson, *Butch Cassidy: My Uncle*, 207, 215.

57. Patterson, *Butch Cassidy*, 316.

58. "Deputy Sheriff Samuel Jenkins," odmp.org, accessed July 29, 2020, http://www.odmp.org/officer/7094-deputy-sheriff-samuel-jenkins.

59. Jameson, *Beyond the Grave*, 88.

60. Betenson, *Butch Cassidy: My Uncle*, 189–190.

61. Ibid., 198–200.

62. Christopher Klein, "The Mysterious Deaths of Butch Cassidy and the Sundance Kid," history.com, accessed August 4, 2020, https://www.history.com/news/the-mysterious-deaths-of-butch-cassidy-and-the-sundance-kid.

63. Ibid.

64. Ibid.

65. Ibid.

66. Betenson, *Butch Cassidy: My Uncle*, 207.

67. Ibid., 216.

68. Ibid., 218.

69. Meadows, *Digging Up Butch and Sundance*, 112.

70. Ibid., 110.

71. Ibid., 109.

72. Betenson, *Butch Cassidy: My Uncle*, 240.

73. Ibid., 242.

74. Ibid., 240.

75. Ibid.

76. Lula Parker Betenson, *Butch Cassidy, My Brother* (New York: Penguin, 1976), 177.

77. Ibid., 196.

78. "Butch Cassidy's Buried Secrets," travelchannel.com, accessed August 7, 2020, https://www.travelchannel.com/shows/mission-declassified/episodes/butch-cassidys-buried-secrets.

79. Ibid.

80. Arthur Chapman, "'Butch' Cassidy," *Elks Magazine*, April 1930, 30; Meadows, *Digging Up Butch and Sundance*, 93.

81. Chapman, "'Butch' Cassidy," 62.

82. Ibid., 62–63.

83. Ibid., 63.

84. Patterson, *Butch Cassidy*, 215; Meadows, *Digging Up Butch and Sundance*, 230, 233.

85. Patterson, *Butch Cassidy*, 215; Meadows, *Digging Up Butch and Sundance*, 230–231, 237, 363.

86. Meadows, *Digging Up Butch and Sundance*, 231.

87. Ibid.

88. Meadows, *Digging Up Butch and Sundance*, 211, 231.

89. Ibid., 163, 164.

90. Ibid., 229, 232.

91. Ibid, 232-233.

92. Meadows, *Digging Up Butch and Sundance*, 134, 135, 233–234, 260.

93. Ibid., 236–237.

94. Betenson, *Butch Cassidy: My Uncle*, 215; Patterson, *Butch Cassidy*, 215.

95. *Corregidor* is a chief magistrate.

96. Meadows, *Digging Up Butch and Sundance*, 266–267.

97. Ibid.

98. Ibid.

99. Ibid.

100. Patterson, *Butch Cassidy*, 216; Meadows, *Digging Up Butch and Sundance*, 136, 264.

101. Meadows, *Digging Up Butch and Sundance*, 264–265, 268.

102. Ibid., 265.

103. Ibid., 265–266.

104. Ibid., 269, 270–271.

105. Ibid., 265.

106. Ibid., 263.

107. Ibid.

108. Ibid., 272–273.

109. Ibid., 182, 214.

110. Ibid., 101, 324–325.

111. Ibid., 134, 260.

112. Hiram Bingham, *Across South America: An Account of A Journey From Buenos Aires to Lima by Way of Potosí* (New York, NY: Houghton Mifflin Company, 1911), 82; Meadows, *Digging Up Butch and Sundance*, 130.

113. Bingham, *Across South America*, 83–84; Meadows, *Digging Up Butch and Sundance*, 131.

114. Ibid., 82.

115. Ibid., 93.

116. Ibid., 93.

117. Ibid.

118. Betenson, *Butch Cassidy: My Uncle*, 220; Meadows, *Digging Up Butch and Sundance*, 80, 127, 128–129.

119. Betenson, *Butch Cassidy: My Uncle*, 220; Meadows, *Digging Up Butch and Sundance*, 136–138, 182.

120. A. G. Francis, "The End of an Outlaw," *Wide World Magazine*, April 1913, 36.

121. Ibid.

122. Ibid.

123. Ibid., 37–39.

124. Ibid., 41–42.

125. Ibid., 42, 43.

126. Ibid., 43.

127. Betenson, *Butch Cassidy: My Uncle*, 85.

128. John H. Mcintosh, "The Evolution of a Bandit," *Wide World Magazine*, September 1910, 565; Chapman, *Elks Magazine*, 62; Bill O'Neal, *Encyclopedia of Western Gunfighters* (Norman: University of Oklahoma Press, 1979), 183–184, 186.

129. Meadows, *Digging Up Butch and Sundance*, 345.

130. Chapman, "'Butch' Cassidy," 30.

131. Ibid., 61.

132. Meadows, *Digging Up Butch and Sundance*, 93, 97–99.

133. Chapman, "'Butch' Cassidy," 60.

134. Ibid., 62.

135. Anne Meadows and Dan Buck, "The Last Days of Butch and Sundance," *Wild West Magazine*, February 1997, 40.

136. Meadows, *Digging Up Butch and Sundance*, 97–99.

137. Francis, "The End of an Outlaw," 39.

138. Chapman, "'Butch' Cassidy," 33.

139. Meadows, *Digging Up Butch and Sundance*, 345.

140. Betenson, *Butch Cassidy, My Brother*, 126; Patterson, *Butch Cassidy*, 138–139.

141. Meadows, *Digging Up Butch and Sundance*, 106.

142. Pinkerton, *Train Robberies*.

143. Ibid., 76.

144. Ibid., 79.

145. Meadows, *Digging Up Butch and Sundance*, 79.

146. Patterson, *Butch Cassidy*, 207; Meadows, *Digging Up Butch and Sundance*, 84.

147. Meadows, *Digging Up Butch and Sundance*, 79, 80.

148. Chris Enss, *Love Lessons from the Old West: Wisdom from Wild Women* (Guilford, CT: Rowman & Littlefield, 2014), 18.

149. Ibid.

150. Mcintosh, "The Evolution of a Bandit," 566; Chapman, "'Butch' Cassidy," 62.

151. Betenson, *Butch Cassidy: My Uncle*, 234–240, 241.

152. Betenson, *Butch Cassidy, My Brother*, 177, 179, 181–194, 195; Betenson, *Butch Cassidy: My Uncle*, 240.

BIBLIOGRAPHY

Books

Abrams, Mac H. *Sioux War Dispatches: Reports from the Field, 1876–1877.* Yardley, PA: Westholme Publishing, 2012.

Ambrose, Stephen E. *Undaunted Courage: Meriwether Lewis, Thomas Jefferson, and the Opening of the American West.* New York, NY: Simon & Schuster, 1996.

Bagley, Will. *So Rugged and Mountainous: Blazing the Trails to Oregon and California, 1812–1848.* Norman, OK: University of Oklahoma Press, 2010.

Bailar, John C. Jr., ed. *General Chemistry,* Boston, MA: Raytheon Education Company, 1968.

Ball, Larry D. *Tom Horn: In Life and Legend.* Norman, OK: University of Oklahoma Press, 2014.

Beebe, Lucius, and Clegg, Charles. *The American West: The Pictorial Epic of a Continent,* New York, NY: E. P. Dutton & Company, 1955.

Betenson, Bill. *Butch Cassidy: My Uncle.* Glendo, WY: High Plains Press, 2012.

Betenson, Lula Parker, and Flack, Dora. *Butch Cassidy, My Brother.* Provo, UT: Brigham Young University, 1975.

Biddle, Nicholas. *The Journals of the Expedition Under the Command of Captains Lewis and Clark,* Vol. 2. Norwalk, CT: The Heritage Press Edition, 1993.

Billington, Ray Allen. *Westward Expansion: A History of the American Frontier,* New York, NY: The MacMillan Company, 1949.

Bingham, Hiram. *Across South America: An Account of a Journey From Buenos Aires to Lima by Way of Potosí,* New York, NY: Houghton Mifflin Company, 1911.

Blair, Robert. *Tales of the Superstitions: The Origins of the Lost Dutchman's Legend.* Tempe, AZ: Arizona Historical Foundation, 1975.

Blewer, Mac. *Wyoming's Outlaw Trail.* Charleston, SC: Arcadia Publishing, 2013.

Bourke, John G. *On the Border with Crook.* New York, NY: Skyhorse Publishing, 2014.

Breihan, Carl W. *Saga of Jesse James.* Caldwell, ID: The Caxton Printers, 1991.

Buel, J. W. *Heroes of the Plains.* Philadelphia, PA: Historical Publishing Co., 1881.

Carlson, Chip. *Tom Horn: Blood on the Moon: Dark History of the Murderous Cattle Detective.* Glendo, WY: High Plains Press, 2001.

Chittenden, Hiram Martin. *The American Fur Trade of the Far West,* Vol. 1. Stanford, CA: Academic Reprints, 1954.

Chronic, Halka. *Roadside Geology of Arizona.* Missoula, MT: Mountain Press Publishing Company, 1983.

Cody, W. F. *Buffalo Bill's Life Story: An Autobiography.* New York, NY: Cosmopolitan Book Corporation, 1920.

Collins, Charles D. Jr. *Atlas of the Sioux Wars*, 2d ed. Fort Leavenworth, KS: Combat Studies Institute Press, 2006.

Conatser, Estee. *The Sterling Legend: The Facts Behind the Lost Dutchman Mine*. Upland, CA: Gem Guide Books, 1972.

Crockett, David A. *Narrative of the Life of David Crockett of the State of Tennessee*. Coppell, TX: CreateSpace, 2016.

Crutchfield, James, Moulton, Candy, and Del Bene, Terry, eds. *The Settlement of America: Encyclopedia of Western Expansion from Jamestown to the Closing of the Frontier*, Vol. 1. Armonk, NY: M. E. Sharp, 2011.

Crutchfield, James, Moulton, Candy, and Del Bene, Terry, eds. *The Settlement of America*, Vol. 2. Armonk, NY: M. E. Sharp, 2011.

Davis, John W. *The Trial of Tom Horn*, Norman: University of Oklahoma Press, 2016.

De Barthe, Joe. *The Life and Adventures of Frank Grouard*. St. Joseph, MO: Combe Printing Company, 1894.

Del Bene, Terry. *Donner Party Cookbook: A Guide to Survival on the Hastings Cutoff*. Norman, OK: Horse Creek Publications, 2003.

DeMallie, Raymond J., vol. ed. *Plains, Handbook of North American Indians*. Volume 13, Part 2, Washington, DC: Smithsonian Institution, 2001.

DeVoto, Bernard. *The Journals of Lewis and Clark*. Boston, MA: Houghton Mifflin Company, 1953.

De Wall, Rob. *The Saga of Sitting Bull's Bones*. Crazy Horse, SD: Korczak's Heritage, 1984.

Di Silvestro, Roger L. *In the Shadow of Wounded Knee: The Untold Final Story of the Indian Wars*. New York: Walker & Company, 2007.

Dixon, Kelly J., Schablitsky, Julie M., and Novak, Shannon A., eds. *An Archaeology of Desperation: Exploring the Donner Party's Alder Creek Camp*. Norman, OK: University of Oklahoma Press, 2011.

Donovan, James. *A Terrible Glory: Custer and the Little Big Horn: The Last Great Battle of the American West*. New York, NY: Little, Brown and Company, 2008.

Donovan, James. *The Blood of Heroes: The 13-Day Struggle for the Alamo—And the Sacrifice that Forged a Nation*. New York, NY: Little, Brown and Company, 2012.

Duncan, Dayton. *Out West: An American Journey*. New York, NY: Viking Penguin 1987.

Edmondson, J. R. *The Alamo Story: From Early History to Current Conflicts*. Plano, TX: Republic of Texas Press, 2000.

Enss, Chris. *Love Lessons from the Old West: Wisdom from Wild Women*. Guilford, CT: Rowman & Littlefield, 2014.

Granger, Byrd Howell. *A Motif Index for Lost Mines and Treasures Applied to Redaction of Arizona Legends, and to Lost Mine and Treasure Legends Exterior to Arizona*. Tucson, AZ: University of Arizona Press, 1977.

Groneman, Bill. *Death of a Legend: The Myth and Mystery Surrounding the Death of Davy Crockett*. Dallas, TX: Republic of Texas Press, 1999.

Groneman, Bill. *Eyewitness to the Alamo*. Lanham, MD: Republic of Texas Press, 2001.

Gwynne, S. C. *Empire of the Summer Moon: Quanah Parker and the Rise and Fall of the Comanches, the Most Powerful Indian Tribe in American History*. New York, NY: Simon & Schuster, 2010.

Hebard, Grace Raymond. *Sacajawea: A Guide and Interpreter of the Lewis and Clark Expedition, with an Account of the Travels of Toussaint Charbonneau, and of Jean Baptiste, The Expedition Papoose.* Mineola, NY: Dover Publications, 1932.

Hedren, Paul L. *Rosebud, June 17, 1876: Prelude to the Little Big Horn.* Norman, OK: University of Oklahoma Press, 2019.

Hellmann, Paul T. *Historical Gazetteer of the United States.* New York, NY: Routledge, 2013.

Horn, Huston. *The Pioneers.* Alexandria, VA: Time-Life Books, 1976.

Horn, Tom. *The Life of Tom Horn, Government Scout and Interpreter.* Scotts Valley, CA: CreateSpace, 2016.

Horsted, Paul, and Grafe, Ernest. *Exploring with Custer: The 1874 Black Hills Expedition.* Custer, SD: Golden Valley Press, 2002.

Huffines, Alan C. *Blood of Noble Men: The Alamo Siege and Battle.* Fort Worth, TX: Eakin Press, 1999.

Hughes, Richard B. Agnes Wright Spring, ed. *Pioneer Years in the Black Hills.* Rapid City, SD: Dakota Alpha Press, 2002.

Hutton, Paul Andrew. *Phil Sheridan and His Army.* Norman: University of Oklahoma Press, 1985.

Jackson, Donald, ed. *The Letters of the Lewis and Clark Expedition with Related Documents, 1783–1854.* Urbana, IL: University of Illinois Press, 1978.

James, Jesse E. *Jesse James, My Father: The First and Only True Story of His Adventures.* Cleveland, OH: Buckeye Publishing Co., 1899.

Jameson, W. C. *Butch Cassidy: Beyond the Grave.* Lanham, MD: Rowman & Littlefield Publishing, 2014.

Johnson, Kristin. *"Unfortunate Emigrants" Narratives of the Donner Party.* Logan, UT: Utah State University Press, 1996.

Jones, Landon Y. *William Clark and the Shaping of the West.* New York, NY: Farrar, Straus and Giroux, 2004.

Kelly, Charles. *The Outlaw Trail: A History of Butch Cassidy and His Wild Bunch.* Lincoln, NE: University of Nebraska Press, 1938, 1959.

Kilgore, Dan. *How Did Davy Die? And Why Do We Care So Much?* comm. ed., Elma Dill Russell Spencer Series in the West and Southwest Commemorative ed., College Station, TX: Texas A&M University Press, 2010.

King, Joseph A. *Winter of Entrapment: A New Look at the Donner Party.* Lafayette, CA: K&K Publications, 1994.

Korns, J. Roderic, and Morgan, Dale L., eds. (revised and updated by Will Bagley and Harold Schindler). *West from Fort Bridger: The Pioneering of the Immigrant Trails across Utah, 1846–1850.* Logan: Utah State University Press, 1994.

Krause, Herbert, and Olson, Gary D. *Prelude to Glory: A Newspaper Accounting of Custer's 1874 Expedition to the Black Hills.* Sioux Falls, SD: Brevet Press, 1974.

Kukla, Jon. *A Wilderness So Immense: The Louisiana Purchase and the Destiny of America.* New York, NY: Alfred A. Knopf, 2003.

LeFors, Joe. *Wyoming Peace Officer: An Autobiography.* Laramie, WY: Laramie Printers, 1953.

Lindley, Thomas Ricks. *Alamo Traces: New Evidence and New Conclusions.* Lanham, MD: Republic of Texas Press, 2000.

Lord, Walter. *A Time to Stand.* Lincoln, NE: University of Nebraska Press, 1961.

Love, Robertus. *The Rise and Fall of Jesse James.* Lincoln, NE: University of Nebraska Press, 1990.

Markley, Bill. *Billy the Kid and Jesse James: Outlaws of the Legendary West,* Guilford, CT: Rowman & Littlefield Publishing, 2019.

Markley, Bill. *Up the Missouri River with Lewis and Clark: From Camp Dubois to the Bad River.* New York, NY: iUniverse, 2005.

Markley, Bill, and Cutsforth, Kellen. *Old West Showdown: Two Authors Wrangle Over the Truth About the Mythic Old West.* Guilford, CT: Rowman & Littlefield, 2018.

Matteoni, Norman E. *Prairie Man: The Struggle between Sitting Bull and Indian Agent James McLaughlin.* Guilford, CT: TwoDot, 2015.

McCord, Monty. *Calling the Brands: Stock Detectives in the Wild West.* Guilford, CT: Rowman & Littlefield Publishing Group, 2018.

McGlashan, Charles. *History of the Donner Party: A Tragedy of the Sierra Nevada,* 11th ed. San Francisco: A Carlisle & Company, 1918.

McLaird, James D. *Calamity Jane: The Woman and the Legend.* Norman, OK: University of Oklahoma Press, 2005.

McLaird, James D. *Wild Bill Hickok and Calamity Jane: Deadwood Legends.* Pierre, SD: South Dakota State Historical Society Press, 2008.

McLaughlin, James. *My Friend the Indian.* Lincoln: University of Nebraska Press, 1989.

Meadows, Anne. *Digging Up Butch and Sundance,* Lincoln, NE: University of Nebraska Press, 2003.

Michno, Gregory F. *Lakota Noon: The Indian Narrative of Custer's Defeat.* Missoula, MT: Mountain Press Publishing Company, 1997.

Milner, Joe E., and Forrest, Earle R. *California Joe: Noted Scout and Indian Fighter.* Lincoln, NE: University of Nebraska Press, 1935.

Morgan, Dale, ed. *Overland in 1846: Diaries and Letters of the California-Oregon Trail.* Vol. 1. Lincoln, NE: University of Nebraska Press, 1963.

Moulton, Gary E., ed. *The Definitive Journals of Lewis and Clark: Up the Missouri River to Fort Mandan,* Vol. 3, Lincoln: University of Nebraska Press, 1987.

Moulton, Gary E., ed. *The Definitive Journals of Lewis and Clark: John Ordway and Charles Floyd,* Vol. 9. Lincoln, NE: University of Nebraska Press, 1995.

Moulton, Gary E., ed. *The Definitive Journals of Lewis and Clark: Patrick Gass,* Vol. 10, Lincoln: University of Nebraska Press, 1996.

Mullen, Frank Jr. *The Donner Party Chronicles: A Day-by-Day Account of a Doomed Wagon Train, 1846–1847,* Reno, NV: Nevada Humanities Committee, 1997.

Nash, Jay Robert. *Encyclopedia of Western Lawmen & Outlaws.* New York, NY: Da Capo Press, 1994.

National Historical Company. *History of Clay and Platte Counties, Missouri.* St. Louis, MO: National Historical Company, 1885.

Nelson, W. Dale. *Interpreters with Lewis and Clark: The Story of Sacagawea and Toussaint Charbonneau.* Denton, TX: University of North Texas Press, 2003.

Nevin, David. *The Texans.* Alexandria, VA: Time-Life Books, 1975.

Nichols, Roger L. *American Indians in U.S. History.* Norman, OK: University of Oklahoma Press, 2003.

Nofi, Albert A. *The Alamo and the Texas War of Independence, September 30, 1835 to April 21, 1836: Heroes, Myths, and History.* Conshohocken, PA: Combined Books, 2001

O'Neal, Bill. *Encyclopedia of Western Gunfighters.* Norman, OK: University of Oklahoma Press, 1979.

Parker, Watson. *Deadwood: The Golden Years.* Lincoln, NE: University of Nebraska Press, 1981.

Parker, Watson. *Gold in the Black Hills.* Pierre, SD: South Dakota Historical Press, 2003.

Patterson, Richard. *Butch Cassidy: A Biography.* Lincoln, NE: University of Nebraska Press, 1998.

Pinkerton, William Allan. *Train Robberies, Train Robbers and the "Holdup" Men.* Erlanger, KY: Andesite Press, 1907.

Pointer, Larry. *In Search of Butch Cassidy.* Norman, OK: University of Oklahoma Press, 1977.

Pollack, Eileen. *Woman Walking Ahead: In Search of Catherine Weldon and Sitting Bull.* Albuquerque: University of New Mexico Press, 2002.

Pope, Dennis C. *Sitting Bull, Prisoner of War.* Pierre, SD: South Dakota State Historical Society Press, 2010.

Porter, Joseph C. *Paper Medicine Man: John Gregory Bourke and his American West.* Norman, OK: University of Oklahoma Press, 1986.

Powers, Thomas. *The Killing of Crazy Horse.* New York: Alfred A. Knopf, 2010.

Rarick, Ethan. *Desperate Passage: The Donner Party's Perilous Journey West.* England: Oxford University Press, 2008.

Rhonda, James P. *Lewis and Clark among the Indians.* Lincoln, NE: University of Nebraska Press, 2002.

Robertson, R. G. *Competitive Struggle: America's Western Fur Trading Posts, 1764–1865.* Boise, ID: Tamarack Books, 1999.

Rosa, Joseph G. *Alias Jack McCall: A Pardon or Death?* Kansas City, MO: Kansas City Posse of the Westerners, 1967.

Rosa, Joseph G. *They Called Him Wild Bill: The Life and Adventures of James Butler Hickok.* Norman, OK: University of Oklahoma Press, 1974.

Rosa, Joseph G. *Wild Bill Hickok, Gunfighter: An Account of Hickok's Gunfights.* Norman, OK: University of Oklahoma Press, 2003.

Rosa, Joseph G. *Wild Bill Hickok: The Man and His Myth.* Lawrence, KS: University Press of Kansas, 1996.

Scott, Robert. *After the Alamo.* Plano, TX: Republic of Texas Press, 2000.

Secrest, William B., ed. *I Buried Hickok: The Memoirs of White Eye Anderson.* College Station, TX: Creative Publishing Co., 1980.

Settle, William A. Jr. *Jesse James Was His Name or, Fact and Fiction Concerning the Careers of the Notorious James Brothers of Missouri.* Lincoln, NE: University of Nebraska Press, 1966.

Sikorsky, Robert. *Fool's Gold: The Facts, Myths and Legends of the Lost Dutchman Mine and the Superstition Mountains.* Phoenix, AZ: Golden West Publishers, 1983.

Smith, Rex Alan. *Moon of the Popping Trees: The Tragedy at Wounded Knee and the End of the Indian Wars.* Lincoln, NE: University of Nebraska Press, 1975.

Steele, Philip. *The Best of NOLA: Outlaws and Lawmen, "James Brothers' Death Hoax."* The National Association for Outlaw and History, 2001.

Stewart, George R. *Ordeal by Hunger: The Story of the Donner Party.* suppl. ed. New York, NY: Houghton Mifflin, 1988.

Stiles, T. J. *Jesse James: Last Rebel of the Civil War.* New York, NY: Random House, 2002.

Stillman, Deanne. *Blood Brothers: The Story of the Strange Friendship between Sitting Bull and Buffalo Bill.* New York, NY: Simon & Schuster, 2017.

Swanson, James, and Kollenborn, Tom. *Superstition Mountain: A Ride Through Time.* Phoenix, AZ: Arrowhead Press, 1981.

Terry, Alfred H. *The Field Diary of General Alfred H. Terry: The Yellowstone Expedition—1876.* 2d ed. Bellevue, NE: Old Army Press, 1970.

Tinkle, Lon. *13 Days to Glory: The Siege of the Alamo.* College Station, TX: Texas A&M University Press, 1958.

Todish, Timothy J., Todish, Terry, and Spring, Ted. *Alamo Sourcebook, 1836: A Comprehensive Guide to the Battle of the Alamo and the Texas Revolution.* Austin, TX: Eakin Press, 1998.

Triplett, Frank. *Jesse James: The Life, Times, and Treacherous Death of the Most Infamous Outlaw of All Time.* New York, NY: Skyhorse, 2013.

Turner, Thad. *Wild Bill Hickok: Deadwood City—End of Trail.* Deadwood, SD: Old West Alive! Publishing, 2001.

Utley, Robert M. *The Lance and the Shield: The Life and Times of Sitting Bull.* New York, NY: Ballantine Books, 1993.

Vaughn, J. W. *Indian Fights: New Facts on Seven Encounters.* Norman, OK: University of Oklahoma Press, 1966.

Vestal, Stanley. *New Sources of Indian History, 1850–1891, the Ghost Dance, the Prairie Sioux, a Miscellany.* Norman, OK: University of Oklahoma Press, 1934.

Vestal, Stanley. *Sitting Bull: Champion of the Sioux.* Norman, OK: University of Oklahoma Press, 1932.

Vikas, Khatri. *World Famous Treasures Lost and Found.* India: Pustak Mahal, 2013.

Waggoner, Josephine. *Witness: A Hunkpapha Historian's Strong-Heart Song of the Lakotas.* Lincoln, NE: University of Nebraska Press, 2013.

Wallis, Michael. *David Crockett: The Lion of the West.* New York, NY: W.W. Norton & Company, 2011.

Warman, Cy. *Frontier Stories, "A Quiet Day in Creed."* New York, NY: Charles Scribner's Sons, 1898.

Wiles, Richard I. Jr. *The Battle of the Rosebud: Crook's Campaign on 1876.* Fort Leavenworth, KS: US Army Command and General Staff College, 1993.

Wilstach, Frank J. *Wild Bill Hickok: The Prince of Pistoleers.* Garden City, NY: Doubleday, Page & Company, 1926.

Woodard, Aaron. *The Revenger: The Life and Times of Wild Bill Hickok.* Guilford, CT: Rowman & Littlefield Publishing Group, 2018.

Yeatman, Ted P. *Frank and Jesse James: The Story Behind the Legend.* Naperville, IL: Sourcebooks 2000.

Young, Harry "Sam." *Hard Knocks: A Life Story of the Vanishing West*. Pierre, SD: South Dakota Historical Society Press, 2005.

Internet Sources

Anderson, Irving W. "Sacagawea: Inside the Corps." pbs.org. Accessed August 29, 2020. pbs.org/lewisandclark/inside/saca.html.

Bicknell, P. C. "One of Arizona's Lost El Dorados." *San Francisco Chronicle*, January 13, 1895. Newspapers.com. Accessed June 14, 2020. newspapers.com/image/27596373/.

Botts, Gene. "Peralta Stones and Lost Dutchman Gold Mine: The Peralta Stones are Fakes!" DesertUSA. Accessed March 23, 2020. desertusa.com/lost-dutchman/peralta-stones-fake.html.

Butterfield, Bonnie. "Sacagawea: What Happened to Sacagawea after the Expedition Returned?" bonniebutterfield.com, accessed September 11, 2020. bonniebutterfield.com/sacagawea-death.html.

Carlson, Chip. "Tom Horn: Wyoming Enigma." wyohistory.org, November 8, 2014. Accessed September 25, 2020. wyohistory.org/encyclopedia/tom-horn-wyoming-enigma#:~:text=Horn%20remains%20controversial%20for%20two,questionable%20nature%20of%20his%20trial.

Chapman, Arthur. "'Butch' Cassidy." *Elks Magazine*, April 1930. Accessed August 11, 2020. elks.org/magazinescans/1930-04A.pdf.

Chelsea, Megan and Brandon, John. "A Brief History of Mobridge, South Dakota." slideshare.net. Accessed April 4, 2020. slideshare.net/argyleist/mobridge-history.

Connor, Seymour V. "New Washington, TX." Texas State Historical Association Handbook of Texas. Accessed October 3, 2020. tshaonline.org/handbook/entries/new-washington-tx.

Coroner's Inquest for William Nickell, Testimony, Part 1-3, (CR4-58 State vs Tom Horn, Laramie County District Court, Wyoming State Archives), 27. Accessed September 5, 2020. drive.google.com/file/d/1a2c1FpuXCv0j1xgZQkJzxfGoUnOFOG17/view.

Digital Horizons. "Sitting Bull's Grave, Fort Yates, N.D." Accessed April 22, 2020. digitalhorizonsonline.org/digital/collection/uw-ndshs/id/5941/.

Donner Houghton, Eliza P. "The Expedition of the Donner Party and Its Tragic Fate." (Chicago, IL: A. C. McClurg & Co., 1911). Accessed June 6, 2020. tile.loc.gov/storage-services//service/gdc/calbk/187.pdf.

Dorsett Duke, Betty. "Fraudulent Jesse James DNA Results?" jessejamesintexas.com. Accessed June 25, 2020. jessejamesintexas.com/2Fraudulent_DNAMedia.pdf.

Frazier Reed, James. "The Snow-Bound, Starved Emigrants of 1846." Pacific Rural Press, Volume 1, Number 13, April 1, 1871. California Digital Newspaper Collection. Accessed June 3, 2020. cdnc.ucr.edu/?a=d&d=PRP18710401.2.5&e=-------en--20--1--txt-txIN--------1.

Fs.gov. "Prospecting, Mining, And Searching for Treasure In Wilderness Areas." Accessed June 13, 2020. fs.usda.gov/detail/tonto/specialplaces/?cid=fsbdev3_018726.

Fs.gov. "Superstition Wilderness Area." Accessed June 9, 2020. fs.usda.gov/detail/tonto/specialplaces/?cid=fsbdev3_018739.

Groneman, William, III. "Davy's Death at the Alamo Is Now a Case Closed—Or Not." *Wild West*. Accessed August 28, 2020. historynet.com/davys-death-at-the-alamo-is-now-a-case-closed-or-not.htm.

History.com. "Indians hammer U.S. soldiers at the Battle of the Rosebud." Accessed May 25, 2020. history.com/this-day-in-history/indians-hammer-u-s-soldiers-at-the-battle-of-the-rosebud.

History.com. "Sitting Bull Killed by Indian Police." Accessed March 25, 2020. history.com/this-day-in-history/sitting-bull-killed-by-indian-police.

Killough, Kevin. "Was Tom Horn Innocent?" county17.com, July 20, 2018. Accessed September 26, 2020. county17.com/2018/07/20/was-tom-horn-innocent-thisweekinwyhistory/.

Klein, Christopher. "The Mysterious Deaths of Butch Cassidy and the Sundance Kid." history.com. Accessed August 4, 2020. history.com/news/the-mysterious-deaths-of-butch-cassidy-and-the-sundance-kid.

Kollenborn, Tom. "An Affliction." *Tom Kollenborn Chronicles*, May 4, 2015. Accessed June 12, 2020. superstitionmountaintomkollenborn.blogspot.com/search?q=gold.

Kollenborn, Tom. "Don't Blame The Thunder God." *Tom Kollenborn Chronicles*, December 16, 2013. Accessed June 9, 2020. superstitionmountaintomkollenborn.blogspot.com/search?q=Apache+Thunder+Gods.

Kollenborn, Tom. "Robert K. Corbin's Legacy." blogspot. Accessed March 16, 2020. superstitionmountaintomkollenborn.blogspot.com/2009/08/robert-k-corbins-legacy.html.

Kollenborn, Tom. "What Dreams Are Made Of." *Tom Kollenborn Chronicles*, September 23, 2013. Accessed June 14, 2020. superstitionmountaintomkollenborn.blogspot.com/2013/09/what-dreams-are-made-of.html?m=1.

Kollenborn, Tom, and the Superstition Mountain Historical Society. "Jacob Waltz 'Lost Dutchman' Exhibit." The Superstition Mountain Lost Dutchman Museum. Accessed June 12, 2020. superstitionmountainmuseum.org/exhibits/jacob-waltz-lost-dutchman-exhibit/.

Lee, Bob. "The Story Behind the Story." *Rapid City Journal*, March 29, 1953. Newspapers.com. Accessed April 22, 2020. newspapers.com/image/351456933.

Legendsofamerica.com. "Goldfield, Arizona – Given a Third Rebirth." Accessed March 15, 2020. legendsofamerica.com/az-goldfield/.

Luttig, John C. "The Journal of a Fur-Trading Expedition on the Upper Missouri 1812–1813, Mountain Men and the Fur Trade." Sources of the Fur Trade in the Rocky Mountain West website. Accessed August 31, 2020. mtmen.org/mtman/html/Luttig/luttig.html.

LyricWiki.org. "Walter Brennan: Dutchman's Gold Lyrics." Accessed June 13, 2020. lyrics.fandom.com/wiki/Walter_Brennan:Dutchman%27s_Gold.

M., Kaspar. "Western Writers of Americas 100 Greatest Westerns." IMDb.com. Accessed July 21, 2020. imdb.com/list/ls006229256/.

Markley, Bill. "Sitting Bull Rests, but is He at Peace?" historynet.com. Accessed April 5, 2020. historynet.com/sitting-bull-rests-peace.htm.

McLaughlin, Mark. "Donner Party Weather." Mic Mac Publishing. Accessed May 14, 2020. thestormking.com/Donner_Party/Donner_Party_Weather/donner_party _weather.html.

Newspapers.com. "N.D.'s Sitting Bull Action Draws Tribal Council Ire." *Rapid City Journal*, March 23, 1953. Accessed April 21, 2020. newspapers.com/image/3514518 43/?article=4ddf931f-cd89-40f3-b399-95d225d65dcc.

Newspapers.com. "S.D. Ghouls Steal Sitting Bull's Bones." *Bismarck Tribune*, April 8, 1953. Accessed April 22, 2020. newspapers.com/image/413317996/?terms=.

Newspapers.com. "Sitting Bull's Body taken to S.D." *Rapid City Journal*, April 8, 1953. Accessed April 22, 2020. newspapers.com/image/351205623/?terms=.

Newspapers.com. "Sitting Bull's Remains." *Chicago Tribune*, December 20, 1890. Accessed April 14, 2020. newspapers.com/image/349506643/?terms=Sitting%2 BBull%2Bdeath%2C.

Newspapers.com. "The War in Texas." *Vermont Chronicle*, May 12, 1836. Accessed September 27, 2020. newspapers.com/image/489182233/?terms=Davy%2BCrockett% 2C&match=2.

Newspapers.com. "Wild Bill: A Sequel to the Tragedy." *Black Hills Weekly Pioneer*, November 11, 1876. Accessed July 19, 2020. newspapers.com/image/262594576/ ?terms=%2C%2BWild%2BBill.

Newspapers.com. "Where's Bull's Body?" *Bismarck Daily Tribune*, December 20, 1890. Accessed April 19, 2020. newspapers.com/image/7414407/?terms=.

odmp.org. "Deputy Sheriff Samuel Jenkins." Accessed July 29, 2020. odmp.org/officer/ 7094-deputy-sheriff-samuel-jenkins.

Roadsideamerica.com. "Sitting Bull, Where Do You Lie?" Accessed March 25, 2020. roadsideamerica.com/story/28961.

Stone, Anne C. 1 Ph.D.; James E. Starrs,2 L.L.M.; and Mark Stoneking, PhD., "LAST WORD SOCIETY Mitochondrial DNA Analysis of the Presumptive Remains of Jesse James." Accessed June 25, 2020. web.archive.org/web/ 20100719085854/http://class.csueastbay.edu/faculty/gmiller/3710/DNA_PDFS/ mtDNA/mtDNA_JesseJames.pdf.

Thomas, Rod. "Sitting Bull's Burials: A History." friendslittleBigHorn.com. Accessed April 4, 2020. friendslittleBigHorn.com/sittingbullsburials.htm.

Thornton, Jessy Quinn. "Oregon and California in 1848, Volume 2." (New York, NY: Harper & Brothers Publishers, 1849), 199. Google Books. Accessed June 1, 2020. books.google.com/books?id=T1pHswEACAAJ&printsec=frontcover&source =gbs_ge_summary_r&cad=0#v=onepage&q&f=false.

travelchannel.com. "Butch Cassidy's Buried Secrets." Accessed August 7, 2020. travel channel.com/shows/mission-declassified/episodes/butch-cassidys-buried-secrets.

Weiser, Kathy. "Jack McCall–Cowardly Killer of Wild Bill Hickok." legendsofamerica .com. Accessed July 18, 2020. legendsofamerica.com/we-jackmccall/.

Periodicals
Anderson, Irving W. "Probing the Riddle of the Bird Woman." *Montana the Magazine of Western History*, Autumn 1973, 16.

Andrews, Thomas F. "Lansford W. Hastings and the Promotion of the Great Salt Lake Cutoff: A Reappraisal." *The Western Historical Quarterly*, 1973.

Burk, Jackson. "The Secret of the Alamo." *Man's Conquest Magazine*, April 1960.

Francis, A.G. "The End of an Outlaw." *Wide World*, April 1913.

"Jesse James is Alive! In Lawton." *The Lawton Constitution*, May 19, 1948.

Jackson, Ron J. Jr. "POW Crockett?" *Wild West Magazine*, February 2020.

Johnson, Kristin. "Donner Party Cannibalism: Did They or Didn't They? (Spoiler alert: They did)." *Wild West*, 2013, 26.

Markley, Bill. "Custer's Gold." *True West*, April 2018.

Mattison, Ray A. "Report on Historical Aspects of the Oahe Reservoir Area, Missouri River, South and North Dakota." *South Dakota Historical Collections and Report, Vol. XXVII*, 1954.

Mcintosh, John H. "The Evolution of a Bandit." *Wide World*, September 1910.

Meadows, Anne and Buck, Dan. "The Last Days of Butch and Sundance." *Wild West*, February 1997.

Palmquist, Bob. "A Home or Perish." *Wild West*, February 2017.

Paul Andrew Hutton, "Out on a Limb," *Wild West*, February 2018.

Woodward, Aaron. "The Coward Who Shot Wild Bill." *Wild West*, August 2019, 40–41.

Manuscripts and Primary Resources

James Swanson personal conversation with Bill Markley at Superstition Mountain Lost Dutchman Museum, March 10, 2020.

"The Lost Dutchman Gold Mine, Jacob Waltz's Mining Tools exhibit," Superstition Mountain Lost Dutchman Museum, viewed by Bill Markley, March 10, 2020.

INDEX

ABOUT THE AUTHORS

Bill Markley is a member of Western Writers of America (WWA) and a staff writer for WWA's *Roundup* magazine. He also writes for *True West* and *Wild West* magazines. This book, *Standoff at High Noon: Another Battle over the Truth in the Mythic Wild West*, is the sequel to the first book that Kellen Cutsforth and Bill wrote together, *Old West Showdown: Two Authors Wrangle over the Truth about the Mythic Old West*, in which Kellen and Bill explore an additional ten controversial stories from the Old West. *Old West Showdown* was a 2019 Will Rogers Medallion Award nonfiction finalist. Bill is writing a series of books called the Legendary West. The first in the series, *Wyatt Earp and Bat Masterson: Lawmen of the Legendary West*, examines the lives of those two well-known Old West characters. His second book in the Legendary West series, *Billy the Kid and Jesse James: Outlaws of the Legendary West*, delves into the lives of the two famous desperados. Both books are 2020 Will Rogers Medallion Award finalists in nonfiction. The third in the series, scheduled for release in May 2021, is *Geronimo and Sitting Bull: Leaders of the Legendary West*, and *Wild Bill and Buffalo Bill: Plainsmen of the Legendary West* is scheduled for release in 2022. The Western Writers of America awarded Bill the 2020 Branding Iron Award for service to WWA.

Bill has written three additional nonfiction books: *Dakota Epic, Experiences of a Reenactor During the Filming of* Dances with Wolves; *Up the Missouri River with Lewis and Clark*; and *American Pilgrim: A Post-September 11th Bus Trip and Other Tales of the Road*. His first historical novel, *Deadwood Dead Men*, was selected by Western Fictioneers as a finalist for its 2014 Peacemaker Award in the category Best First Western Novel. Bill wrote the "Military Establishment" chapter and thirty entries for the *Encyclopedia of Western Expansion*. He was a member of Toastmasters International for twenty years. He earned a bachelor's degree in Biology and a master's degree in Environmental Sciences and Engineering at Virginia Tech, worked on two Antarctic field teams, and worked forty years with the South Dakota Department of Environment and Natural Resources. Raised on a farm near Valley Forge, Pennsylvania, Bill has always loved history. He has reenacted Civil War infantry and frontier cavalry and has participated in the films *Dances with Wolves*, *Son of the Morning Star*, *Far and Away*, *Gettysburg*, and *Crazy Horse*. Bill and his wife, Liz, live in Pierre, South Dakota, where they raised two children and currently have three grandchildren.

Kellen Cutsforth has published numerous books on the history of the American West, including *Buffalo Bill, Boozers, Brothels, and Bare-Knuckle Brawlers*; *Buffalo Bill's Wild West Coloring Book*; the co-authored and award-winning volume *Old West Showdown: Two Authors Wrangle over the Truth about the Mythic Old West*; and the upcoming *Buffalo Bill and the Birth of American Celebrity* (2021). Kellen has also worked as a ghostwriter on numerous projects. He has published over forty articles in such magazines as *Wild West* and *True West* and is a featured columnist for Western Writers of America's *Roundup* magazine. Kellen is a professional speaker and is an active member of the Western Writers of America and served as a Spur Award judge and panelist at numerous WWA conventions.

Kellen is currently the Western Writers Twitter account manager and a past president of the Western history group Denver Posse of Westerners. He was a finalist for the Will Rogers 2019 Medallion award, and he was honored in 2018 by the Denver Posse of Westerners with the group's prestigious Rosenstock Lifetime Achievement Award. Kellen was also the co-chairman for the Denver Posse of Westerner's 75th Anniversary *Brand Book* committee. He can be found online at patreon.com/kellencutsforth, facebook.com/kellencutsforth, and on twitter @western_writers.